THE DASH DIET COOKBOOK

Over 1000 Recipes to Lower Blood Pressure with 28-Day Complete Meal Plan Recipes to Lose Weight and Decrease Hypertension.

By
Sophia Cooper

DASH Shopping List

PICK ORGANIC, EAT A RAINBOW OF PRODUCE, & GO RAW

Vegetables

- [ ] Spinach
- [ ] Kale
- [ ] Collard Greens
- [ ] Broccoli
- [ ] Cucumber
- [ ] Arugula
- [ ] Asparagus
- [ ] Brussels Sprouts
- [ ] Cauliflower
- [ ] Cabbage
- [ ] Parsnips
- [ ] Leeks
- [ ] Celery
- [ ] Radishes
- [ ] Sweet Potatoes
- [ ] Onions
- [ ] Garlic
- [ ] Scallions
- [ ] Eggplant
- [ ] Carrots
- [ ] Bell Peppers
- [ ] Beets & Beet Greens
- [ ] Zucchini
- [ ] Pumpkin
- [ ] Butternut Squash
- [ ] Leafy Salad Greens
- [ ] Watercress
- [ ] Microgreens
- [ ] Sprouted Greens
- [ ] Swiss Chard

Other

- [ ] Kimchee
- [ ] Sauerkraut
- [ ] Wheatgrass
- [ ] Aloe

Fruits

- [ ] Blueberries
- [ ] Cranberries
- [ ] Blackberries
- [ ] Raspberries
- [ ] Oranges
- [ ] Lemons
- [ ] Limes
- [ ] Passion Fruit
- [ ] Peaches
- [ ] Cherries
- [ ] Plums
- [ ] Mulberries
- [ ] Coconut
- [ ] Jujube
- [ ] Persimmon
- [ ] Mangosteen
- [ ] Nectarines
- [ ] Apples
- [ ] Pears
- [ ] Grapefruit
- [ ] Bananas
- [ ] Melon
- [ ] Honeydew
- [ ] Avocado
- [ ] Tomatoes
- [ ] Watermelon
- [ ] Kiwi
- [ ] Figs
- [ ] Papaya
- [ ] Pomegranate

Sweeteners

- [ ] Raw Honey
- [ ] Stevia Leaf
- [ ] Monkfruit

Nuts & Seeds
No More Than 4 oz Daily

- [ ] Chia Seeds
- [ ] Sesame Seeds
- [ ] Sunflower Seeds
- [ ] Macadamia Nuts
- [ ] Flaxseed
- [ ] Hempseed
- [ ] Pumpkin Seeds
- [ ] Pecans
- [ ] Walnuts
- [ ] Pine Nuts
- [ ] Brazil Nuts
- [ ] Hazelnuts
- [ ] Pistachios
- [ ] Almonds

Healthy Oils
No More Than 1 oz Daily

- [ ] Extra Virgin Olive Oil
- [ ] Avocado Oil
- [ ] Flaxseed Oil
- [ ] Sesame Oil
- [ ] Walnut Oil
- [ ] Coconut Oil
- [ ] Grapeseed Oil

Beverages

- [ ] Distilled Water
- [ ] Green Tea
- [ ] Hibiscus Tea
- [ ] Jasmine Tea
- [ ] Herbal Tea
- [ ] Organic Coffee
- [ ] Nut Milks
- [ ] Kombucha
- [ ] Fresh Pressed Fruit Juice
- [ ] Fresh Pressed Green Juice

Table of Contents

Introduction 1

CHAPTER 1: The Dietary Approach to Stop
Hypertension (DASH) Basics 2

CHAPTER 2: Benefits of Dash Diet 4

CHAPTER 3: Breakfast 7

Spinach, Egg, And Cheese Breakfast Quesadillas 7
Apple Pancakes 7
Super-Simple Granola 7
Savory Yogurt Bowls 8
Energy Sunrise Muffins 8
Simple Cheese and Broccoli Omelets 8
Creamy Avocado and Egg Salad Sandwiches 9
Blueberry Waffles 9
Breakfast Hash 9
Hearty Breakfast Casserole 10
Sweet Potato Toast Three Ways 10
Creamy Apple-Avocado Smoothie 11
Strawberry, Orange, and Beet Smoothie 11
Blueberry-Vanilla Yogurt Smoothie 11
Creamy Oats, Greens & Blueberry Smoothie 11
Banana & Cinnamon Oatmeal 11
Bagels Made Healthy 11
Greek Yogurt Oat Pancakes 12
Scrambled Egg and Veggie Breakfast Quesadillas 12
Stuffed Breakfast Peppers 12
Apple-Apricot Brown Rice Breakfast Porridge 12
Carrot Cake Overnight Oats 13
Steel-Cut Oatmeal with Plums and Pear 13
French Toast with Applesauce 13
Banana-Peanut Butter and Greens Smoothie 13
Baking Powder Biscuits 14
Oatmeal Banana Pancakes with Walnuts 14
Cereal with Cranberry-Orange Twist 14
No Cook Overnight Oats 14
Avocado Cup with Egg 15
Mediterranean Toast 15
Instant Banana Oatmeal 15
Almond Butter-Banana Smoothie 15
Salmon and Egg Scramble 15
Breakfast Banana Split 16
Easy Veggie Muffins 16

Carrot Muffins 16
Pineapple Oatmeal 16
Spinach Muffins 17
Chia Seeds Breakfast Mix 17
Breakfast Fruits Bowls 17
Pumpkin Cookies 17
Veggie Scramble 17
Mushrooms and Turkey Breakfast 18
Mushrooms and Cheese Omelet 18
Pumpkin Muffins 18
Sweet Berries Pancake 19
Zucchini Pancakes 19
Egg White Breakfast Mix 19
Pesto Omelet 19
Quinoa Bowls 19
Strawberry Sandwich 19
Apple Quinoa Muffins 20
Very Berry Muesli 20
Veggie Quiche Muffins 20
Turkey Sausage and Mushroom Strata 20
Jack-o-Lantern Pancakes 21
Fruit Pizza 21
Flax Banana Yogurt Muffins 21
Bacon Bits 21
Steel Cut Oat Blueberry Pancakes 22
Brown Sugar Cinnamon Oatmeal 22
Buckwheat Pancakes with Vanilla Almond Milk 22
Spinach, Mushroom, and Feta Cheese Scramble 22
Red Velvet Pancakes with Cream Cheese Topping 23
Peanut Butter & Banana Breakfast Smoothie 23
No-Bake Breakfast Granola Bars 23
Mushroom Shallot Frittata 23

CHAPTER 4: Lunch 25

Creamy Chicken Breast 25
Indian Chicken Stew 25
Sweet Potatoes and Zucchini Soup 25
Lemongrass and Chicken Soup 25
Easy Lunch Salmon Steaks 26
Chicken, Bamboo, and Chestnuts Mix 26
Salsa Chicken 26
Rice with Chicken 26
Tomato Soup 26
Cod Soup 27
Sweet Potato Soup 27

Light Balsamic Salad..27

Purple Potato Soup..28

Leeks Soup..28

Cauliflower Lunch Salad...................................28

CHAPTER 5: Dinner 29

Quinoa and Scallops Salad................................29

Squid and Shrimp Salad...................................29

Parsley Seafood Cocktail..................................29

Shrimp and Onion Ginger Dressing....................30

Lime Shrimp and Kale......................................30

Parsley Cod Mix...30

Fruit Shrimp Soup...31

Mussels and Chickpea Soup..............................31

Shrimp Cocktail..31

Fish Stew..32

Shrimp and Broccoli Soup.................................32

Coconut Turkey Mix..32

Salmon and Cabbage Mix..................................32

CHAPTER 6: Mains...34

Spicy Tofu Burrito Bowls with Cilantro Avocado Sauce 34

Sweet Potato Cakes with Classic Guacamole 34

Chickpea Cauliflower Tikka Masala 34

Lentil Avocado Tacos.......................................35

Eggplant Parmesan Stacks.................................35

Tofu & Green Bean Stir-Fry...............................36

Peanut Vegetable Pad Thai................................36

Roasted Vegetable Enchiladas............................36

Tomato & Olive Orecchiette with Basil Pesto 37

Italian Stuffed Portobello Mushroom Burgers.............37

Gnocchi with Tomato Basil Sauce........................38

Creamy Pumpkin Pasta.....................................38

Mexican-Style Potato Casserole 38

Black Bean Stew with Cornbread.........................39

Vegetarian Lasagna 39

Carrot Cakes..40

Vegan Chili...40

Tuna Sandwich...40

Fruited Quinoa Salad.......................................40

Aromatic Whole Grain Spaghetti.........................41

Chunky Tomatoes 41

Baked Falafel 41

Paella..41

Mushroom Cakes..42

Glazed Eggplant Rings.....................................42

Sweet Potato Balls..42

Chickpea Curry..42

Pan-Fried Salmon with Salad.............................42

Veggie Variety...43

Vegetable Pasta..43

Vegetable Noodles with Bolognese 43

Harissa Bolognese with Vegetable Noodles...............44

Curry Vegetable Noodles with Chicken....................44

Sweet and Sour Vegetable Noodles 45

Turkey Wrap..45

Chicken Wrap..45

Mushroom Florentine 45

Hassel back Eggplant.......................................46

Vegetarian Kebabs..46

White Beans Stew...46

Veggie Wrap..46

Salmon Wrap...47

Dill Chicken Salad...47

CHAPTER 7: Side Dishes 48

Turmeric Endives..48

Parmesan Endives...48

Lemon Asparagus..48

Lime Carrots..48

Creamy Cauliflower Mash..................................48

Avocado, Tomato, and Olives Salad.....................49

Radish and Olives Salad....................................49

Spinach and Endives Salad 49

Basil Olives Mix...49

Arugula Salad 49

Spanish Rice..50

Sweet Potatoes and Apples................................50

Roasted Turnips..50

No-Mayo Potato Salad......................................51

Zucchini Tomato Bake......................................51

Creamy Broccoli Cheddar Rice 51

Smashed Brussels Sprouts 52

Cilantro Lime Rice..52

Corn Salad with Lime Vinaigrette 52

Tex-Mex Cole Slaw...53

Garlic Potato Pan..53

Balsamic Cabbage 53

Chili Broccoli 54

Sweet Butternut..54

Mushroom Sausages 54

Parsley Red Potatoes..54

Jalapeno Black-Eyed Peas Mix............................55

Sour Cream Green Beans...................................55

Cumin Brussels Sprouts 55

Hot Brussels Sprouts 55

Paprika Brussels Sprouts 55

Roasted Okra 56

Brown Sugar Glazed Carrots 56

Oven-Roasted Beets with Honey Ricotta........................56

Easy Carrots Mix 56

Tasty Grilled Asparagus 57

Roasted Carrots 57

Oven Roasted Asparagus 57

Baked Potato with Thyme 57

Spicy Brussels Sprouts 57

Baked Cauliflower with Chili 58

Baked Broccoli 58

Slow Cooked Potatoes with Cheddar 58

Squash Salad with Orange 58

Colored Iceberg Salad 59

Fennel Salad with Arugula 59

Corn Mix 59

Persimmon Salad 59

Avocado Side Salad..60

Spiced Broccoli Florets 60

Lima Beans Dish 60

Mediterranean Chickpea Salad 60

Italian Roasted Cabbage 61

Soy Sauce Green Beans 61

Butter Corn 61

Stevia Peas with Marjoram 61

Pilaf with Bella Mushrooms 62

Parsley Fennel 62

Peach and Carrots 62

Tasty Cauliflower 62

Artichoke and Spinach Dip...63

Baby Spinach and Grains Mix 63

Quinoa Curry 63

Lemon and Cilantro Rice 63

Chili Beans 63

Bean Spread 64

Stir-Fried Steak, Shiitake, and Asparagus 64

Chickpeas and Curried Veggies......................................64

Brussels Sprouts Casserole 65

Apple Salsa..65

CHAPTER 8: Fish and Seafood 66

Cod and Cauliflower Chowder 66

Sardine Bruschetta with Fennel and Lemon Crema.......66

Chopped Tuna Salad 66

Citrus-Glazed Salmon with Zucchini Noodles................67

Salmon Cakes with Bell Pepper Plus Lemon Yogurt......67

Halibut in Parchment with Zucchini, Shallots, and Herbs............68

Flounder with Tomatoes and Basil..................................68

Grilled Mahi-Mahi with Artichoke Caponata 68

Monkfish with Sautéed Leeks, Fennel, and Tomatoes 69

Caramelized Fennel and Sardines with Penne...............69

Cioppino 69

Green Goddess Crab Salad with Endive 70

Seared Scallops with Blood Orange Glaze.....................70

Air-Fryer Fish Cakes 70

Pesto Shrimp Pasta 71

Quick Shrimp Scampi 71

Poached Salmon with Creamy Piccata Sauce................72

Tuscan-Style Tuna Salad 72

Tuna Salad-Stuffed Tomatoes with Arugula 72

Herbed Seafood Casserole 73

Lemon Herb Baked Salmon 73

Baked Salmon Foil Packets with Vegetables 74

Lemon Garlic Shrimp 74

Shrimp Fra Diavolo 74

Fish Amandine..75

Baked Fish & Potatoes...75

Steamed Salmon Teriyaki 75

Easy Steamed Alaskan Cod 76

Dill and Lemon Cod Packets 76

Steamed Fish Mediterranean Style................................76

Coconut Curry Sea Bass 76

Stewed Cod Filet with Tomatoes 77

Lemony Parmesan Shrimps 77

Tuna and Carrots Casserole 77

Sweet-Ginger Scallops...77

Savory Lobster Roll 77

Garlic and Tomatoes on Mussels 78

Lemon Salmon with Kaffir Lime 78

Baked Fish Served with Vegetables................................78

Fish in A Vegetable Patch 79

Easy Shrimp..79

Steamed Blue Crabs...79

Steamed Veggie and Lemon Pepper Salmon 80

Steamed Fish with Scallions and Ginger........................80

Steamed Tilapia with Green Chutney 80

Creamy Haddock with Kale...80

Ginger Sesame Salmon 80

Sicilian Spaghetti with Tuna...81

CHAPTER 9: Poultry 82

Rosemary Roasted Chicken..82

Artichoke and Spinach Chicken 82

Pumpkin and Black Beans Chicken................................82

Chicken Thighs and Apples Mix 82

Thai Chicken Thighs 82

Falling "Off" The Bone Chicken 83

Feisty Chicken Porridge..83

The Ultimate Faux-Tisserie Chicken 83

Oregano Chicken Thighs...84

Pesto Chicken Breasts with Summer Squash..................84

Chicken, Tomato and Green Beans 84

Chicken Tortillas 84

Chicken with Potatoes Olives & Sprouts 84

Garlic Mushroom Chicken 85

Grilled Chicken 85

Delicious Lemon Chicken Salad 85

Healthy Chicken Orzo 85

Lemon Garlic Chicken 86

Baked Chicken 86

Garlic Pepper Chicken...86

Mustard Chicken Tenders..87

Salsa Chicken Chili 87

Honey Crusted Chicken...87

Paella with Chicken, Leeks, and Tarragon 87

Southwestern Chicken and Pasta 88

Parmesan and Chicken Spaghetti Squash 88

Apricot Chicken 88

Oven-Fried Chicken Breasts..88

Stuffed Chicken Breasts 89

Buffalo Chicken Salad Wrap...89

Chicken Sliders 89

White Chicken Chili...90

Sweet Potato-Turkey Meatloaf 90

Oaxacan Chicken...90

Spicy Chicken with Minty Couscous...............................91

Chicken, Pasta and Snow Peas 91

Chicken with Noodles 91

Teriyaki Chicken Wings..92

Hot Chicken Wings 92

Crispy Cashew Chicken 92

Chicken Tortellini Soup 93

Chicken Divan...93

Creamy Chicken Fried Rice 93

Chicken Tikka 94

Honey Spiced Cajun Chicken..94

Italian Chicken 94

Simple Mediterranean Chicken 95

Roasted Chicken Thighs..95

Mediterranean Turkey Breast..95

Olive Capers Chicken 95

Chicken with Mushrooms 96

Lemon-Parsley Chicken Breast.......................................96

CHAPTER 10: Vegetables 97

Moroccan-Inspired Tagine with Chickpeas & Vegetables 97

Roasted Brussels Sprouts.. 97

Broccoli with Garlic and Lemon 97

Brown Rice Pilaf... 98

Chunky Black-Bean Dip 98

Sweet Potato Rice with Spicy Peanut Sauce 98

Vegetable Red Curry 98

Black Bean Burgers 99

Summer Barley Pilaf with Yogurt Dill Sauce 99

Lentil Quinoa Gratin with Butternut Squash................... 100

Brown Rice Casserole with Cottage Cheese 100

Quinoa-Stuffed Peppers.. 100

Greek Flatbread with Spinach, Tomatoes & Feta............ 101

Mushroom Risotto with Peas 101

Loaded Tofu Burrito with Black Beans 102

Southwest Tofu Scramble.. 102

Black-Bean and Vegetable Burrito 102

Baked Eggs in Avocado 103

Red Beans and Rice 103

Hearty Lentil Soup.. 103

Black-Bean Soup... 104

Loaded Baked Sweet Potatoes 104

White Beans with Spinach and Pan-Roasted Tomatoes 104

Spaghetti Squash with Maple Glaze & Tofu Crumbles................. 104

Stuffed Tex-Mex Baked Potatoes 105

Lentil-Stuffed Zucchini Boats... 105

Baked Eggplant Parmesan 106

Black-Eyed Peas and Greens Power Salad....................... 106

Butternut-Squash Macaroni and Cheese 106

Pasta with Tomatoes and Peas 107

Healthy Vegetable Fried Rice 107

Portobello-Mushroom Cheeseburgers............................. 107

Baked Chickpe -And-Rosemary Omelet.......................... 108

Chilled Cucumber-And-Avocado Soup with Dill 108

Southwestern Bean-And-Pepper Salad 108

Cauliflower Mashed Potatoes.. 108

Classic Hummus.. 109

Crispy Potato Skins... 109

Roasted Chickpeas... 109

Carrot-Cake Smoothie 109

Vegetable Cheese Calzone... 110

Mixed Vegetarian Chili 110

Zucchini Pepper Kebabs 110

Asparagus Cheese Vermicelli 111

Corn Stuffed Peppers 111

Stuffed Eggplant Shells 111

Southwestern Vegetables Tacos 112

CHAPTER 11: Soups 113

Soup for The Day 113

Chipotle Squash Soup 113

Kale Verde 113

Escarole with Bean Soup 113

Chicken Squash Soup 114

Veggie and Beef Soup 114

Collard, Sweet Potato and Pea Soup 114

Bean Soup 115

Brown Rice and Chicken Soup 115

Broccoli Soup 115

Hearty Ginger Soup 116

Tasty Tofu and Mushroom Soup 116

Ingenious Eggplant Soup 116

Loving Cauliflower Soup 116

Garlic and Lemon Soup 117

Italian Wedding Soup 117

Taco Soup 117

Italian Sausage & Fennel Soup 117

Beef & Barley Soup 118

Cucumber Soup 118

Roasted Garlic Soup 118

Roasted Carrot Soup 118

Pumpkin Soup 119

Coconut Avocado Soup 119

Coconut Arugula Soup 119

Cabbage Soup 119

Ginger Zucchini Avocado Soup 119

Greek Lemon and Chicken Soup 120

Garlic and Pumpkin Soup 120

Golden Mushroom Soup..120

Minestrone 120

Butternut Squash Soup 121

Black Bean Soup 121

Chickpea & Kale Soup 121

Clam Chowder 122

Chicken & Rice Soup 122

Tom Kha Gai 122

Chicken Corn Chowder 122

Turkey Ginger Soup 123

Chicken and Tortilla Soup 123

Stuffed Pepper Soup 123

Ham and Pea Soup 123

Pea Soup 124

CHAPTER 12: Salads 125

Bean Salad with Orange Vinaigrette 125

Fresh Corn, Pepper, and Avocado Salad 125

Garlic Potato Salad 125

Creamy Low-Sodium Coleslaw 126

Southwestern Beet Slaw 126

Warm Kale Salad 126

Tabouleh Salad 127

Tart Apple Salad with Fennel and Honey Yogurt Dressing 127

Orchid Salad 127

Thai Pasta Salad 127

Whole-Wheat Couscous Salad with Citrus and Cilantro 128

Salad Niçoise 128

Simple Green Salad 129

Kale-Poppy Seed Salad 129

Edamame Salad with Corn and Cranberries 129

Warm Asian Slaw 130

Tangy Three-Bean Salad with Barley 130

Wedge Salad with Creamy Blue Cheese Dressing 130

Southwestern Bean Salad with Creamy Avocado Dressing 131

Cobb Pasta Salad 131

CHAPTER 13: Snacks...132

Mediterranean Pop Corn Bites 132

Hearty Buttery Walnuts 132

Refreshing Watermelon Sorbet 132

Garlic Cottage Cheese Crispy 132

Lemon Fat Bombs 132

Chocolate Coconut Bombs 133

Espresso Fat Bombs 133

Crispy Coconut Bombs 133

Pumpkin Pie Fat Bombs 133

Sweet Almond and Coconut Fat Bomb 133

Almond and Tomato Balls 133

Avocado Tuna Bites...134

Faux Mac and Cheese 134

Banana Custard...134

Healthy Tahini Buns 134

CHAPTER 14: Desserts...136

Chocolate Truffles 136

Grilled Pineapple Strips..136
Raspberry Peach Pancake...136
Mango Rice Pudding..137
Choco Banana Cake...137
Zesty Zucchini Muffins..137
Blueberry Oat Muffins...138
Banana Bread..138
Poached Pears...138
Pumpkin with Chia Seeds Pudding.............................139
Milk Chocolate Pudding..139
Minty Lime and Grapefruit Yogurt Parfait...................139
Peach Tarts..140
Raspberry Nuts Parfait..140
Strawberry Bruschetta...140
Vanilla Cupcakes with Cinnamon-Fudge Frosting.......140
Chocolate Cupcakes with Vanilla Frosting...................141
Chocolate Chip Banana Muffin Top Cookies...............141
Lemon Cookies 142
Peanut Butter Chocolate Chip Blondies 142
Ginger Snaps...142
Carrot Cake Cookies 143
Chewy Pumpkin Oatmeal Raisin Cookies 143
Easy Apple Crisp...143
Mango Crumble...144
Homemade Banana Ice Cream 144
Vegan Rice Pudding...144
Beetroot and Berry Smoothie 144
Berry Blast 145
Oats and Fruit Bar Cracker...145
Colorful Pops...145
Pumpkin Pie Recipe 145
Walnut and Oatmeal Chocolate Chip Cookies............146
Apple Dumplings 146
Berries Marinated in Balsamic Vinegar.......................147
Lemon Pudding Cakes...147
Mixed Berry Whole-Grain Coffee Cake.......................147
Strawberries and Cream Cheese Crepes 147
Healthy Blueberry & Banana Muffins...........................148

Tart Raspberry Crumble Bar.......................................148
Easy Strawberry Sheet Cake......................................148
Easy Coconut-Carrot Cake Balls 149
Banana Delight..149
Healthy Banana-Choco Ice Cream..............................149
Healthy Chocolate Mousse 150
Almond Rice Pudding...150
Apples and Cream Shake..150
Baked Stuffed Apples 150
Carrot-Cake Smoothie...150
Easy Cinnamon Baked Apples.....................................151
Chocolate Cake in A Mug..151
Peanut Butter Banana "Ice Cream".............................151
Banana-Cashew Cream Mousse..................................152
Grilled Plums with Vanilla Bean Frozen Yogurt 152
Key Lime Cherry "Nice" Cream....................................152
Oatmeal Dark Chocolate Chip Peanut Butter Cookies.................152
Peach Crumble Muffins 153
Karen's Apple Kugel..153
Peach Cobbler...154
Blueberry Pudding Cake..154
Peanut Butter Banana Bread Bites 154
Toasted Almond Ambrosia 155
Apricot Biscotti..155
Apple & Berry Cobbler..156
Mixed Fruit Compote Cups..156

28-Day Meal Plan – Average Calories: 1074 157

Appendix 1   Measurement Conversion Chart........... 159

Appendix 2   Dirty Dozen and Clean Fifteen 160

Appendix 3   Index 161

Introduction

In the mid-1990s, dietary approaches to stop hypertension (DASH) was designed to lower blood pressure through a healthy diet, not a drug. Scientists have been studying the effect of diet on blood pressure for some time. The time has come to put this knowledge into practice. The researchers also observed that diets rich in calcium and potassium and, to a lesser extent, magnesium had helped lower blood pressure. Logically, it seemed that taking these dietary supplements would lower blood pressure.

Much research has been done, but unfortunately, most showed little or no benefit from calcium, potassium, or magnesium supplements, so the approach went back to the diet. As we have seen, it has been observed that, in general, vegetarians living in the United States had lower blood pressure and lower heart disease mortality rates than people who consumed a more traditional western diet. But few Americans would be willing to give up meat, even if it meant reducing the risk of a heart attack.

Frustrated by the inability of supplements to provide an easy solution for hypertension, the researchers decided to create a diet rich in foods that contain these nutrients. The menu was rich in plant foods such as fruits, vegetables, beans, nuts, seeds, mainly whole grains, and heart-healthy oils. Low-fat dairy products were an essential part of the diet, as were limited quantities of lean meat, poultry, and fish. It was based on the knowledge acquired in vegetarian diets. The first research on the DASH diet was published in 1997. It is a study that aimed to evaluate the effect of the dietary pattern on blood pressure, and it did it very effectively.

The DASH diet reduced blood pressure and first-line medications in just fourteen days. Surprisingly, the rise in blood pressure occurred even though researchers did not allow participants to lose weight. It contained many carbohydrates, mainly to prevent weight loss because if the participants had also lost weight, the researchers would not have known if weight loss or diet would have been helpful. As reported and stated by the New England Journal of Medicine: "DASH is particularly effective in people with hypertension (variation of SBP and DBP: -10.7- and -4.7-mm Hg, respectively)." 8 In the late 1980s and 1990s, most heart specialists, recommended replacing saturated fat. (SFA) with so-called complex carbohydrates.

Another study (Omni-Heart) was conducted to evaluate whether the results of measuring blood pressure in the DASH diet would be better if, instead of replacing SFA with carbohydrates (particularly refined), SFAs were replaced with monounsaturated fats (MUFA) or protein. And actually, they have seen better results. 9, 10 both approaches reduced total cholesterol, but MUFA did not increase triglycerides (TG) or "good" cholesterol (HDL). Maintaining a higher HDL value and a lower TG is very beneficial for heart health. It is a vital sign that you are successfully managing or reducing the risk of metabolic syndrome. A particular advantage was that appetite seemed to be much easier to control. Instead of needing drugs with very unwanted side effects, participants can have very positive "side effects." Wouldn't you like to check your blood pressure with food instead of medications? Have you ever heard of the DASH diet before reading this book? Many people don't. So why isn't DASH adoption universal? Why didn't it explode?

Most educational material, including the National Heart, Lung, and Blood Institute (NHLBI), makes monitoring DASH difficult. Based on the complex information in this literature, many doctors believed that it would be tough for patients to follow them, so they did not. Don't even bother to recommend; what a pity! We thought this food model was too important to be a research curiosity. We made this cookbook about the Dash diet to show people how easy it is to take a life formula. And it worked. People have found that they can continue with this and that their health has improved significantly. So, let's follow the latest DASH improvements and include all the recipes here to make it the best plan in the world! And the best flavor!

CHAPTER 1:

The Dietary Approach to Stop Hypertension (DASH) Basics

Unlike the regular diets out there, DASH is a tad bit different. It means Dietary Approaches to Stop Hypertension. Yes, you read that right. Finally, a diet that focuses on one of the greatest killers of the 21st century- hypertension. According to recent studies, one out of three adults suffers from hypertension or high blood pressure. It keeps increasing with age, with almost two-thirds of the population suffering from it from the age of 65. High blood pressure is not a single stroke disease- it brings heart trouble, kidney diseases, and even diabetes.

Our sedentary lifestyles, coupled with unhealthy eating habits, have fueled several hypertension-related diseases. Most can be corrected by following a healthy diet, which is what DASH aims at. This diet comprises foods and recipes that promote lower sodium levels and higher potassium, calcium, fiber, and magnesium levels in the body. It also helps lower the overall blood pressure to an optimum level without harming the body processes. When this happens, disorders related to hypertension disappear, such as osteoporosis, diabetes, and kidney failure.

The original diet plan aimed to lower blood pressure through natural foods and without medication aid. It was sponsored and endorsed by the US National Institute of Health. When the trials of the first DASH diet came out, it was found that lowering the blood pressure helped maintain the level even with some excess sodium in the blood. Not only this, but the diet was also found to be beneficial in keeping the extra pounds off and prevent many disorders related to hypertension.

Who Should Follow This Diet?

Is the diet for me? Or is it only for people with existing hypertension

problems? According to the Dietary Guidelines for Americans, the DASH diet is a healthy eating model that anyone can follow. Of course, since the diet's primary objective is to lower blood pressure, people suffering from hypertension become the primary beneficiaries of the diet. But anyone who wishes to get healthy and scientifically lose weight can follow it, children included.

This diet works while other diets fail miserably because the body is kept full with the required nutrition. The fundamental nutrients, such as calcium, magnesium, and potassium, are elevated in the body through a wholesome diet plan, and sodium levels are also kept in control. And it is all done in a controlled, scientific, and disciplined manner without any crashes or spikes in the metabolism, ensuring a healthier you.

The Improved DASH Diet Plan

When research into diet plans for hypertension began, they did not focus too much on weight loss. They were more concerned with getting the blood pressure levels regulated. But soon, the researchers realized that healthy weight loss was the need of the hour, and therefore there were an additional need to create a systematic weight loss plan and reduced blood pressure levels. So, after a lot of deliberation, the DASH diet for weight loss was also formulated, including nuts, cereals, whole fruits and vegetables, and seeds.

Unlike other flyby diets, which are more word of mouth than scientific, the DASH diet is primarily based on scientific principles of good health. The research on DASH diets indicates that it is not merely a tool for reducing your blood pressure by eating a low sodium diet. The plan is designed for each person, keeping their specific needs in mind, and comprises wholesome foods, such as fruits, vegetables, grains, fresh produce, etc. which keeps the body in fighting fit condition. Top rung research institutes such as the American Heart Association, Dietary Guidelines for Americans, the National Heart, Lung, and Blood Institute- all endorse this diet plan.

Several more corroborating research reports after, the DASH diet was further improved to optimize health and reduce hypertension by increasing the protein intake and cutting down on empty carbs and bad fats. The DASH diet's primary hypothesis is based on sound scientific principles of attainable and sustainable weight loss. The meals and snacks prescribed in the diet plan comprise bulky, fibrous foods, which keep you filled for hours and do not let

you snack mindlessly. They are designed to keep your blood sugar levels regulated, instead of the spike and crash cycles, as seen with other diets. By following this diet, you keep your blood sugar levels on an even keel, defeat other diseases like diabetes, reduce your triglycerides, melt your stubborn belly fat, lower your LDL, improve your HDL numbers, and generally feel healthier on average. Of course, a significant portion of the diet is protein- rich, so you build your muscle and lose body fat, and in the process, you avoid slowing your metabolism, which aids in sustaining your current weight.

Even if you're is not suffering from hypertension, you can adopt the DASH diet to keep your internal systems healthy and robust. In this part of your journey, you will learn how you can make this diet work for you.

Rome wasn't built in a day. Similarly, your body will not take too kindly to change if you do it suddenly. It will protest, and you will soon return to square one. To avoid that discomfort, take baby steps. Do not jump into the diet headlong. Try the meal plan for two days a week, then increase it to three times, and when you are comfortable with it, adopt it ultimately. You might already be eating some DASH diet foods and snacks and not be aware of it. Make a list and see which food items correspond to the diet's meal plan. And do not be under the impression that the DASH diet goes for a toss while dining out. There are plenty of options and strategies you can adopt while eating out. You need to be careful and select healthy choices.

Beginning the DASH Diet

Now that you are supplied with the necessary background information on the DASH diet let us see first what it entails. This meal plan is rich in vegetables, fruits, dairy products, whole grains, lean meats, poultry, fish, and legumes such as peas and beans. Additionally, it contains low fat from natural sources and high fiber from sweet potatoes, cabbage, and leafy vegetables. It adheres to the US guidelines about the sodium and potassium content. It is a flexible eating plan designed to meet the needs of a variety of people and keeps in mind their food preferences. There is a healthy alternative to almost any kind of food craving. It is what a typical DASH diet comprises:

Type of Food	Number of servings (1600-3000 calorie plan)	Number of servings (1500-2000 calorie plan)
Whole grains or meals made out of whole grains	6-12	7-9
Fresh fruits (not fruit juice)	4-5	4-6
Farm fresh vegetables (try avoiding store bought ones)	4-6	4-6
Dairy products (low fat)	3-4	2-4
Poultry, fish, lean meats	2-3	3-4
Legumes, seeds and nuts	3-5	4-5
Desserts, natural fats	2-3	2

CHAPTER 2:

Benefits of Dash Diet

Although you're likely to go for the DASH diet because of a slimmer waist and better health, there are more reasons to consider the DASH diet. They include the following:

Weight Loss

DASH advocates for much less fat than you'd find in a typical American diet. It means that it's lower in calories. This diet eliminates and reduces unhealthy fats, fast food, fried foods, as well as foods that are highly processed. Instead, it emphasizes healthy fats like saturated fats and healthy saturated fats like omega 3 fats that are good for your body and help weight loss. These are mostly present in foods with lower calories. The high fiber content in most of the foods recommended under the DASH diet is another great contributor to weight loss because fibers help you have a feeling of satiety while also aiding digestion so your body can eliminate wastes while slowing down the absorption of sugar and fat. It promotes efficient regulation and response to insulin, limiting the risk of and symptoms of metabolic syndrome.

The high absorption or consumption of fresh vegetables and fruits translates to high vitamin c and antioxidants levels. Vitamin C is instrumental in reducing the stress that reduces the amount of stress hormone, cortisol, produced. This hormone is also responsible for the storage of fat in the area around the abdomen. Therefore, what you eat will not be stored as fat in your abdomen. Additionally, vitamin C is a building block of L-carnitine that is instrumental in the transportation of fat. When your body receives a signal or cue that you no longer need the fat, it is turned to glucose for use as energy. The body needs sufficient amounts of vitamin C to make L-carnitine naturally. It means you need to consume vitamin C daily to contribute to weight loss because the primary role of vitamin C is fighting infection and rebuilding damaged cells.

The DASH diet also advocates for caloric intake that differs from one person to another, considering your weight loss goals, current weight, body shape,

and activity level. This diet avoids consuming very few calories that eventually puts you at risk of losing lean muscle tissue instead of fat while ensuring you're getting enough nutrients to support your level of activity.

Heart Disease

When you have a combination of high blood pressure, metabolic syndrome, and type 2 diabetes, you're likely to end up with heart disease. The fact that the DASH diet addresses all these conditions means that it can also eliminate your risk of heart disease. This diet is an excellent option even when you're not already experiencing any of these conditions. Heart disease records the most significant number of deaths among Americans. Health professionals recommend a diet low in unhealthy fats and high in healthy fats, and fiber will positively influence your heart health. The American Heart Association recommends DASH because it's a heart-healthy diet. Apart from improved heart health, this diet also reduces the risk of developing kidney stones and improving colon and digestive health.

Metabolic Syndrome

The term metabolic syndrome is used for a group of symptoms associated with insulin and obesity. This syndrome is sometimes known as pre-diabetes because when not checked, it results in type 2 diabetes. Some of the typical metabolic syndrome markers include high blood sugar, large waist size, elevated HDL, and high triglycerides. The DASH diet can eliminate these unwanted symptoms. The DASH diet consists of reduced amounts of bad fats and an increase in the consumption of good fats and fiber, helping lower triglyceride levels and HDL cholesterol. The nutrients you obtain from the DASH diet with the fat loss you experience around the abdomen, account for a significant reduction in metabolic syndrome, helping you experience optimal health.

Type 2 Diabetes

The DASH diet was rated as the best diet or battling Type 2 diabetes and for anyone facing the risk of developing diabetes by the U.S. News and World Report. It has been demonstrated that this diet is capable of lessening the symptoms and the severity of diabetes significantly. In some cases, the dietary change associated with this diet has helped in reversing the condition. The reason behind this is simple. The foods incorporated into the DASH diet help in improving the health of people who have diabetes. For instance, nuts help controlling glucose in people with diabetes. Simultaneously, the high fiber content will slow down the absorption of sugar, which helps prevent blood sugar levels. All the vegetables and fruits in the DASH diet are packed with antioxidants that help prevent and reduce or lower complications related to Type 2 diabetes. The DASH diet can also help reduce type 2 diabetes by promoting weight loss, especially abdominal fat, that triggers insulin insensitivity.

Controlled Blood Pressure

It is the main benefit of the DASH diet and the reason why nutritionists and physicians recommend it. Following DASH lets you keep your blood pressure in check. This diet is ideal for anyone who is taking medication to control blood pressure and those with prehypertension symptoms and are looking for better ways of managing these symptoms. DASH is specially designed to help tame blood pressure and has been scientifically proven to work.

Healthy Eating

Let's face it. One of the grounds or reasons why most people experience high blood pressure is that being overweight or obese is associated with poor eating choices. Following the DASH diet helps you make a lifestyle change to healthy eating. Thus, you will be spending more time in the kitchen preparing fresh food instead of grabbing processed food on the go. You will also enjoy your mealtimes because your plate will be filled with more nutritious foods. DASH also stretches you a little to try out new vegetables and fruits and experiment with various seasonings that are salt-free to create meals that you will enjoy.

Reduced Risk of Osteoporosis

The majority of dietary approaches to preventing and treating osteoporosis include increasing your intake of calcium and vitamin D that is found in abundance in foods recommended for the DASH diet. It, coupled with reduced sodium intake, is proof that the DASH diet is quite beneficial for bone health. Some studies found a notable decline in bone turnover for people who followed the DASH diet. When sustained over a more extended period, the DASH diet is instrumental in improving bone mineral status. Other nutrients in abundance in the DASH diet and are excellent at promoting bone health over time include vitamin C, antioxidants,

magnesium, and polyphenols.

Healthy Cholesterol Levels

Since most of the fruits, beans, nuts, whole grains, and vegetables recommended under the DASH diet have high fiber content, you can eat them alongside fish and lean meat while limiting or regulating your intake of refined carbohydrates and sweets. It goes a long way in improving your cholesterol levels.

Healthier Kidneys

The DASH diet lowers the risk for kidney stones and kidney disease because of the abundance of magnesium, potassium, calcium, and fiber present in the foods encouraged. The focus on reducing sodium intake is also an advantage if you face developing kidney disease. Even then, the DASH diet should be restricted to patients who have chronic kidney disease and those undergoing dialysis without close guidance of qualified health care professionals.

Decreased Risk of Certain Cancers

Researchers have studied the relationship between the DASH diet and certain types of cancers and found a positive association that relates to reducing salt intake and monitoring dietary fat consumption. The diet is also low in red meant that it is linked to cancer of the rectum, colon, esophagus, lung, stomach, kidney, and prostate. Eating plenty of fresh produce helps prevent various cancers while emphasizing dairy products that are low in fat contributes to a drop in the risk of colon cancer.

Better Mental Health

The DASH diet will boost your mood while decreasing symptoms of mental health disorders like anxiety or depression. It is associated with various lifestyle changes that include avoiding cigarettes, moderating alcohol consumption, and exercising regularly. Moreover, the inclusion of nutrient- rich foods in the diet also helps balance hormones and chemicals in the brain and body, thus contributing to improved mental health and overall well- being.

Anti-Aging Properties

Many people who follow the DASH diet have attested to the fact that this diet helps avoid some effects of aging so that they keep them feeling and looking younger. Increasing your consumption of fresh vegetables and fruits that are

full of antioxidants will rejuvenate your hair and skin, revitalize and strengthen your joints, muscles, and bones, help you lose weight, and leave you feeling healthier.

Reduced Risk of Developing Heart Disease

The DASH diet's ability to keep your blood pressure in check is instrumental in strengthening the body's resistance to heart disease. According to a 2010 study, DASH can substantially lower the risk of heart disease. It is particularly remarkable given the persistent and enormous burden of coronary heart disease. It is attributed to the fact that lowered blood pressure lets the heart function efficiently and effectively. Moreover, it can also be beneficial for those who are not struggling with hypertension but are keen on preventing the onset of heart disease.

CHAPTER 3: Breakfast

Spinach, Egg, And Cheese Breakfast Quesadillas

Preparation time: 15 minutes Cooking time: 15 minutes Servings: 4

Ingredients:

- 1½ tablespoons extra-virgin olive oil
- ½ medium onion, diced
- 1 medium red bell pepper, diced 4 large eggs
- 1/8 teaspoon salt
- 1/8 teaspoon freshly ground black pepper 4 cups baby spinach
- ½ cup crumbled feta cheese Nonstick cooking spray
- 4 (6-inch) whole-wheat tortillas, divided 1 cup shredded part-skim low-moisture mozzarella cheese, divided

Directions:

Warm-up oil over medium heat in a large skillet. Add the onion and bell pepper and sauté for about 5 minutes, or until soft.

1. Mix the eggs, salt, and black pepper in a medium bowl. Stir in the spinach and feta cheese. Put the egg batter in the skillet and scramble for about 2 minutes, or until the eggs are cooked. Remove from the heat.

2. Coat a clean skillet with cooking spray and add 2 tortillas. Place one- quarter of the spinach-egg mixture on one side of each tortilla. Sprinkle each with ¼ cup of mozzarella cheese. Fold the other halves of the tortillas down to close the quesadillas and brown for about 1 minute.

3. Turnover and cook again in a minute on the other side. Repeat with the remaining 2 tortillas and ½ cup of mozzarella cheese. Cut each quesadilla in half or wedges. Divide among 4 storage containers or reusable bags.

Nutrition: Calories: 453 Fat: 28g
Carbohydrates: 28g Fiber: 4.5g
Protein: 23g Potassium: 205mg Sodium: 837mg

Apple Pancakes

Preparation time: 15 minutes Cooking time: 5 minutes Servings: 16

Ingredients:

- ¼ cup extra-virgin olive oil, divided 1 cup whole wheat flour
- 2 teaspoons baking powder
- 1 teaspoon baking soda
- teaspoon ground cinnamon 1 cup 1% milk
- large eggs
- medium Gala apple, diced 2 tablespoons maple syrup
- ¼ cup chopped walnuts

Directions:

1. Set aside 1 teaspoon of oil to use for greasing a griddle or skillet. In a large bowl, stir the flour, baking powder, baking soda, cinnamon, milk, eggs, apple, and the remaining oil.

2. Warm griddle or skillet on medium-high heat and coat with the reserved oil. Working in batches, pour in about ¼ cup of the batter for each pancake. Cook until browned on both sides.

3. Place 4 pancakes into each of 4 medium storage containers and the maple syrup in 4 small containers. Put each serving with 1 tablespoon of walnuts and drizzle with ½ tablespoon of maple syrup.

Nutrition: Calories: 378 Fat: 22g
Carbohydrates: 39g
Protein: 10g Sodium: 65mg

Super-Simple Granola

Preparation time: 15 minutes Cooking time: 25 minutes Servings: 8

Ingredients:

- ¼ cup extra-virgin olive oil
- ¼ cup honey
- ½ teaspoon ground cinnamon
- ½ teaspoon vanilla extract
- ¼ teaspoon salt
- cups rolled oats
- ½ cup chopped walnuts

½ cup slivered almonds
Directions:

1. Preheat the oven to 350°F. Mix the oil, honey, cinnamon, vanilla, and salt in a large bowl. Add the oats, walnuts, and almonds. Stir to coat. Put the batter out onto the prepared sheet pan. Bake for 20 minutes. Let cool.

Nutrition: Calories: 254 Fat: 16g
Carbohydrates: 25g Fiber: 3.5g
Protein: 5g Potassium: 163mg Sodium: 73mg

Savory Yogurt Bowls

Preparation time: 15 minutes Cooking time: 0 minutes Servings:4

Ingredients:
- 1 medium cucumber, diced
- ½ cup pitted Kalamata olives, halved 2 tablespoons fresh lemon juice
- tablespoon extra-virgin olive oil 1 teaspoon dried oregano
- ¼ teaspoon freshly ground black pepper
- cups nonfat plain Greek yogurt
- ½ cup slivered almonds

Directions:
1. In a small bowl, mix the cucumber, olives, lemon juice, oil, oregano, and pepper. Divide the yogurt evenly among 4 storage containers. Top with the cucumber-olive mix and almonds.

Nutrition: Calories: 240 Fat: 16g
Carbohydrates: 10g Protein: 16g Potassium: 353mg
Sodium: 350mg

Energy Sunrise Muffins

Preparation time: 15 minutes Cooking time: 25 minutes Servings: 16

Ingredients:
- Nonstick cooking spray 2 cups whole wheat flour 2 teaspoons baking soda
- teaspoons ground cinnamon 1 teaspoon ground ginger
- ¼ teaspoon salt
- large eggs
- ½ cup packed brown sugar
- 1/3 cup unsweetened applesauce
- ¼ cup honey
- ¼ cup vegetable or canola oil 1 teaspoon grated orange zest Juice of 1 medium orange
- 2 teaspoons vanilla extract 2 cups shredded carrots
- 1 large apple, peeled and grated

- ½ cup golden raisins
- ½ cup chopped pecans
- ½ cup unsweetened coconut flakes

Directions:
1. If you can fit two 12-cup muffin tins side by side in your oven, then leave a rack in the middle, then preheat the oven to 350°F.

2. Coat 16 cups of the muffin tins with cooking spray or line with paper liners. Mix the flour, baking soda, cinnamon, ginger, and salt in a large bowl. Set aside.

3. Mix the eggs, brown sugar, applesauce, honey, oil, orange zest, orange juice, and vanilla until combined in a medium bowl. Add the carrots and apple and whisk again.

4. Mix the dry and wet ingredients with a spatula. Fold in the raisins, pecans, and coconut. Mix everything once again, just until well combined. Put the batter into the prepared muffin cups, filling them to the top.

5. Bake within 20 to 25 minutes, or until a wooden toothpick inserted into the middle of the center muffin comes out clean (switching racks halfway through if baking on 2 racks). Cool for 5 minutes in the tins, then transfers to a wire rack to cool for an additional 5 minutes. Cool completely before storing in containers.

Nutrition: Calories: 292 Fat: 14g
Carbohydrates: 42g Protein: 5g Sodium: 84mg

Simple Cheese and Broccoli Omelets

Preparation time: 15 minutes Cooking time: 10 minutes Servings: 4
Ingredients:
- 3 tablespoons extra-virgin olive oil, divided 2 cups chopped broccoli
- 8 large eggs
- ¼ cup 1% milk
- ½ teaspoon freshly ground black pepper
- 8 tablespoons shredded reduced-fat Monterey Jack cheese, divided

Directions:
1. In a nonstick skillet, heat 1 tablespoon of oil over medium-high heat. Add the broccoli and sauté, occasionally stirring,

for 3 to 5 minutes, or until the broccoli turns bright green. Scrape into a bowl.Mix the eggs, milk, plus pepper in a small bowl. Wipe out the skillet and heat ½ tablespoon of oil. Add one-quarter of the egg mixture and tilt the skillet to ensure an even layer. Cook for 2 minutes and then add 2 tablespoons of cheese and one-quarter of the broccoli. Use a spatula to fold into an omelet.

2. Repeat step 3 with the remaining 1½ tablespoons of oil, remaining egg mixture, 6 tablespoons of cheese, and remaining broccoli to make a total of 4 omelets. Divide into 4 storage containers.

Nutrition: Calories: 292 Fat: 23g
Carbohydrates: 4g Fiber: 1g
Protein: 18g Potassium: 308mg
Sodium: 282mg

Creamy Avocado and Egg Salad Sandwiches

Preparation time: 15 minutes Cooking time: 15 minutes Servings: 4
Ingredients:
- 2 small avocados, halved and pitted
- 2 tablespoons nonfat plain Greek yogurt Juice of 1 large lemon
- ¼ teaspoon salt
- ½ teaspoon freshly ground black pepper
- 8 large eggs, hardboiled, peeled, and chopped 3 tablespoons finely chopped fresh dill
- 3 tablespoons finely chopped fresh parsley 8 whole wheat bread slices (or your choice)

Directions:

1. Scoop the avocados into a large bowl and mash. Mix in the yogurt, lemon juice, salt, and pepper. Add the eggs, dill, and parsley and combine.

2. Store the bread and salad separately in 4 reusable storage bags and 4 containers and assemble the night before or serving. To serve, divide the mixture evenly among 4 of the bread slices and top with the other slices to make sandwiches.

Nutrition: Calories: 488 Fat: 22g
Carbohydrates: 48g Fiber: 8g
Protein: 23g Potassium: 469mg
Sodium: 597mg

Blueberry Waffles

Preparation time: 15 minutes Cooking time: 15 minutes Servings: 8

Ingredients:
- 2 cups whole wheat flour
- tablespoon baking powder 1 teaspoon ground cinnamon 2 tablespoons sugar
- large eggs
- tablespoons unsalted butter, melted
- 3 tablespoons nonfat plain Greek yogurt 1½ cups 1% milk
- 2 teaspoons vanilla extract
- 4 ounces blueberries Nonstick cooking spray
- ½ cup maple almond butter

Directions:

1. Preheat waffle iron. Mix the flour, baking powder, cinnamon, plus sugar in a large bowl. Mix the eggs, melted butter, yogurt, milk, and vanilla in a small bowl. Combine well.

2. Put the wet fixing to the dry mix and whisk until well combined. Do not over whisk; it's okay if the mixture has some lumps. Fold in the blueberries.

3. Oiled the waffle iron with cooking spray, then cook 1/3 cup of the batter until the waffles are lightly browned and slightly crisp. Repeat with the rest of the batter.

4. Place 2 waffles in each of 4 storage containers. Store the almond butter in 4 condiment cups. To serve, top each warm waffle with 1 tablespoon of maple almond butter.

Nutrition: Calories: 647 Fat: 37g
Carbohydrates: 67g Protein: 22g Sodium: 156mg

Breakfast Hash

Preparation time: 15 minutes Cooking time: 25 minutes Servings: 4
Ingredients:
- Nonstick cooking spray
- 2 large sweet potatoes, ½-inch cubes 1 scallion, finely chopped
- ¼ teaspoon salt
- ½ teaspoon freshly ground black pepper
- 8 ounces extra-lean ground beef (96% or leaner) 1 medium onion, diced

- 2 garlic cloves, minced 1 red bell pepper, diced
- ¼ teaspoon ground cumin
- ¼ teaspoon paprika
- 2 cups coarsely chopped kale leaves
- ¾ cup shredded reduced-fat Cheddar cheese 4 large eggs

Directions:

1. Oiled a large skillet with cooking spray and heat over medium heat. Add the sweet potatoes, scallion, salt, and pepper. Sauté for 10 minutes, stirring often.

2. Add the beef, onion, garlic, bell pepper, cumin, and paprika. Sauté, frequently stirring, for about 4 minutes, or until the meat browns. Add the kale to the skillet and stir until wilted. Sprinkle with the Cheddar cheese.

3. Make four wells in the hash batter and crack an egg into each. Cover and let the eggs cook until the white is fully cooked and the yolk is to your liking. Divide into 4 storage containers.

Nutrition: Calories: 323 Fat: 15g
Carbohydrates: 23g Fiber: 4g
Protein: 25g Potassium: 676mg Sodium: 587mg

Hearty Breakfast Casserole

Preparation time: 15 minutes Cooking time: 30 minutes Servings: 4

Ingredients:
- Nonstick cooking spray
- 1 large green bell pepper, diced
- 8 ounces cremini mushrooms, diced
- ½ medium onion, diced 3 garlic cloves, minced
- 1 large sweet potato, grated
- 1 cup baby spinach 12 large eggs
- 3 tablespoons 1% milk
- 1 teaspoon mustard powder 1 teaspoon paprika
- 1 teaspoon freshly ground black pepper
- ½ teaspoon salt
- ½ cup shredded reduced-fat Colby-Jack cheese

Directions:

1. Preheat the oven to 350°F. Oiled at a 9- by-13-inch baking dish with cooking spray. Coat a large skillet with cooking spray and heat over medium heat. Add the bell pepper, mushrooms, onion, garlic, and sweet potato.

2. Sauté, frequently stirring, for 3 to 4 minutes, or until the onion is translucent. Add the spinach and continue to sauté while stirring, until the spinach has wilted. Remove, then set aside to cool slightly.

3. Mix the eggs, milk, mustard powder, paprika, black pepper, and salt in a large bowl. Add the sautéed vegetables. Put the batter into the prepared baking dish.

4. Bake for 30 minutes. Remove from the oven, sprinkle with the Colby- Jack cheese, return to the oven, and bake again within 5 minutes to melt the cheese. Divide into 4 storage containers.

Nutrition: Calories: 378 Fat: 25g
Carbohydrates: 17g
Fiber: 3g Protein: 26g
Potassium: 717mg
Sodium: 658mg

Sweet Potato Toast Three Ways

Preparation time: 15 minutes Cooking time:2 5 minutes Servings:
Ingredients:
- 1 large sweet potato, unpeeled Topping Choice #1:
- 4 tablespoons peanut butter
- 1 ripe banana, sliced Dash ground cinnamon Topping Choice #2:
- ½ avocado, peeled, pitted, and mashed 2 eggs (1 per slice)
- Topping Choice #3:
- 4 tablespoons nonfat or low-fat ricotta cheese 1 tomato, sliced
- Dash black pepper

Directions:

1. Slice the sweet potato lengthwise into ¼-inch thick slices. Place the sweet potato slices in a toaster on high for about 5 minutes or until cooked through.

2. Repeat multiple times, if necessary, depending on your toaster settings. Top with your desired topping choices and

enjoy.
Nutrition: Calories: 137 Fat: 0g Sodium: 17mg
Potassium: 265mg
Carbohydrates: 32g Fiber: 4g
Sugars: 0g
Protein: 2g

Creamy Apple-Avocado Smoothie

Preparation time: 15 minutes Cooking time: 0
minutes Servings: 2
Ingredients:

- ½ medium avocado, peeled and pitted 1
  medium apple, chopped
- 1 cup baby spinach leaves
- 1 cup nonfat vanilla Greek yogurt
- ½ to 1 cup of water 1 cup ice
- Freshly squeezed lemon juice (optional)

Directions:

1. Blend all of the fixing using a blender, and
   blend until smooth and creamy. Put a
   squeeze of lemon juice on top if desired,
   and serve immediately.

Nutrition: Calories: 200 Fat: 7g Sodium: 56mg
Potassium: 378mg Carbohydrates: 27g Fiber: 5g
Sugars: 20g Protein: 10g

Strawberry, Orange, and Beet Smoothie

Preparation time: 5 minutes Cooking time: 0
minutes Servings: 2
Ingredients:

- 1 cup nonfat milk
- 1 cup of frozen strawberries
- 1 medium beet, cooked, peeled, and cubed
  1 orange, peeled and quartered
- 1 frozen banana, peeled and chopped 1 cup
  nonfat vanilla Greek yogurt
- 1 cup ice

Directions:
1.   In a blender, combine all of the fixings,
and blend until smooth. Serve immediately.
Nutrition: Calories: 266 Fat: 0g Cholesterol: 7mg
Sodium: 104mg
Carbohydrates: 51g
Fiber: 6g Sugars: 34g Protein: 15g

Blueberry-Vanilla Yogurt Smoothie

Preparation time: 5 minutes Cooking time: 0
minutes Servings: 2
Ingredients:

- 1½ cups frozen blueberries
- 1 cup nonfat vanilla Greek yogurt 1 frozen

banana, peeled and sliced
- ½ cup nonfat or low-fat milk 1 cup ice

Directions:
1.   In a blender, combine all of the fixing
listed, and blend until smooth and creamy. Serve
immediately.
Nutrition: Calories: 228 Fat: 1g Sodium: 63mg
Potassium: 470mg Carbohydrates: 45g Fiber: 5g
Sugars: 34g
Protein: 12g

Creamy Oats, Greens & Blueberry Smoothie

Preparation time: 4 minutes Cooking time: 0
minutes Servings: 1
Ingredients:

- 1 c. cold
- Fat-free milk
- c. salad greens
- ½ c. fresh frozen blueberries
- ½ c. frozen cooked oatmeal 1 tbsp.
  sunflower seeds

Directions:
1.   Blend all ingredients using a powerful
blender until smooth and creamy. Serve and enjoy.
Nutrition: Calories: 280 Fat:6.8 g Carbs:44.0 g
Protein:14.0 g Sugars:32 g Sodium:141 mg

Banana & Cinnamon Oatmeal

Preparation time: 5 minutes Cooking time: 0
minutes Servings: 6
Ingredients:

- c. quick-cooking oats 4 c. Fat-free milk
- tsp. ground cinnamon
- chopped large ripe banana 4 tsp. Brown
  sugar
- Extra ground cinnamon

Directions:

1. Place milk in a skillet and bring to boil.
   Add oats and cook over medium heat until
   thickened, for two to four minutes.

2. Stir intermittently. Add cinnamon, brown
   sugar, and banana and stir to combine. If
   you want, serve with the extra cinnamon
   and milk.   Enjoy!

Nutrition: Calories: 215 Fat:2 g Carbs:42 g
Protein:10 g Sugars:1 g Sodium:40 mg

Bagels Made Healthy

Greek Yogurt Oat Pancakes

Preparation time: 15 minutes Cooking time: 10 minutes Servings: 2
Ingredients:

- 6 egg whites (or ¾ cup liquid egg whites) 1 cup rolled oats
- 1 cup plain nonfat Greek yogurt
- 1 medium banana, peeled and sliced 1 teaspoon ground cinnamon
- teaspoon baking powder

Directions:

1. Blend all of the listed fixing using a blender. Warm a griddle over medium heat. Spray the skillet with nonstick cooking spray.

2. Put 1/3 cup of the mixture or batter onto the griddle. Allow to cook and flip when bubbles on the top burst, about 5 minutes. Cook again within a minute until golden brown. Repeat with the remaining batter. Divide between two serving plates and enjoy.

Nutrition: Calories: 318 Fat: 4g Sodium: 467mg Potassium: 634mg Carbohydrates: 47g Fiber: 6g Sugars: 13g Protein: 28g

Scrambled Egg and Veggie Breakfast Quesadillas

Preparation time: 15 minutes Cooking time: 15 minutes Servings: 2
Ingredients:

- eggs
- 2 egg whites
- 2 to 4 tablespoons nonfat or low-fat milk
- ¼ teaspoon freshly ground black pepper 1 large tomato, chopped
- 2 tablespoons chopped cilantro
- ½ cup canned black beans, rinsed and drained 1½ tablespoons olive oil, divided
- 4 corn tortillas
- ½ avocado, peeled, pitted, and thinly sliced

Directions:

1. Mix the eggs, egg whites, milk, and black pepper in a bowl. Using an

2. electric mixer, beat until smooth. To the same bowl, add the tomato, cilantro, and black beans, and fold into the eggs with a spoon.

3. Warm-up half of the olive oil in a medium pan over medium heat. Add the scrambled egg mixture and cook for a few minutes, stirring, until cooked through. Remove from the pan.

4. Divide the scrambled-egg mixture between the tortillas, layering only on one half of the tortilla. Top with avocado slices and fold the tortillas in half.

5. Heat the remaining oil over medium heat, and add one of the folded tortillas to the pan. Cook within 1 to 2 minutes on each side or until browned. Repeat with remaining tortillas. Serve immediately.

Nutrition: Calories: 445
Fat: 24g Sodium: 228mg
Potassium: 614mg

Carbohydrates: 42g Fiber: 11g
Sugars: 2g
Protein: 19g

Stuffed Breakfast Peppers

Preparation time: 15 minutes Cooking time: 45 minutes Servings: 4
Ingredients:

- 4 bell peppers (any color)
- 1 (16-ounce) bag frozen spinach 4 eggs
- ¼ cup shredded low-fat cheese (optional) Freshly ground black pepper

Directions:

1. Preheat the oven to 400°F. Line a baking dish with aluminum foil. Cut the tops off the pepper, then discard the seeds. Discard the tops and seeds. Put the peppers in the baking dish, and bake for about 15 minutes.

2. While the peppers bake, defrost the spinach and drain off the excess moisture. Remove the peppers, then stuff the bottoms evenly with the defrosted spinach.

3. Crack an egg over the spinach inside each pepper. Top each egg with a tablespoon of the cheese (if using) and season with black pepper to taste. Bake within 15 to 20 minutes, or until the egg whites are set and opaque.

Nutrition: Calories: 136 Fat: 5g Sodium: 131mg Potassium: 576mg Carbohydrates: 15g Protein: 11g

Apple-Apricot Brown Rice Breakfast Porridge

Preparation time: 15 minutes Cooking time: 8 minutes Servings: 4

Ingredients:
- 3 cups cooked brown rice
- 1¾ cups nonfat or low-fat milk
- 2 tablespoons lightly packed brown sugar 4 dried apricots, chopped
- 1 medium apple, cored and diced
- ¾ teaspoon ground cinnamon
- ¾ teaspoon vanilla extract

Directions:
1. Combine the rice, milk, sugar, apricots, apple, and cinnamon in a medium saucepan. Boil it on medium heat, lower the heat down slightly and cook within 2 to 3 minutes. Turn it off, then stir in the vanilla extract. Serve warm.

Nutrition: Calories: 260 Fat: 2g Sodium: 50mg Potassium: 421mg Carbohydrates: 57g Fiber: 4g Sugars: 22g Protein: 7g

Carrot Cake Overnight Oats

Preparation time: overnight Cooking time: 2 minutes Servings: 1

Ingredients:
½ cup rolled oats
½ cup plain nonfat or low-fat Greek yogurt
½ cup nonfat or low-fat milk
¼ cup shredded carrot 2 tablespoons raisins
½ teaspoon ground cinnamon
to 2 tablespoons chopped walnuts (optional)

Directions:
1.   Mix all of the fixings in a lidded jar, shake well, and refrigerate overnight. Serve.

Nutrition: Calories: 331 Fat: 3g Sodium: 141mg Carbohydrates: 59g Fiber: 8g
Sugars: 26g
Protein: 22g

Steel-Cut Oatmeal with Plums and Pear

Preparation time: 15 minutes Cooking time: 25 minutes Servings: 4

Ingredients:
- cups of water
- 1 cup nonfat or low-fat milk 1 cup steel-cut oats
- 1 cup dried plums, chopped
- medium pear, cored, and skin removed, diced 4 tablespoons almonds, roughly chopped

Directions:
1. Mix the water, milk, plus oats in a medium pot and bring to a boil over high heat. Reduce the heat and cover. Simmer for about 10 minutes, stirring occasionally.

2. Add the plums and pear, and cover. Simmer for another 10 minutes. Turn off the heat and let stand within 5 minutes until all of the liquid is absorbed. To serve, top each portion with a sprinkling of almonds.

Nutrition: Calories: 307 Fat: 6g Sodium: 132mg Potassium: 640mg Carbohydrates: 58g Fiber: 9g Sugars: 24g Protein: 9g

French Toast with Applesauce

Preparation time: 5 minutes Cooking time: 5 minutes Servings: 6

Ingredients:
- ¼ c. unsweetened applesauce
- ½ c. skim milk 2 packets Stevia
- eggs
- 6 slices whole-wheat bread 1 tsp. ground cinnamon

Directions:
1. Mix well applesauce, sugar, cinnamon, milk, and eggs in a mixing bowl. Soak the bread into the applesauce mixture until wet. On medium fire, heat a large nonstick skillet.

2. Add soaked bread on one side and another on the other side. Cook in a single layer within 2-3 minutes per side on medium-low fire or until lightly browned. Serve and enjoy.

Nutrition: Calories: 122.6 Fat:2.6 g Carbs:18.3 g Protein:6.5 g Sugars:14.8 g Sodium: 11mg

Banana-Peanut Butter and Greens Smoothie

Preparation time: 5 minutes Cooking time: 0 minutes Servings: 1

Ingredients:
- 1 c. chopped and packed Romaine lettuce 1 frozen medium banana
- 1 tbsp. all-natural peanut butter
- 1 c. cold almond milk

Directions:
1.   In a heavy-duty blender, add all ingredients. Puree until smooth and creamy. Serve and enjoy.

Nutrition: Calories: 349.3 Fat:9.7 g Carbs:57.4 g Protein:8.1 g Sugars:4.3 g Sodium:18 mg

Baking Powder Biscuits

Preparation time: 5 minutes Cooking time: 5 minutes Servings: 1
Ingredients:

- 1 egg white
- 1 c. white whole-wheat flour
- 4 tbsps. Non-hydrogenated vegetable shortening 1 tbsp. sugar
- 2/3 c. low-Fat milk
- 1 c. unbleached all-purpose flour 4 tsp.
- Sodium-free baking powder

Directions:

1. Warm oven to 450°F. Put the flour, sugar, plus baking powder into a mixing bowl and mix. Split the shortening into the batter using your fingers until it resembles coarse crumbs. Put the egg white plus milk and stir to combine.

2. Put the dough out onto a lightly floured surface and knead 1 minute. Roll dough to ¾ inch thickness and cut into 12 rounds. Place rounds on the baking sheet. Bake 10 minutes, then remove the baking sheet and place biscuits on a wire rack to cool.

Nutrition: Calories: 118 Fat:4 g Carbs:16 g
Protein:3 g Sugars:0.2 g Sodium: 6 mg

Oatmeal Banana Pancakes with Walnuts

Preparation time: 15 minutes Cooking time: 5 minutes Servings: 8
Ingredients:

- 1 finely diced firm banana
- 1 c. whole wheat pancake mix 1/8 c. chopped walnuts
- ¼ c. old-fashioned oats Directions:
- Make the pancake mix, as stated in the directions on the package. Add
- walnuts, oats, and chopped banana. Coat a griddle with cooking spray. Add about ¼ cup of the pancake batter onto the griddle when hot.
- Turn pancake over when bubbles form on top. Cook until golden brown. Serve immediately.

Nutrition: Calories: 155 Fat:4 g Carbs:28 g
Protein:7 g Sugars:2.2 g Sodium:16 mg
Preparation time: 5 minutes Cooking time: 40 minutes Servings: 8
Ingredients:

- ½ c. warm water 1 ¼ c. bread flour 2 tbsps.

Honey
- c. whole wheat flour 2 tsp. Yeast
- 1 ½ tbsps. Olive oil
- 1 tbsp. vinegar

Directions:

1. In a bread machine, mix all ingredients, and then process on dough

2. cycle. Once done, create 8 pieces shaped like a flattened ball. Create a donut shape using your thumb to make a hole at the center of each ball.

3. Place donut-shaped dough on a greased baking sheet then covers and let it rise about ½ hour. Prepare about 2 inches of water to boil in a large pan.

4. In boiling water, drop one at a time the bagels and boil for 1 minute, then turn them once. Remove them and return to the baking sheet and bake at 350oF for about 20 to 25 minutes until golden brown.

Nutrition: Calories: 228 Fat:3.7 g Carbs:41.8 g
Protein:6.9 g Sugars:0 g
Sodium:15 mg

Cereal with Cranberry-Orange Twist

Preparation time: 5 minutes Cooking time: 0 minutes Servings: 1
Ingredients:

- ½ c. water
- ½ c. orange juice 1/3 c. oat bran
- ¼ c. dried cranberries Sugar
- Milk

Directions:
1. In a bowl, combine all ingredients. For about 2 minutes, microwave the bowl, then serve with sugar and milk. Enjoy!
Nutrition: Calories: 220 Fat:2.4 g Carbs:43.5 g
Protein:6.2 g Sugars:8 g Sodium:1 mg

No Cook Overnight Oats

Preparation time: 5 minutes Cooking time: 0 minutes Servings: 1
Ingredients:

- 1 ½ c. low-fat milk
- 5 whole almond pieces 1 tsp. chia seeds
- 2 tbsps. Oats
- 1 tsp. sunflower seeds 1 tbsp. Craisins

Directions:

1. In a jar or mason bottle with a cap, mix all

ingredients. Refrigerate overnight. Enjoy for breakfast.

Nutrition: Calories: 271 Fat:9.8 g Carbs:35.4 g Protein:16.7 g Sugars:9 Sodium:103 mg

Avocado Cup with Egg

Preparation time: 5 minutes Cooking time: 0 minutes Servings: 4

Ingredients:
- 4 tsp. parmesan cheese 1 chopped stalk scallion 4 dashes pepper
- 4 dashes paprika
- 2 ripe avocados
- 4 medium eggs

Directions:

1. Preheat oven to 375 0F. Slice avocadoes in half and discard the seed. Slice the rounded portions of the avocado to make it level and sit well on a baking sheet.

2. Place avocadoes on a baking sheet and crack one egg in each hole of the avocado o. Season each egg evenly with pepper and paprika. Bake within 25 minutes or until eggs is cooked to your liking. Serve with a sprinkle of parmesan.

Nutrition: Calories: 206 Fat:15.4 g Carbs:11.3 g Protein:8.5 g Sugars:0.4 g Sodium:21 mg

Mediterranean Toast

Preparation time: 10 minutes Cooking time: 0 minutes Servings: 2

Ingredients:
- 1 ½ tsp. reduced-Fat crumbled feta 3 sliced Greek olives
- ¼ mashed avocado
- 1 slice good whole wheat bread
- 1 tbsp. roasted red pepper hummus 3 sliced cherry tomatoes
- 1 sliced hardboiled egg

Directions:
1. First, toast the bread and top it with ¼ mashed avocado and 1 tablespoon hummus. Add the cherry tomatoes, olives, hardboiled egg, and feta. To taste, season with salt and pepper.

Nutrition: Calories: 333.7 Fat:17 g Carbs:33.3 g Protein:16.3 g Sugars:1 g Sodium:19 mg

Instant Banana Oatmeal

Preparation time: 1 minute Cooking time: 2 minutes Servings: 1

Ingredients:

- 1 mashed ripe banana
- ½ c. water
- ½ c. quick oats

Directions:

1. Measure the oats and water into a microwave-safe bowl and stir to combine. Place bowl in microwave and heat on high for 2 minutes. Remove the bowl, then stir in the mashed banana and serve.

Nutrition: Calories: 243 Fat:3 g Carbs:50 g Protein:6 g Sugars:20 g Sodium:30 mg

Almond Butter-Banana Smoothie

Preparation time: 5 minutes Cooking time: 0 minutes Servings: 1

Ingredients:
- 1 tbsp. Almond butter
- ½ c. ice cubes
- ½ c. packed spinach
- 1 peeled and a frozen medium banana 1 c. Fat-free milk

Directions:
1. Blend all the listed fixing above in a powerful blender until smooth and creamy. Serve and enjoy.

Nutrition: Calories: 293 Fat:9.8 g Carbs:42.5 g Protein:13.5 g Sugars:12 g Sodium:40 mg

Salmon and Egg Scramble

Preparation time: 15 minutes Cooking time: 4 minutes Servings: 4

Ingredients:
- 1 teaspoon of olive oil 3 organic whole eggs 3 tablespoons of water 1 minced garlic
- 6 Oz. Smoked salmon, sliced 2 avocados, sliced
- Black pepper to taste
- 1 green onion, chopped

Directions:

1. Warm-up olive oil in a large skillet and sauté onion in it. Take a medium bowl and whisk eggs in it, add water and make a scramble with the help of a fork. Add to the skillet the smoked salmon along with garlic and black pepper.

2. Stir for about 4 minutes until all ingredients get fluffy. At this stage, add the egg mixture. Once the eggs get firm, serve on a plate with a garnish of avocados.

Nutrition: Calories: 120 Carbs: 3g Fat: 4g Protein: 19g

Sodium: 898 mg Potassium: 129mg
Preparation time: 15 minutes Cooking time: 10
minutes Servings: 4
Ingredients:

- 4 large zucchinis
- 4 green onions, diced 1/3 cup of milk
- organic egg
- Sea Salt, just a pinch Black pepper, grated
- tablespoons of olive oil

Directions:

1. First, wash the zucchinis and grate it with a cheese grater. Mix the egg and add in the grated zucchinis and milk in a large bowl. Warm oil in a skillet and sauté onions in it

2. Put the egg batter into the skillet and make pancakes. Once cooked from both sides. Serve by sprinkling salt and pepper on top.

Nutrition: Calories: 70 Carbs: 8g Fat: 3g Protein: 2g
Cholesterol: 43 mg
Sodium: 60 m
g Potassium: 914mg

Breakfast Banana Split

Preparation time: 15 minutes Cooking time: 0
minutes Servings: 3
Ingredients:

- 2 bananas, peeled 1 cup oats, cooked
- 1/2 cup low-fat strawberry yogurt
- 1/3 teaspoon honey, optional 1/2 cup pineapple, chunks

Directions:

1. Peel the bananas and cut lengthwise. Place half of the banana in each separate bowl. Spoon strawberry yogurt on top and pour cooked oats with pineapple chunks on each banana. Serve immediately with a glaze of honey of liked.

Nutrition: Calories: 145 Carbs: 18g Fat: 7g Protein:
3g Sodium:2 mg
Potassium: 380 mg

Easy Veggie Muffins

Preparation time: 10 minutes Cooking time: 40
minutes Servings: 4
Ingredients:

- ¾ cup cheddar cheese, shredded 1 cup green onion, chopped
- 1 cup tomatoes, chopped
- 1 cup broccoli, chopped 2 cups non-fat milk
- 1 cup biscuit mix
- 4 eggs Cooking spray

- 1 teaspoon Italian seasoning
- A pinch of black pepper

Directions:

1. Grease a muffin tray with cooking spray and divide broccoli, tomatoes,

2. cheese, and onions in each muffin cup.

3. n a bowl, combine green onions with milk, biscuit mix, eggs, pepper, and Italian seasoning, whisk well and pour into the muffin tray as well.

4. Cook the muffins in the oven at 375 degrees F for 40 minutes, divide them between plates, and serve.

Nutrition: Calories: 80 Carbs: 3g Fat: 5g Protein: 7g
Sodium: 25 mg

Carrot Muffins

Preparation time: 10 minutes Cooking time: 30
minutes Servings: 5
Ingredients:

- 1 and ½ cups whole wheat flour
- ½ cup stevia
- 1 teaspoon baking powder
- ½ teaspoon cinnamon powder
- ½ teaspoon baking soda
- ¼ cup natural apple juice
- ¼ cup olive oil 1 egg
- cup fresh cranberries
- carrots, grated
- 2 teaspoons ginger, grated
- ¼ cup pecans, chopped Cooking spray

Directions:

1. Mix the flour with the stevia, baking powder, cinnamon, and baking soda in a large bowl. Add apple juice, oil, egg, cranberries, carrots, ginger, and pecans and stir well.

2. Oiled a muffin tray with cooking spray, divide the muffin mix, put in the oven, and cook at 375 degrees F within 30 minutes. Divide the muffins between plates and serve for breakfast.

Nutrition: Calories: 34 Carbs: 6g Fat: 1g
Protein: 0g Sodium: 52 mg

Pineapple Oatmeal

Preparation time: 10 minutes Cooking time: 25
minutes Servings: 4
Ingredients:

- 2 cups old-fashioned oats 1 cup walnuts,

chopped 2 cups pineapple, cubed
- tablespoon ginger, grated 2 cups non-fat milk
- eggs
- 2 tablespoons stevia
- 2 teaspoons vanilla extract

Directions:

1. In a bowl, combine the oats with the pineapple, walnuts, and ginger, stir and divide into 4 ramekins. Mix the milk with the eggs, stevia, and vanilla in a bowl and pour over the oats mix. Bake at 400 degrees F within 25 minutes. 4. Serve for breakfast.

Nutrition: Calories: 200 Carbs: 40g Fat: 1g Protein: 3g
Sodium: 275 mg

Spinach Muffins

Preparation time: 10 minutes Cooking time: 30 minutes Servings: 6
Ingredients:

- 6 eggs
- ½ cup non-fat milk
- cup low-fat cheese, crumbled 4 ounces spinach
- ½ cup roasted red pepper, chopped 2 ounces prosciutto, chopped Cooking spray

Directions:

1. Mix the eggs with the milk, cheese, spinach, red pepper, and prosciutto in a bowl. Greas a muffin tray with cooking spray, divide the muffin mix, introduce in the oven, and bake at 350 degrees F within 30 minutes. Divide between plates and serve for breakfast.

Nutrition: Calories: 112 Carbs: 19g Fat: 3g Protein: 2g
Sodium: 274 mg

Chia Seeds Breakfast Mix

Preparation time: 8 hours Cooking time: 0 minutes
Servings: 4
Ingredients:

- cups old-fashioned oats 4 tablespoons chia seeds
- 4 tablespoons coconut sugar
- 3 cups of coconut milk
- 1 teaspoon lemon zest, grated 1 cup blueberries

Directions:

1. In a bowl, combine the oats with chia seeds, sugar, milk, lemon zest, and blueberries, stir, divide into cups and keep in the fridge for 8 hours. 2. Serve for breakfast.

Nutrition: Calories: 69 Carbs: 0g Fat: 5g Protein: 3g
Sodium: 0 mg

Breakfast Fruits Bowls

Preparation time: 10 minutes Cooking time: 0 minutes Servings: 2
Ingredients:

- 1 cup mango, chopped 1 banana, sliced
- 1 cup pineapple, chopped
- cup almond milk

Directions:

1. Mix the mango with the banana, pineapple, and almond milk in a bowl, stir, divide into smaller bowls, and serve.

Nutrition: Calories: 10 Carbs: 0g Fat: 1g Protein: 0g
Sodium: 0mg

Pumpkin Cookies

Preparation time: 10 minutes Cooking time: 25 minutes Servings: 6
Ingredients:

- cups whole wheat flour 1 cup old-fashioned oats 1 teaspoon baking soda
- 1 teaspoon pumpkin pie spice 15 ounces pumpkin puree
- 1 cup coconut oil, melted
- 1 cup of coconut sugar 1 egg
- ½ cup pepitas, roasted
- ½ cup cherries, dried

Directions:

1. Mix the flour the oats, baking soda, pumpkin spice, pumpkin puree, oil,

sugar, egg, pepitas, and cherries in a bowl, stir well, shape medium cookies out of this mix, arrange them all on a baking sheet, then bake within 25 minutes at 350 degrees F. Serve the cookies for breakfast.

Nutrition: Calories: 150 Carbs: 24g Fat: 8g Protein: 1g
Sodium: 220 mg

Veggie Scramble

Preparation time: 10 minutes Cooking time: 2 minutes Servings: 1
Ingredients:

- 1 egg

- 1 tablespoon water
- ¼ cup broccoli, chopped
- ¼ cup mushrooms, chopped A pinch of black pepper
- 1 tablespoon low-fat mozzarella, shredded
- 1 tablespoon walnuts, chopped Cooking spray

Directions:

1. Grease a ramekin with cooking spray, add the egg, water, pepper, mushrooms, and broccoli, and whisk well. Introduce in the microwave and cook for 2 minutes. Add mozzarella and walnuts on top and serve for breakfast.

Nutrition: Calories: 128 Carbs: 24g Fat: 0g Protein: 9g
Sodium: 86 mg

Mushrooms and Turkey Breakfast

Preparation time: 10 minutes Cooking time: 1 hour and 5 minutes Servings: 12
Ingredients:

- 8 ounces whole-wheat bread, cubed 12 ounces turkey sausage, chopped 2 cups fat-free milk
- 5 ounces low-fat cheddar, shredded 3 eggs
- ½ cup green onions, chopped
- cup mushrooms, chopped
- ½ teaspoon sweet paprika A pinch of black pepper
- tablespoons low-fat parmesan, grated

Directions:

1. Put the bread cubes on a prepared lined baking sheet, bake at 400

2. degrees F for 8 minutes. Meanwhile, heat a pan over medium-high heat, add turkey sausage, stir, and brown for 7 minutes.

3. In a bowl, combine the milk with the cheddar, eggs, parmesan, black pepper, and paprika and whisk well.

4. Add mushrooms, sausage, bread cubes, and green onions stir, pour into a baking dish, bake at 350 degrees F within 50 minutes. 5. Slice, divide between plates and serve for breakfast.

Nutrition: Calories: 88 Carbs: 1g Fat: 9g Protein: 1g
Sodium: 74 mg

Mushrooms and Cheese Omelet

Preparation time: 10 minutes Cooking time: 15

minutes Servings: 4
Ingredients:

- tablespoons olive oil A pinch of black pepper
- ounces mushrooms, slicedcup baby spinach, chopped 3 eggs, whisked
- tablespoons low-fat cheese, grated
- 1 small avocado, peeled, pitted, and cubed 1 tablespoons parsley, chopped

Directions:

1. Add mushrooms, stir, cook them for 5 minutes and transfer to a bowl on a heated pan with the oil over medium-high heat.

2. Heat-up the same pan over medium-high heat, add eggs and black pepper, spread into the pan, cook within 7 minutes, and transfer to a plate.

3. Spread mushrooms, spinach, avocado, and cheese on half of the omelet, fold the other half over this mix, sprinkle parsley on top, and serve.

Nutrition: Calories: 136 Carbs: 5g Fat: 5g Protein: 16g
Sodium: 192 mg

Pumpkin Muffins

Preparation time: 15 minutes Cooking time: 20 minutes Servings: 4
Ingredients:

- 4 cups of almond flour
- cups of pumpkin, cooked and pureed 2 large whole organic eggs
- teaspoons of baking powder
- 2 teaspoons of ground cinnamon 1/2 cup raw honey
- 4 teaspoons almond butter

Directions:

1. Preheat the oven at 400-degree F. Line the muffin paper on the muffin tray.

2. Mix almond flour, pumpkin puree, eggs, baking powder, cinnamon, almond butter, and honey in a large bowl.

3. Put the prepared batter into a muffin tray and bake within 20 minutes. Once golden-brown, serve, and enjoy.

Nutrition: Calories: 136 Carbs: 22g Fat: 5g Protein: 2g
Sodium: 11 mg
Potassium: 699 mg

Sweet Berries Pancake

Preparation time: 15 minutes Cooking time: 15 minutes Servings: 4
Ingredients:
- 4 cups of almond flour Pinch of sea salt
- 2 organic eggs
- 4 teaspoons of walnut oil
- 1 cup of strawberries, mashed 1 cup of blueberries, mashed 1 teaspoon baking powder Honey for topping, optional

Directions:
1. Take a bowl and add almond flour, baking powder, and sea salt. Take another bowl and add eggs, walnut oil, strawberries, and blueberries mash. Combine ingredients of both bowls.
2. Heat a bit of walnut oil in a cooking pan and pour the spoonful mixture to make pancakes. Once the bubble comes on the top, flip the pancake to cook from the other side. Once done, serve with the glaze of honey on top.

Nutrition: Calories: 161 Carbs: 23g Fat: 6g Protein: 3g
Cholesterol: 82 mg
Sodium: 91 mg Potassium: 252mg

Zucchini Pancakes

Egg White Breakfast Mix

Preparation time: 10 minutes Cooking time: 10 minutes Servings: 4
Ingredients:
- 1 yellow onion, chopped 3 plum tomatoes, chopped
- 10 ounces spinach, chopped
- A pinch of black pepper 2 tablespoons water
- 12 egg whites
- Cooking spray

Directions:
1. Mix the egg whites with water and pepper in a bowl. Grease a pan with cooking spray, heat up over medium heat, add ¼ of the egg whites, spread into the pan, and cook for 2 minutes.
2. Spoon ¼ of the spinach, tomatoes, and onion, fold, and add to a plate. 4. Serve for

breakfast. Enjoy!
Nutrition: Calories: 31 Carbs: 0g Fat: 2g Protein: 3g
Sodium: 55 mg

Pesto Omelet

Preparation time: 10 minutes Cooking time: 6 minutes Servings: 2
Ingredients:
- 2 teaspoons olive oil
- Handful cherry tomatoes, chopped 3 tablespoons pistachio pesto
- A pinch of black pepper 4 eggs

Directions:
1. In a bowl, combine the eggs with cherry tomatoes, black pepper, and pistachio pesto and whisk well. Add eggs mix, spread into the pan, cook for 3 minutes, flip, cook for 3 minutes more, divide between 2 plates, and serve on a heated pan with the oil over medium-high heat.

Nutrition: Calories: 240 Carbs: 23g Fat: 9g Protein: 17g
Sodium: 292 mg

Quinoa Bowls

Preparation time: 10 minutes Cooking time: 20 minutes Servings: 2
Ingredients:
- 1 peach, sliced
- 1/3 cup quinoa, rinsed 2/3 cup low-fat milk
- ½ teaspoon vanilla extract 2 teaspoons brown sugar 12 raspberries
- 14 blueberries

Directions:
1. Mix the quinoa with the milk, sugar, and vanilla in a small pan, simmer over medium heat, cover the pan, cook for 20 minutes and flip with a fork. Divide this mix into 2 bowls, top each with raspberries and blueberries and serve for breakfast.

Nutrition: Calories: 170 Carbs: 31g Fat: 3g Protein: 6g
Sodium: 120 mg

Strawberry Sandwich

Preparation time: 10 minutes Cooking time: 0 minutes Servings: 4
Ingredients:
- 8 ounces low-fat cream cheese, soft 1 tablespoon stevia
- 1 teaspoon lemon zest, grated

- 4 whole-wheat English muffins, toasted 2 cups strawberries, sliced

Directions:

1. In your food processor, combine the cream cheese with the stevia and lemon zest and pulse well. Spread 1 tablespoon of this mix on 1 muffin half and top with some of the sliced strawberries. Repeat with the rest of the muffin halves and serve for breakfast. Enjoy!

Nutrition: Calories: 150 Carbs: 23g Fat: 7g Protein: 2g
Sodium: 70 mg

Apple Quinoa Muffins

Preparation time: 10 minutes Cooking time: 35 minutes Servings: 4
Ingredients:

- ½ cup natural, unsweetened applesauce 1 cup banana, peeled and mashed
- cup quinoa
- and ½ cups old-fashioned oats
- ½ cup almond milk 2 tablespoons stevia
- 1 teaspoon vanilla extract 1 cup of water
- Cooking spray
- 1 teaspoon cinnamon powder
- 1 apple, cored, peeled, and chopped

Directions:

1. Put the water in a small pan, bring to a simmer over medium heat, add quinoa, cook within 15 minutes, fluff with a fork, and transfer to a bowl.

2. Add all ingredients, stir, divide into a muffin pan greases with cooking spray, introduce in the oven, and bake within 20 minutes at 375 degrees

F. Serve for breakfast. Nutrition:
Calories: 241 Carbs: 31g Fat: 11g Protein: 5g
Sodium: 251 mg

Very Berry Muesli

Preparation time: 15 minutes Cooking time: 0 minutes Servings: 2
Ingredients:

- 1 c. Oats
- 1 c. Fruit flavored Yogurt
- ½ c. Milk 1/8 tsp. Salt
- ½ c dried Raisins
- ½ c. Chopped Apple
- ½ c. Frozen Blueberries

- ¼ c. chopped Walnuts

Directions:

1. Combine your yogurt, salt, and oats in a medium bowl, mix well, and then cover it tightly. Fridge for at least 6 hours. Add your raisins and apples the gently fold. Top with walnuts and serve. Enjoy!

Directions: Nutrition: Calories: 195 Protein 6g Carbs 31g Fat 4g Sodium 0mg

Veggie Quiche Muffins

Preparation time: 15 minutes Cooking time: 40 minutes Servings: 12
Ingredients:

- ¾ c. shredded Cheddar
- 1 c. chopped Green Onion 1 c. chopped Broccoli
- 1 c. diced Tomatoes 2 c. Milk
- 4 Eggs
- 1 c. Pancake mix 1 tsp. Oregano
- ½ tsp. Salt
- ½ tsp. Pepper

Directions:

Preheat your oven to 375 0F, and lightly grease a 12-cup muffin tin with
oil. Sprinkle your tomatoes, broccoli, onions, and cheddar into your muffin cups.

1. Combine your remaining ingredients in a medium, whisk to combine, then pour evenly on top of your veggies.

2. Set to bake in your preheated oven for about 40 minutes or until golden brown. Allow to cool slightly (about 5 minutes), then serve. Enjoy!

Nutrition: Calories: 58.5
Protein 5.1 g
Carbs 2.9 g
Fat 3.2 g
Sodium 340 mg

Turkey Sausage and Mushroom Strata

Preparation time: 15 minutes Cooking time: 8 minutes Servings: 12
Ingredients:

- 8 oz. cubed Ciabatta bread
- 12 oz. chopped turkey sausage 2 c. Milk
- 4 oz. shredded Cheddar 3 large Eggs
- 12 oz. Egg substitute
- ½ c. chopped Green onion 1 c. diced Mushroom

- ½ tsp. Paprika
- ½ tsp. Pepper
- 2 tbsps. grated Parmesan cheese

Directions:

1. Set oven to preheat to 400 0F. Lay your bread cubes flat on a baking tray and set it to toast for about 8 min. Meanwhile, add a skillet over medium heat with sausage and cook while stirring, until fully brown and crumbled.

2. Mix salt, pepper, paprika, parmesan cheese, egg substitute, eggs, cheddar cheese, and milk in a large bowl. Add in your remaining ingredients and toss well to incorporate.

3. Transfer mixture to a large baking dish (preferably a 9x13-inch), then tightly cover and allow to rest in the refrigerator overnight. Set your oven to preheat to 3500F, remove the cover from your casserole, and set to bake until golden brown and cooked through. Slice and serve.

Nutrition: Calories: 288.2
Protein 24.3g Carbs 18.2g Fat. 12.4g Sodium 355 mg

Jack-o-Lantern Pancakes

Preparation time: 15 minutes Cooking time: 5 minutes Servings: 8
Ingredients:
Egg
- ½ c. Canned pumpkin 1¾c. Low-fat milk
- tbsps. Vegetable oil 2 c. Flour
- 2 tbsps. Brown sugar
- 1 tbsp. Baking powder 1 tsp. Pumpkin pie spice 1 tsp. Salt

Directions:

1. In a mixing bowl, mix milk, pumpkin, eggs, and oil. Add dry ingredients to egg mixture. Stir gently. Coat skillet lightly with cooking spray and heat on medium.

2. When the skillet is hot, spoon (using a dessert spoon) batter onto the skillet. When bubbles start bursting, flip pancakes over and cook until it's a nice golden-brown color.

Nutrition: Calories: 313 Protein 15g Carbs 28g Fat 16g Sodium 1 mg

Fruit Pizza

Preparation time: 15 minutes Cooking time: 0 minutes Servings: 2
Ingredients:
- English muffin
- tbsps. Fat-free cream cheese 2 tbsps. sliced strawberries
- 2 tbsps. blueberries
- 2 tbsps. crushed pineapple

Directions:

1. Cut English muffin in half and toast halves until slightly browned. Coat both halves with cream cheese. Arrange fruits atop cream cheese on muffin halves. Serve soon after preparation. Any leftovers refrigerate within 2 hours.

Nutrition: Calories: 119 Protein 6g Carbs 23g Fat 1g
Sodium 288 mg

Flax Banana Yogurt Muffins

Preparation time: 15 minutes Cooking time: 20 minutes Servings: 12
Ingredients:
- 1 c. Whole wheat flour
- c. Old-fashioned rolled oats 1 tsp. Baking soda
- tbsps. Ground flaxseed 3 large ripe bananas
- ½ c. Greek yogurt
- ¼ c. Unsweetened applesauce
- ¼ c. Brown sugar
- 2 tsp. Vanilla extract

Directions:

1. Set oven at 355 0F and preheat. Prepare muffin tin, or you can use cooking spray or cupcake liners. Combine dry ingredients in a mixing bowl.

2. In a separate bowl, mix yogurt, banana, sugar, vanilla, and applesauce. Combine both mixtures and mix. Do not over mix. The batter should not be smooth but lumpy. Bake for 20 mins, or when inserted, toothpick comes out clean.

Nutrition: Calories: 136 Protein 4g Carbs 30g Fat 2g
Sodium 242 mg

Bacon Bits

Preparation time: 15 minutes Cooking time: 60 minutes Servings: 4
Ingredients:
- 1 c. Millet

- 5 c. Water
- 1 c. diced Sweet potato 1 tsp. ground Cinnamon 2 tbsps. Brown sugar
- 1 medium diced Apple
- ¼ c. Honey

Directions:

1. In a deep pot, add your sugar, sweet potato, cinnamon, water, and millet, then stir to combine, then boil on high heat. After that, simmer on low.

2. Cook like this for about an hour, until your water is fully absorbed and millet is cooked. Stir in your remaining ingredients and serve.

Nutrition: Calories: 136 Protein 3.1g Carbs 28.5g
Fat 1.0g
Sodium 120 mg

Steel Cut Oat Blueberry Pancakes

Preparation time: 15 minutes Cooking time: 15 minutes Servings: 4
Ingredients:

- 1½ c. Water
- ½ c. steel-cut oats 1/8 tsp. Salt
- 1 c. Whole wheat Flour
- ½ tsp. Baking powder
- ½ tsp. Baking soda 1 Egg
- 1 c. Milk
- ½ c. Greek yogurt
- c. Frozen Blueberries
- ¾ c. Agave Nectar

Directions:

1. Combine your oats, salt, and water in a medium saucepan, stir, and allow to come to a boil over high heat. Adjust the heat to low, and allow to simmer for about 10 min, or until oats get tender. Set aside.

2. Combine all your remaining ingredients, except agave nectar, in a medium bowl, then fold in oats. Preheat your skillet, and lightly grease it. Cook ¼ cup of milk batter at a time for about 3 minutes per side. Garnish with Agave Nectar.

Nutrition: Calories: 257 Protein 14g Carbs 46g Fat 7g
Sodium 123 mg

Brown Sugar Cinnamon Oatmeal

Preparation time: 1 minute Cooking time: 3 minutes

Servings: 4
Ingredients:

- ½ tsp. ground cinnamon
- 1 ½ tsp pure vanilla extract
- ¼ c. light brown sugar 2 c. low- Fat milk
- 1 1/3 c. quick oats

Directions:

1. Put the milk plus vanilla into a medium saucepan and boil over medium- high heat.

2. Lower the heat to medium once it boils. Mix in oats, brown sugar, plus cinnamon, and cook, stirring2–3 minutes. Serve immediately.

Nutrition: Calories: 208 Fat:3 g Carbs:38 g
Protein:8 g Sugars:15 g Sodium:33 mg

Buckwheat Pancakes with Vanilla Almond Milk

Preparation time: 10 minutes Cooking time: 10 minutes Servings: 1
Ingredients:

- ½ c. unsweetened vanilla almond milk 2-4 packets natural sweetener
- 1/8 tsp salt
- ½ cup buckwheat flour
- ½ tsp. double-acting baking powder

Directions:

1. Prepare a nonstick pancake griddle and spray with the cooking spray, place over medium heat. Whisk the buckwheat flour, salt, baking powder, and stevia in a small bowl and stir in the almond milk after.

2. Onto the pan, scoop a large spoonful of batter, cook until bubbles no longer pop on the surface and the entire surface looks dry and (2-4 minutes). Flip and cook for another 2-4 minutes. Repeat with all the remaining batter.

Nutrition: Calories: 240 Fat:4.5 g Carbs:2 g
Protein:11 g Sugars:17 g Sodium:38 mg

Spinach, Mushroom, and Feta Cheese Scramble

Preparation time: 15 minutes Cooking time: 4 minutes Servings: 1
Ingredients:

- Olive oil cooking spray
- ½ c. sliced Mushroom 1 c. chopped

Spinach 3 Eggs
- tbsps. Feta cheese Pepper

Directions:

1. Set a lightly greased, medium skillet over medium heat. Add spinach and mushrooms, and cook until spinach wilts.

2. Combine egg whites, cheese, pepper, and whole egg in a medium bowl, whisk to combine. Pour into your skillet and cook, while stirring, until set (about 4 minutes). Serve.

Nutrition: Calories: 236.5 Protein 22.2g Carbs 12.9g Fat 11.4g
Sodium 405 mg

Red Velvet Pancakes with Cream Cheese Topping

Preparation time: 15 minutes Cooking time: 10 minutes Servings: 2
Ingredients:
- Cream Cheese Topping: 2 oz. Cream cheese 3 tbsps. Yogurt
- tbsps. Honey
- 1 tbsp. Milk Pancakes:
- ½ c. Whole wheat Flour
- ½ c. all-purpose flour 2¼tsps. Baking powder
- ½ tsp. Unsweetened Cocoa powder
- ¼ tsp. Salt
- ¼ c. Sugar 1 large Egg
- 1 c. + 2 tbsps. Milk
- 1 tsp. Vanilla
- 1 tsp. Red paste food coloring

Directions:

1. Combine all your topping ingredients in a medium bowl, and set aside. Add all your pancake ingredients in a large bowl and fold until combined. Set a greased skillet over medium heat to get hot.

2. Add ¼ cup of pancake batter onto the hot skillet and cook until bubbles begin to form on the top. Flip and cook until set. Repeat until your batter is done well. Add your toppings and serve.

Nutrition:
Calories: 231 Protein 7g Carbs 43g Fat 4g Sodium 0mg

Peanut Butter & Banana Breakfast Smoothie

Preparation time: 15 minutes Cooking time: 0 minutes Servings: 1
Ingredients:
- 1 c. Non-fat milktbsp. Peanut butter 1 Banana
- ½ tsp. Vanilla

Directions:

1. Place non-fat milk, peanut butter, and banana in a blender. Blend until smooth.

Nutrition: Calories: 295 Protein 133g Carbs 42g Fat 8.4g
Sodium 100 mg

No-Bake Breakfast Granola Bars

Preparation time: 15 minutes Cooking time: 0 minutes Servings: 18
Ingredients:
- c. Old fashioned oatmeal
- ½ c. Raisins
- ½ c. Brown sugar
- 2½ c. Corn rice cereal
- ½ c. Syrup
- ½ c. Peanut butter
- ½ tsp. Vanilla

Directions:

1. In a suitable size mixing bowl, mix using a wooden spoon, rice cereal, oatmeal, and raisins. In a saucepan, combine corn syrup and brown sugar. On a medium-high flame, continuously stir the mixture and bring to a boil.

2. On boiling, take away from heat. In a saucepan, stir vanilla and peanut into the sugar mixture. Stir until very smooth.

3. Spoon peanut butter mixture on the cereal and raisins into the mixing bowl and combine — shape mixture into a 9 x 13 baking tin. Allow to cool properly, then cut into bars (18 pcs).

Nutrition: Calories: 152 Protein 4g Carbs 26g Fat 4.3g
Sodium 160 mg

Mushroom Shallot Frittata

Preparation time: 15 minutes Cooking time: 25 minutes Servings: 4
Ingredients:
- 1 tsp. butter
- 4 chopped shallots
- ½ lb. chopped mushrooms 2 tsp. chopped

parsley

- 1 tsp. dried thyme Black pepper
- 3 medium Eggs
- 5 large Egg whites 1 tbsp. Milk
- ¼ c. grated parmesan cheese

Directions:

1. Heat oven to 350 0F. In a suitable size oven-proof skillet, heat butter

2. over medium flame. Add shallots and sauté for about 5 mins. or until golden brown. Add to pot, thyme, parsley, chopped mushroom, and black pepper to taste.

3. Whisk milk, egg whites, parmesan, and eggs into a bowl. Pour mixture into the skillet, ensuring the mushroom is covered completely. Transfer the skillet to the oven as soon as the edges begin to set.

4. Bake until frittata is cooked (15-20 mins). Should be served warm, cut into equal wedges (4 pcs).

Nutrition: Calories: 346 Protein 19.1g Carbs 48.3g Fat 12g
Sodium 218 mg

CHAPTER 4: Lunch

Creamy Chicken Breast

Preparation time: 10 minutes Cooking time: 20 minutes Servings: 4

Ingredients:

- tablespoon olive oil
- A pinch of black pepper
- pounds chicken breasts, skinless, boneless, and cubed 4 garlic cloves, minced
- 2 and ½ cups low-sodium chicken stock 2 cups coconut cream
- ½ cup low-fat parmesan, grated 1 tablespoon basil, chopped

Directions:

1. Heat-up a pan with the oil over medium-high heat, add chicken cubes, and brown them for 3 minutes on each side. Add garlic, black pepper, stock, and cream, toss, cover the pan and cook everything for 10 minutes more. Add cheese and basil, toss, divide between plates and serve for lunch. Enjoy!

Nutrition: Calories 221 Fat 6g
Fiber 9g Carbs 14g Protein 7g
Sodium 197 mg

Indian Chicken Stew

Preparation time: 1 hour Cooking time: 20 minutes Servings: 4

Ingredients:

- 1-pound chicken breasts, skinless, boneless, and cubed 1 tablespoon garam masala
- 1 cup fat-free yogurt
- 1 tablespoon lemon juice A pinch of black pepper
- ¼ teaspoon ginger, ground
- 15 ounces tomato sauce, no-salt-added 5 garlic cloves, minced
- ½ teaspoon sweet paprika

Directions:

1. In a bowl, mix the chicken with garam masala, yogurt, lemon juice, black pepper, ginger, and fridge for 1 hour. Heat-up a pan over medium heat, add chicken mix, toss and cook for 5-6 minutes.

2. Add tomato sauce, garlic and paprika, toss,

cook for 15 minutes, divide between plates and serve for lunch. Enjoy!

Nutrition: Calories 221 Fat 6g
Fiber 9g Carbs 14g Protein 16g Sodium 4 mg

Sweet Potatoes and Zucchini Soup

Preparation time: 10 minutes Cooking time: 20 minutes Servings: 8

Ingredients:

- 4 cups veggie stock
- 2 tablespoons olive oil
- 2 sweet potatoes, peeled and cubed 8 zucchinis, chopped
- 2 yellow onions, chopped 1 cup of coconut milk
- A pinch of black pepper
- 1 tablespoon coconut aminos 4 tablespoons dill, chopped
-
- ½ teaspoon basil, chopped

Directions:

1. Heat-up a pot with the oil over medium heat, add onion, stir and cook

2. for 5 minutes. Add zucchinis, stock, basil, potato, and pepper, stir and cook for 15 minutes more. Add milk, aminos, and dill, pulse using an immersion blender, ladle into bowls and serve for lunch.

Nutrition: Calories: 270 Carbs: 50g Fat: 4g Protein: 11g
Sodium 416 mg

Lemongrass and Chicken Soup

Preparation time: 10 minutes Cooking time: 25 minutes Servings: 4

Ingredients:

- 4 lime leaves, torn
- 4 cups veggie stock, low-sodium 1 lemongrass stalk, chopped
- 1 tablespoon ginger, grated
- 1-pound chicken breast, skinless, boneless, and cubed 8 ounces mushrooms, chopped
- 4 Thai chilies, chopped
- 13 ounces of coconut milk
- ¼ cup lime juice
- ¼ cup cilantro, chopped A pinch of black pepper

Directions:

1. Put the stock into a pot, bring to a simmer over medium heat, add lemongrass, ginger, and lime leaves, stir, cook for 10 minutes, strain into another pot, and heat up over medium heat again.

2. Add chicken, mushrooms, milk, cilantro, black pepper, chilies, and lime juice, stir, simmer for 15 minutes, ladle into bowls and serve.

Nutrition: Calories: 105 Carbs: 1g Fat: 2g Protein: 15g
Sodium 200 mg

Easy Lunch Salmon Steaks

Chicken, Bamboo, and Chestnuts Mix

Preparation time: 10 minutes Cooking time: 20 minutes Servings: 4
Ingredients:
- 1-pound chicken thighs, boneless, skinless, and cut into medium chunks
- cup low-sodium chicken stock 1 tablespoon olive oil
- tablespoons coconut aminos 1-inch ginger, grated
- carrot, sliced
- garlic cloves, minced
- 8 ounces canned bamboo shoots, no-salt-added and drained 8 ounces water chestnuts

Directions:

1. Heat-up a pan with the oil over medium-high heat, add chicken, stir, and brown for 4 minutes on each side. Add the stock, aminos, ginger, carrot, garlic, bamboo, and chestnuts, toss, cover the pan, and cook everything over medium heat for 12 minutes. Divide everything between plates and serve. Enjoy!

Nutrition: Calories 281 Fat 7g
Fiber 9g
Carbs 14g Protein 14g Sodium 125mg

Salsa Chicken

Preparation time: 10 minutes Cooking time: 25 minutes Servings: 4
Ingredients:
- 1 cup mild salsa, no-salt-added
- ½ teaspoon cumin, ground Black pepper to the taste
- tablespoon chipotle paste
- 1-pound chicken thighs, skinless and boneless 2 cups corn
- Juice of 1 lime
- tablespoon olive oil
- tablespoons cilantro, chopped 1 cup cherry tomatoes, halved
- 1 small avocado, pitted, peeled, and cubed

Directions:

1. In a pot, combine the salsa with the cumin, black pepper, chipotle paste, chicken thighs, and corn, toss, bring to a simmer and cook over medium heat for 25 minutes. Add lime juice, oil, cherry tomatoes, and avocado, toss, divide into bowls and serve for lunch. Enjoy!

Nutrition: Calories 269 Fat 6g
Fiber 9g Carbs 18g Protein 7g
Sodium 500 mg

Rice with Chicken

Preparation time: 10 minutes Cooking time: 30 minutes Servings: 4
Ingredients:
- ½ cup coconut aminos 1/3 cup rice wine vinegar 2 tablespoons olive oil
- chicken breast, skinless, boneless, and cubed
- ½ cup red bell pepper, chopped A pinch of black pepper
- garlic cloves, minced
- ½ teaspoon ginger, grated
- ½ cup carrots, grated 1 cup white rice
- cups of water

Directions:

1. Heat-up a pan with the oil over medium-high heat, add the chicken, stir and brown for 4 minutes on each side. Add aminos, vinegar, bell pepper, black pepper, garlic, ginger, carrots, rice and stock, stock, cover the pan and cook over medium heat for 20 minutes. Divide everything into bowls and serve for lunch. Enjoy!

Nutrition: Calories: 70 Carbs: 13g Fat: 2g Protein: 2g Sodium 5 mg

Tomato Soup

Preparation time: 10 minutes Cooking time: 20 minutes Servings: 4
Ingredients:
- garlic cloves, minced 1 yellow onion,

chopped 3 carrots, chopped

- 15 ounces tomato sauce, no-salt-added 1 tablespoon olive oil
- 15 ounces roasted tomatoes, no-salt-added
- 1 cup low-sodium veggie stock
- 1 tablespoon tomato paste, no-salt-added 1 tablespoon basil, dried
- ¼ teaspoon oregano, dried 3 ounces coconut cream A pinch of black pepper

Directions:

1. Heat-up a pot with the oil over medium heat, add garlic and onion, stir and cook for 5 minutes. Add carrots, tomato sauce, tomatoes, stock, tomato paste, basil, oregano, and black pepper, stir, bring to a simer, cook for 15 minutes, add cream, blend the soup using an immersion blender, divide into bowls and serve for lunch. Enjoy!

Nutrition: Calories: 90 Carbs: 20g Fat: 0g Protein: 2g
Sodium 480 mg

Cod Soup

Preparation time: 10 minutes Cooking time: 25 minutes Servings: 4
Ingredients:

- 1 yellow onion, chopped
- 12 cups low-sodium fish stock 1-pound carrots, sliced
- tablespoon olive oil Black pepper to the taste
- tablespoons ginger, minced
- 1 cup of water
- 1-pound cod, skinless, boneless, and cut into medium chunks

Directions:

1. Heat-up a pot with the oil over medium-high heat, add onion, stir and cook for 4 minutes. Add water, stock, ginger, and carrots, stir and cook for 10 minutes more.

2. Blend soup using an immersion blender, add the fish and pepper, stir, cook for 10 minutes more, ladle into bowls and serve. Enjoy!

Nutrition: Calories: 344 Carbs: 35g Fat: 4g Protein: 46g
Sodium 334 mg

Sweet Potato Soup

Preparation time: 10 minutes Cooking time: 1 hour

and 40 minutes Servings: 6
Ingredients:

- 4 big sweet potatoes 28 ounces veggie stock
- A pinch of black pepper
- ¼ teaspoon nutmeg, ground
- 1/3 cup low-sodium heavy cream

Directions:

1. Put the sweet potatoes on a lined baking sheet, bake them at 350 degrees F for 1 hour and 30 minutes, cool them down, peel, roughly chop them, and put them in a pot.

2. Add stock, nutmeg, cream, and pepper pulse well using an immersion blender, heat the soup over medium heat, cook for 10 minutes, ladle into bowls and serve. Enjoy!

Nutrition: Calories: 110 Carbs: 23g Fat: 1g Protein: 2g
Sodium 140 mg
Preparation time: 10 minutes Cooking time: 20 minutes Servings: 4
Ingredients:

- 1 big salmon fillet, cut into 4 steaks 3 garlic cloves, minced
- 1 yellow onion, chopped
- Black pepper to the taste 2 tablespoons olive oil
- ¼ cup parsley, chopped
- Juice of 1 lemon
- 1 tablespoon thyme, chopped 4 cups of water

Directions:

1. Heat a pan with the oil on medium-high heat, cook onion and garlic within 3 minutes.

2. Add black pepper, parsley, thyme, water, and lemon juice, stir, bring to a gentle boil, add salmon steaks, cook them for 15 minutes, drain, divide between plates and serve with a side salad for lunch.

Nutrition: Calories: 110 Carbs: 3g Fat: 4g Protein: 15g
Sodium 330 mg

Light Balsamic Salad

Preparation time: 10 minutes Cooking time: 0 minutes Servings: 3
Ingredients:

- 1 orange, cut into segments 2 green onions, chopped
- 1 romaine lettuce head, torn

- 1 avocado, pitted, peeled, and cubed
- ¼ cup almonds, sliced For the salad dressing:
- teaspoon mustard
- ¼ cup olive oil
- tablespoons balsamic vinegar Juice of ½ orange
- Salt and black pepper

Directions:

1. In a s

2. Alad

3. bowl, mix oranges with avocado, lettuce, almonds, and green onions. In another bowl, mix olive oil with vinegar, mustard, orange juice, salt, and pepper, whisk well, add this to your salad, toss and serve.

Nutrition: Calories: 35 Carbs: 5g Fat: 2g Protein: 0g Sodium 400 mg

Purple Potato Soup

Preparation time: 10 minutes Cooking time: 1 hour and 15 minutes Servings: 6
Ingredients:

- 6 purple potatoes, chopped
- 1 cauliflower head, florets separated Black pepper to the taste
- 4 garlic cloves, minced 1 yellow onion, chopped 3 tablespoons olive oil
- tablespoon thyme, chopped 1 leek, chopped
- shallots, chopped
- 4 cups chicken stock, low-sodium

Directions:

1. In a baking dish, mix potatoes with onion, cauliflower, garlic, pepper,

2. thyme, and half of the oil, toss to coat, introduce in the oven and bake for 45 minutes at 400 degrees F.

3. Heat a pot with the rest of the oil over medium-high heat, add leeks and shallots, stir and cook for 10 minutes.

4. Add roasted veggies and stock, stir, bring to a boil, cook for 20 minutes, transfer soup to your food processor, blend well, divide into bowls, and serve.

Nutrition: Calories: 70 Carbs: 15g Fat: 0g Protein: 2g
Sodium 6 mg

Leeks Soup

Preparation time: 10 minutes Cooking time: 1 hour and 15 minutes Servings: 6
Ingredients:

- 2 gold potatoes, chopped 1 cup cauliflower florets Black pepper to the taste 5 leeks, chopped
- garlic cloves, minced 1 yellow onion, chopped 3 tablespoons olive oil
- Handful parsley, chopped
-
- 4 cups low-sodium chicken stock

Directions:

1. Heat-up a pot with the oil over medium-high heat, add onion and garlic, stir and cook for 5 minutes.

2. Add potatoes, cauliflower, black pepper, leeks, and stock, stir, bring to a simmer, cook over medium heat for 30 minutes, blend using an immersion blender, add parsley, stir, ladle into bowls and serve.

Nutrition: Calories: 125 Carbs: 29g Fat: 1g Protein: 4g Sodium 52 mg

Cauliflower Lunch Salad

Preparation time: 2 hours Cooking time: 10 minutes Servings: 4
Ingredients:

- 1/3 cup low-sodium veggie stock 2 tablespoons olive oil
- 6 cups cauliflower florets, grated
- Black pepper to the taste
-
- ¼ cup red onion, chopped 1 red bell pepper, chopped Juice of ½ lemon
-
- cup kalamata olives halved 1 teaspoon mint, chopped
-
- tablespoon cilantro, chopped

Directions:

1. Heat-up a pan with the oil over medium-high heat, add cauliflower, pepper and stock, stir, cook within 10 minutes, transfer to a bowl, and keep in the fridge for 2 hours. Mix cauliflower with olives, onion, bell pepper, black pepper, mint, cilantro, and lemon juice, toss to coat, and serve.

Nutrition: Calories: 102 Carbs: 3g Fat: 10g Protein: 0g
Sodium 97 mg

CHAPTER 5: Dinner

Quinoa and Scallops Salad

Preparation time:10 minutes Cooking time:35 minutes Servings: 6

Ingredients:
- 12 ounces dry sea scallops 4 tablespoons canola oil
- 2 teaspoons canola oil
- 4 teaspoons low sodium soy sauce 1 and ½ cup quinoa, rinsed
- teaspoons garlic, minced
- cups of water
- 1 cup snow peas, sliced diagonally 1 teaspoon sesame oil
- 1/3 cup rice vinegar
- 1 cup scallions, sliced
- 1/3 cup red bell pepper, chopped
-
- ¼ cup cilantro, chopped

Directions:

1. In a bowl, mix scallops with 2 teaspoons soy sauce, stir gently, and leave aside for now. Heat a pan with 1 tablespoon canola oil over medium- high heat, add the quinoa, stir and cook for 8 minutes. Put garlic, stir and cook within 1 more minute.

2. Put the water, boil over medium heat, stir, cover, and cook for 15 minutes. Remove from heat and leave aside covered for 5 minutes. Add snow peas, cover again and leave for 5 more minutes.

3. Meanwhile, in a bowl, mix 3 tablespoons canola oil with 2 teaspoons soy sauce, vinegar, and sesame oil and stir well. Add quinoa and snow peas to this mixture and stir again. Add scallions, bell pepper, and stir again.

4. Pat dry the scallops and discard marinade. Heat another pan with 2 teaspoons canola oil over high heat, add scallops, and cook for 1 minute on each side. Add them to the quinoa salad, stir gently, and serve with chopped cilantro.

Nutrition: Calories: 181 Carbs: 12g Fat: 6g Protein: 13g
Sodium: 153 mg

Squid and Shrimp Salad

Preparation time: 10 minutes Cooking time:15 minutes Servings: 4
Ingredients:
- 8 ounces squid, cut into medium pieces 8 ounces shrimp, peeled and deveined 1 red onion, sliced
- cucumber, chopped
- tomatoes, cut into medium wedges 2 tablespoons cilantro, chopped
- 1 hot jalapeno pepper, cut in rounds 3 tablespoons rice vinegar
- 3 tablespoons dark sesame oil
- Black pepper to the taste

Directions:

1. In a bowl, mix the onion with cucumber, tomatoes, pepper, cilantro,

2. shrimp, and squid and stir well. Cut a big parchment paper in half, fold it in half heart shape and open. Place the seafood mixture in this parchment piece, fold over, seal edges, place on a baking sheet, and introduce in the oven at 400 degrees F for 15 minutes.

3. Meanwhile, in a small bowl, mix sesame oil with rice vinegar and black pepper and stir very well. Take the salad out of the oven, leave to cool down for a few minutes, and transfer to a serving plate. Put the dressing over the salad and serve right away.

Nutrition: Calories: 235 Carbs: 9g Fat: 8g
Protein: 30g Sodium: 165 mg

Parsley Seafood Cocktail

Preparation time: 2 hours and 10 minutes Cooking time: 1 hour and 30 minutes Servings: 4
Ingredients:
- big octopus, cleaned 1-pound mussels
- pounds clams
- 1 big squid cut in rings 3 garlic cloves, chopped
- 1 celery rib, cut crosswise into thirds
- ½ cup celery rib, sliced
- 1 carrot, cut crosswise into 3 pieces 1 small white onion, chopped
- bay leaf

- ¾ cup white wine
- cups radicchio, sliced 1 red onion, sliced
- 1 cup parsley, chopped 1 cup olive oil
- 1 cup red wine vinegar Black pepper to the taste

Directions:

1. Put the octopus in a pot with celery rib cut in thirds, garlic, carrot, bay leaf, white onion, and white wine. Add water to cover the octopus, cover with a lid, bring to a boil over high heat, reduce to low, and simmer within 1 and ½ hours.

2. Drain octopus, reserve boiling liquid, and leave aside to cool down. Put

3. ¼ cup octopus cooking liquid in another pot, add mussels, heat up over medium-high heat, cook until they open, transfer to a bowl, and leave aside.

4. Add clams to the pan, cover, cook over medium-high heat until

   they open, transfer to the bowl with mussels, and leave aside. Add squid to the pan, cover and cook over medium-high heat for 3 minutes, transfer to the bowl with mussels and clams.

5. Meanwhile, slice octopus into small pieces and mix with the rest of the seafood. Add sliced celery, radicchio, red onion, vinegar, olive oil, parsley, salt, and pepper, stir gently, and leave aside in the fridge within 2 hours before serving.

Nutrition: Calories: 102 Carbs: 7g Fat: 1g Protein: 16g Sodium: 0mg

Shrimp and Onion Ginger Dressing

Preparation time: 10 minutes Cooking time: 5 minutes Servings: 2
Ingredients:

- 8 medium shrimp, peeled and deveined 12 ounces package mixed salad leaves 10 cherry tomatoes, halved

- 2 green onions, sliced

- 2 medium mushrooms, sliced 1/3 cup rice vinegar

- ¼ cup sesame seeds, toasted

- tablespoon low-sodium soy sauce 2 teaspoons ginger, grated

- teaspoons garlic, minced 2/3 cup canola oil

- 1/3 cup sesame oil

Directions:

1. In a bowl, mix rice vinegar with sesame seeds, soy sauce, garlic, ginger, and stir well. Pour this into your kitchen blender, add canola oil and sesame oil, pulse very well, and leave aside. Brush shrimp with 3 tablespoons of the ginger dressing you've prepared.

2. Heat your kitchen grill over high heat, add shrimp and cook for 3 minutes, flipping once. In a salad bowl, mix salad leaves with grilled shrimp, mushrooms, green onions, and tomatoes. Drizzle ginger dressing on top and serve right away!

Nutrition: Calories: 360 Carbs: 14g Fat: 11g Protein: 49g Sodium: 469 mg

Lime Shrimp and Kale

Preparation time: 10 minutes Cooking time: 20 minutes Servings: 4
Ingredients:

- 1-pound shrimp, peeled and deveined 4 scallions, chopped
- 1 teaspoon sweet paprika
- 1 tablespoon olive oil Juice of 1 lime
- Zest of 1 lime, grated
- A pinch of salt and black pepper 2 tablespoons parsley, chopped

Directions:

1. Bring the pan to medium heat, add the scallions and sauté for 5 minutes. Add the shrimp and the other ingredients, toss, cook over medium heat for 15 minutes more, divide into bowls and serve.

Nutrition: Calories: 149 Carbs: 12g Fat: 4g Protein: 21g
Sodium: 250 mg

Parsley Cod Mix

Preparation time: 10 minutes Cooking time: 20 minutes Servings: 4
Ingredients:

- 1 tablespoon olive oil 2 shallots, chopped
- 4 cod fillets, boneless and skinless
- 2 garlic cloves, minced
- 2 tablespoons lemon juice 1 cup chicken stock
- A pinch of salt and black pepper

Directions:

1. Bring the pan to medium heat -high heat, add the shallots and the garlic and sauté for 5 minutes. Add the cod and the other ingredients, cook everything for 15 minutes more, divide between plates and serve for lunch.

Nutrition: Calories: 216 Carbs: 7g Fat: 5g Protein: 34g
Sodium: 380 mg

Fruit Shrimp Soup

Preparation time:10 minutes Cooking time:25 minutes Servings: 6
Ingredients:
- 8 ounces shrimp, peeled and deveined 1 stalk lemongrass, smashed
- 2 small ginger pieces, grated
- 6 cup chicken stock 2 jalapenos, chopped
- 4 lime leaves
- 1 and ½ cups pineapple, chopped
- cup shiitake mushroom caps, chopped 1 tomato, chopped
- ½ bell pepper, cubed
- tablespoons fish sauce 1 teaspoon sugar
- ¼ cup lime juice
- 1/3 cup cilantro, chopped 2 scallions, sliced

Directions:

1. In a pot, mix ginger with lemongrass, stock, jalapenos, and lime leaves, stir, boil over medium heat, cook within 15 minutes. Strain liquid in a bowl and discard solids.

2. Return soup to the pot again, add pineapple, tomato, mushrooms, bell pepper, sugar, and fish sauce, stir, boil over medium heat, cook for 5 minutes, add shrimp and cook for 3 more minutes. Remove from heat, add lime juice, cilantro, and scallions, stir, ladle into soup bowls and serve.

Nutrition: Calories: 290 Carbs: 39g Fat: 12g
Protein: 7g
Sodium: 21 mg

Mussels and Chickpea Soup

Preparation time: 10 minutes Cooking time:10 minutes Servings: 6
Ingredients:
- garlic cloves, minced 2 tablespoons olive oil A pinch of chili flakes
- 1 and ½ tablespoons fresh mussels, scrubbed 1 cup white wine
- 1 cup chickpeas, rinsed
- 1 small fennel bulb, sliced Black pepper to the taste Juice of 1 lemon
- 3 tablespoons parsley, chopped

Directions:

1. Heat a big saucepan with the olive oil over medium-high heat, add garlic and chili flakes, stir and cook within a couple of minutes. Add white wine and mussels, stir, cover, and cook for 3-4 minutes until mussels open.

2. Transfer mussels to a baking dish, add some of the cooking liquid over them, and fridge until they are cold enough. Take mussels out of the fridge and discard shells.

3. Heat another pan over medium-high heat, add mussels, reserved cooking liquid, chickpeas, and fennel, stir well, and heat them. Add black pepper to the taste, lemon juice, and parsley, stir again, divide between plates and serve.

Nutrition: Calories: 286 Carbs: 49g
Fat: 4g Protein: 14g
Sodium: 145mg

Shrimp Cocktail

Preparation time: 10 minutes Cooking time: 5 minutes Servings: 8
Ingredients:
- pounds big shrimp, deveined 4 cups of water
- 2 bay leaves
- 1 small lemon, halved
- Ice for cooling the shrimp Ice for serving
- medium lemon sliced for serving
- ¾ cup tomato passata
- and ½ tablespoons horseradish, prepared
- ¼ teaspoon chili powder 2 tablespoons lemon juice

Directions:

1. Pour the 4 cups water into a large pot, add lemon and bay leaves. Boil over medium-high heat, reduce temperature, and boil for 10 minutes. Put shrimp, stir and cook within 2 minutes. Move the shrimp to a bowl filled with ice and leave aside for 5 minutes.

2. In a bowl, mix tomato passata with

horseradish, chili powder, and lemon juice and stir well. Place shrimp in a serving bowl filled with ice, with lemon slices, and serve with the cocktail sauce you've prepared.

Nutrition: Calories: 276 Carbs: 0g Fat: 8g Protein: 25g
Sodium: 182 mg

Fish Stew

Preparation time: 10 minutes Cooking time: 30 minutes Servings: 4
Ingredients:

- red onion, sliced
- tablespoons olive oil
- 1-pound white fish fillets, boneless, skinless, and cubed 1 avocado, pitted and chopped
- tablespoon oregano, chopped 1 cup chicken stock
- tomatoes, cubed
- teaspoon sweet paprika
- A pinch of salt and black pepper 1 tablespoon parsley, chopped Juice of 1 lime

Directions:

1. Warm-up oil in a pot over medium heat, add the onion, and sauté within 5 minutes. Add the fish, the avocado, and the other ingredients, toss, cook over medium heat for 25 minutes more, divide into bowls and serve for lunch.

Nutrition: Calories: 78 Carbs: 8g Fat: 1g Protein: 11g
Sodium: 151 mg

Shrimp and Broccoli Soup

Preparation time: 5 minutes Cooking time: 25 minutes Servings: 4
Ingredients:

- tablespoons olive oil
- 1 yellow onion, chopped 4 cups chicken stock Juice of 1 lime
- 1-pound shrimp, peeled and deveined
- ½ cup coconut cream
- ½ pound broccoli florets
- 1 tablespoon parsley, chopped

Directions:

1. Heat a pot with the oil over medium heat,

add the onion and sauté for 5 minutes. Add the shrimp and the other ingredients, simmer over medium heat for 20 minutes more. Ladle the soup into bowls and serve.

Nutrition: Calories: 220 Carbs: 12g Fat: 7g Protein: 26g
Sodium: 577 mg

Coconut Turkey Mix

Preparation time: 10 minutes Cooking time: 30 minutes Servings: 4
Ingredients:

- yellow onion, chopped
- 1-pound turkey breast, skinless, boneless, and cubed 2 tablespoons olive oil
- garlic cloves, minced 1 zucchini, sliced
- 1 cup coconut cream
- A pinch of sea salt black pepper

Directions:

1. Bring the pan to medium heat, add the onion and the garlic and sauté for 5 minutes. Put the meat and brown within 5 minutes more. Add the rest of the ingredients, toss, bring to a simmer and cook over medium heat for 20 minutes more. Serve for lunch.

Nutrition: Calories 200 Fat 4g
Fiber 2g Carbs 14g Protein 7g
Sodium 111mg

Salmon and Cabbage Mix

Preparation time: 5 minutes Cooking time: 25 minutes Servings: 4
Ingredients:

- 4 salmon fillets, boneless 1 yellow onion, chopped 2 tablespoons olive oil
- 1 cup red cabbage, shredded 1 red bell pepper, chopped
- 1 tablespoon rosemary, chopped
- 1 tablespoon coriander, ground 1 cup tomato sauce
- A pinch of sea salt
- black pepper

Directions:

1. Bring the pan to medium heat, add the onion and sauté for 5 minutes.

2. Put the fish and sear it within 2 minutes on each side. Add the cabbage and the remaining ingredients, toss, cook over medium heat for 20 minutes more, divide between plates and serve.

Nutrition: Calories: 130 Carbs: 8g Fat: 6g Protein: 12g   Sodium: 345 mg

CHAPTER 6:

Mains

Spicy Tofu Burrito Bowls with Cilantro Avocado Sauce

Preparation time: 15 minutes Cooking time: 15 minutes Servings: 4
Ingredients:

- For the sauce:
- ¼ cup plain nonfat Greek yogurt
- ½ cup fresh cilantro leaves
- ½ ripe avocado, peeled Zest and juice of 1 lime 2 garlic cloves, peeled
- ¼ teaspoon kosher or sea salt 2 tablespoons water

For the burrito bowls:1 (14-ounce) package extra-firm tofu 1 tablespoon canola oil

- yellow or orange bell pepper, diced
- tablespoons Taco Seasoning
- ¼ teaspoon kosher or sea salt 2 cups Fluffy Brown Rice
- (15-ounce) can black beans, drained

Directions:

1. Place all the sauce ingredients in the bowl of a food processor or blender and purée until smooth. Taste and adjust the seasoning, if necessary. Refrigerate until ready for use.

2. Put the tofu on your plate lined with a kitchen towel. Put another kitchen towel over the tofu and place a heavy pot on top, changing towels if they become soaked. Let it stand within 15 minutes to remove the moisture. Cut the tofu into 1-inch cubes.

3. Warm-up canola oil in a large skillet over medium heat. Add the tofu and bell pepper and sauté, breaking up the tofu into smaller pieces for 4 to 5 minutes. Stir in the taco seasoning, salt, and ¼ cup of water. Evenly divide the rice and black beans among 4 bowls. Top with the tofu/bell pepper mixture and top with the cilantro avocado sauce.

Nutrition: Calories: 383 Fat: 13g Sodium: 438mg Carbohydrate: 48g Protein: 21g

Sweet Potato Cakes with Classic Guacamole

Preparation time: 15 minutes Cooking time: 20 minutes Servings: 4
Ingredients:
For the guacamole:

- ripe avocados, peeled and pitted
- ½ jalapeño, seeded and finely minced
- ¼ red onion, peeled and finely diced
- ¼ cup fresh cilantro leaves, chopped Zest and juice of 1 lime
  ¼ teaspoon kosher or sea salt For the cakes
- sweet potatoes, cooked and peeled
- ½ cup cooked black beans 1 large egg
- ½ cup panko bread crumbs
- teaspoon ground cumin 1 teaspoon chili powder
- ½ teaspoon kosher or sea salt
- ¼ teaspoon ground black pepper 2 tablespoons canola oil

Directions:

1. Mash the avocado, then stir in the jalapeño, red onion, cilantro, lime zest and juice, and salt in a bowl. Taste and adjust the seasoning, if necessary.

2. Put the cooked sweet potatoes plus black beans in a bowl and mash until a paste form. Stir in the egg, bread crumbs, cumin, chili powder, salt, and black pepper until combined.

3. Warm-up canola oil in a large skillet at medium heat. Form the sweet potato mixture into 4 patties, place them in the hot skillet, and cook within 3 to 4 minutes per side, until browned and crispy. Serve the sweet potato cakes with guacamole on top.

Nutrition: Calories: 369 Fat: 22g Sodium: 521mg Carbohydrate: 38g Protein: 8g

Chickpea Cauliflower Tikka Masala

Preparation time: 15 minutes Cooking time: 40 minutes Servings: 6

Ingredients:

- tablespoons olive oil
- 1 yellow onion, peeled and diced 4 garlic cloves, peeled and minced
- 1-inch piece fresh ginger, peeled and minced 2 tablespoons Garam Masala
- teaspoon kosher or sea salt
- ½ teaspoon ground black pepper
- ¼ teaspoon ground cayenne pepper
- ½ small head cauliflower, small florets
- (15-ounce) cans no-salt-added chickpeas, rinsed and drained 1 (15-ounce) can no-salt-added petite diced tomatoes, drained 1½ cups unsalted vegetable broth
- ½ (15-ounce) can coconut milk Zest and juice of 1 lime
- ½ cup fresh cilantro leaves, chopped, divided
- 1½ cups cooked Fluffy Brown Rice, divided

Directions:

1. Warm-up olive oil over medium heat, then put the onion and sauté within 4 to 5 minutes in a large Dutch oven or stockpot. Stir in the garlic, ginger, garam masala, salt, black pepper, and cayenne pepper and toast for 30 to 60 seconds, until fragrant.

2. Stir in the cauliflower florets, chickpeas, diced tomatoes, and vegetable broth and increase to medium-high. Simmer within 15 minutes, until the cauliflower is fork-tender.

3. Remove, then stir in the coconut milk, lime juice, lime zest, and half of the cilantro. Taste and adjust the seasoning, if necessary. Serve over the rice and the remaining chopped cilantro.

Nutrition: Calories: 323 Fat: 12g Sodium: 444mg Carbohydrate: 44g Protein: 11g

Lentil Avocado Tacos

Preparation time: 15 minutes Cooking time: 35 minutes Servings: 6
Ingredients:

- 1 tablespoon canola oil
- ½ yellow onion, peeled and diced 2-3 garlic cloves, minced
- 1½ cups dried lentils
- ½ teaspoon kosher or sea salt
- 3 to 3½ cups unsalted vegetable or chicken stock
- 2½ tablespoons Taco Seasoning or store-bought low-sodium taco seasoning
- 16 (6-inch) corn tortillas, toasted 2 ripe avocados, peeled and sliced

Directions:

1. Heat-up the canola oil in a large skillet or Dutch oven over medium heat. Cook the onion within 4 to 5 minutes, until soft. Mix in the garlic and cook within 30 seconds until fragrant. Then add the lentils, salt, and stock. Bring to a simmer for 25 to 35 minutes, adding additional stock if needed.

2. When there's only a small amount of liquid left in the pan, and the lentils are al dente, stir in the taco seasoning and let simmer for 1 to 2 minutes. Taste and adjust the seasoning, if necessary. Spoon the lentil mixture into tortillas and serve with the avocado slices.

Nutrition: Calories: 400 Fat: 14g Sodium: 336mg Carbohydrate: 64g

Eggplant Parmesan Stacks

Preparation time: 15 minutes Cooking time: 20 minutes Servings: 4
Ingredients:

- 1 large eggplant, cut into thick slices 2 tablespoons olive oil, divided
- ¼ teaspoon kosher or sea salt
- ¼ teaspoon ground black pepper 1 cup panko bread crumbs
- ¼ cup freshly grated Parmesan cheese
- 5 to 6 garlic cloves, minced
- ½ pound fresh mozzarella, sliced 1½ cups lower-sodium marinara
- ½ cup fresh basil leaves, torn

Directions:

1. Preheat the oven to 425°F. Coat the eggplant slices in 1 tablespoon olive oil and sprinkle with the salt and black pepper. Put on a large baking sheet, then roast for 10 to 12 minutes, until soft with crispy edges. Remove the eggplant and set the oven to a low broil.

2. In a bowl, stir the remaining tablespoon of olive oil, bread crumbs, Parmesan cheese, and garlic. Remove the cooled eggplant from the baking sheet and clean it.

3. Create layers on the same baking sheet by stacking a roasted eggplant slice with a slice of mozzarella, a tablespoon of marinara, and a tablespoon of the bread crumb mixture, repeating with 2 layers of each ingredient. Cook under the broiler within 3 to 4 minutes until the cheese is melted and bubbly.

Nutrition: Calories: 377
Fat: 22g Sodium: 509mg
Carbohydrate: 29g
Protein: 16g

Tofu & Green Bean Stir-Fry

Preparation time: 15 minutes Cooking time: 20 minutes Servings: 4
Ingredients:

- (14-ounce) package extra-firm tofu 2 tablespoons canola oil
- 1-pound green beans, chopped
- carrots, peeled and thinly sliced
- ½ cup Stir-Fry Sauce or store-bought lower-sodium stir-fry sauce 2 cups Fluffy Brown Rice
- 2 scallions, thinly sliced
- 2 tablespoons sesame seeds

Directions:

1. Put the tofu on your plate lined with a kitchen towel, put separate

2. kitchen towel over the tofu, and place a heavy pot on top, changing towels every time they become soaked. Let sit within 15 minutes to remove the moisture. Cut the tofu into 1-inch cubes.

3. Heat the canola oil in a large wok or skillet to medium-high heat. Add the tofu cubes and cook, flipping every 1 to 2 minutes, so all sides become browned. Remove from the skillet and place the green beans and carrots in the hot oil. Stir-fry for 4 to 5 minutes,
occasionally tossing, until crisp and slightly tender.

4. While the vegetables are cooking, prepare the Stir-Fry Sauce (if using homemade). Place the tofu back in the skillet. Put the sauce over the tofu and vegetables and let simmer for 2 to 3 minutes. Serve over rice, then top with scallions and sesame seeds.

Nutrition: Calories: 380 Fat: 15g
Sodium: 440mg Potassium: 454mg Carbohydrate:

45g Protein: 16g

Peanut Vegetable Pad Thai

Preparation time: 15 minutes Cooking time: 20 minutes Servings: 6
Ingredients:

- 8 ounces brown rice noodles 1/3 cup natural peanut butter
- 3 tablespoons unsalted vegetable broth
- tablespoon low-sodium soy sauce 2 tablespoons of rice wine vinegar 1 tablespoon honey
- teaspoons sesame oil
- 1 teaspoon sriracha (optional) 1 tablespoon canola oil
- red bell pepper, thinly sliced 1 zucchini, cut into matchsticks
- large carrots, cut into matchsticks
- large eggs, beaten
- ¾ teaspoon kosher or sea salt
- ½ cup unsalted peanuts, chopped
- ½ cup cilantro leaves, chopped

Directions:

1. Boil a large pot of water. Cook the rice noodles as stated in package directions. Mix the peanut butter, vegetable broth, soy sauce, rice wine vinegar, honey, sesame oil, and sriracha in a bowl. Set aside.

2. Warm-up canola oil over medium heat in a large nonstick skillet. Add the red bell pepper, zucchini, and carrots, and sauté for 2 to 3 minutes, until slightly soft. Stir in the eggs and fold with a spatula until scrambled. Add the cooked rice noodles, sauce, and salt. Toss to combine. Spoon into bowls and evenly top with the peanuts and cilantro.

Nutrition: Calories: 393 Fat: 19g Sodium: 561mg Carbohydrate: 45g Protein: 13g

Roasted Vegetable Enchiladas

Preparation time: 15 minutes Cooking time: 45 minutes Servings: 8
Ingredients:

- 2 zucchinis, diced
- red bell pepper, seeded and sliced 1 red onion, peeled and sliced
- ears corn
- 2 tablespoons canola oil

- can no-salt-added black beans, drained 1½ tablespoons chili powder
- teaspoon ground cumin
- 1/8 teaspoon kosher or sea salt
- ½ teaspoon ground black pepper 8 (8-inch) whole-wheat tortillas
- 1 cup Enchilada Sauce or store-bought enchilada sauce
- ½ cup shredded Mexican-style cheese
- ½ cup plain nonfat Greek yogurt
- ½ cup cilantro leaves, chopped

Directions:

1. Preheat oven to 400°F. Place the zucchini, red bell pepper, and red onion on a baking sheet. Place the ears of corn separately on the same baking sheet. Drizzle all with the canola oil and toss to coat. Roast for 10 to 12 minutes, until the vegetables are tender. Remove and reduce the temperature to 375°F.

2. Cut the corn from the cob. Transfer the corn kernels, zucchini, red bell pepper, and onion to a bowl and stir in the black beans, chili powder, cumin, salt, and black pepper until combined

3. Oiled a 9-by-13-inch baking dish with cooking spray. Line up the tortillas in the greased baking dish. Evenly distribute the vegetablebean filling into each tortilla. Pour half of the enchilada Sauce

4. e and sprinkle half of the shredded cheese on top of the filling.

5. Roll each tortilla into enchilada shape and place them seam-side down. Pour the remaining enchilada sauce and sprinkle the remaining cheese over the enchiladas. Bake for 25 minutes until the cheese is melted and bubbly. Serve the enchiladas with Greek yogurt and chopped cilantro.

Nutrition: Calories: 335 Fat: 15g Sodium: 557mg Carbohydrate: 42g Protein: 13g Fiber: 15g Protein: 16g

Tomato & Olive Orecchiette with Basil Pesto

Preparation time: 15 minutes Cooking time: 25 minutes Servings: 6
Ingredients:
- 12 ounces orecchiette pasta 2 tablespoons olive oil

- 1-pint cherry tomatoes, quartered
- ½ cup Basil Pesto or store-bought pesto
- ¼ cup kalamata olives, sliced
- tablespoon dried oregano leaves
- ¼ teaspoon kosher or sea salt
- ½ teaspoon freshly cracked black pepper
- ¼ teaspoon crushed red pepper flakes
- tablespoons freshly grated Parmesan cheese

Directions:

1. Boil a large pot of water. Cook the orecchiette, drain and transfer the pasta to a large nonstick skillet.

2. Put the skillet over medium-low heat, then heat the olive oil. Stir in the cherry tomatoes, pesto, olives, oregano, salt, black pepper, and crushed red pepper flakes. Cook within 8 to 10 minutes, until heated throughout. Serve the pasta with the freshly grated Parmesan cheese.

Nutrition: Calories: 332 Fat: 13g Sodium: 389mg Carbohydrate: 44g Protein: 9g

Italian Stuffed Portobello Mushroom Burgers

Preparation time: 15 minutes Cooking time: 25 minutes Servings: 4
Ingredients:
- 1 tablespoon olive oil
- 4 large portobello mushrooms, washed and dried
- ½ yellow onion, peeled and diced 4 garlic cloves, peeled and minced 1 can cannellini beans, drained
- ½ cup fresh basil leaves, torn
- ½ cup panko bread crumbs 1/8 teaspoon kosher or sea salt
- ¼ teaspoon ground black pepper
- 1 cup lower-sodium marinara, divided
- ½ cup shredded mozzarella cheese 4 whole-wheat buns, toasted
- cup fresh arugula

Directions:

1. Heat-up the olive oil in a large skillet to medium-high heat. Sear the mushrooms for 4 to 5 minutes per side, until slightly soft. Place on a baking sheet. Preheat the oven to a low broil.

2. Put the onion in the skillet and cook for 4 to 5 minutes, until slightly soft. Mix in the garlic then cooks within 30 to 60 seconds.

Move the onions plus garlic to a bowl. Add the cannellini beans and smash with the back of a fork to form a chunky paste. Stir in the basil, bread crumbs, salt, and black pepper and half of the marinara. Cook for 5 minutes.

3. Remove the bean mixture from the stove and divide among the mushroom caps. Spoon the remaining marinara over the stuffed mushrooms and top each with the mozzarella cheese. Broil within 3 to 4 minutes, until the cheese is melted and bubbly. Transfer the burgers to the toasted whole-wheat buns and top with the arugula.

Nutrition: Calories: 407 Fat: 9g Sodium: 575mg Carbohydrate: 63g Protein: 25g

Gnocchi with Tomato Basil Sauce

Preparation time: 15 minutes Cooking time: 25 minutes Servings: 6
Ingredients:

- tablespoons olive oil
- ½ yellow onion, peeled and diced 3 cloves garlic, peeled and minced
- (32-ounce) can no-salt-added crushed San Marzano tomatoes
- ¼ cup fresh basil leaves
- teaspoons Italian seasoning
- ½ teaspoon kosher or sea salt 1 teaspoon granulated sugar
- ½ teaspoon ground black pepper
- 1/8 teaspoon crushed red pepper flakes 1 tablespoon heavy cream (optional) 12 ounces gnocchi
- ¼ cup freshly grated Parmesan cheese

Directions:

1. Heat-up the olive oil in a Dutch oven or stockpot over medium heat.

2. Add the onion and sauté for 5 to 6 minutes, until soft. Stir in the garlic and stir until fragrant, 30 to 60 seconds. Then stir in the tomatoes, basil, Italian seasoning, salt, sugar, black pepper, and crushed red pepper flakes.

3. Bring to a simmer for 15 minutes. Stir in the heavy cream, if desired. For a smooth, puréed sauce, use an immersion blender or transfer sauce to a blender and purée until smooth. Taste and adjust the seasoning, if necessary.

4. While the sauce simmers, cook the gnocchi according to the package instructions, remove with a slotted spoon, and transfer to 6 bowls. Pour the sauce over the gnocchi and top with the Parmesan cheese.

Nutrition: Calories: 287 Fat: 7g Sodium: 527mg Carbohydrate: 41g Protein: 10g

Creamy Pumpkin Pasta

Preparation time: 15 minutes Cooking time: 30 minutes Servings: 6
Ingredients:

- 1-pound whole-grain linguine 1 tablespoon olive oil
- garlic cloves, peeled and minced
- 2 tablespoons chopped fresh sage 1½ cups pumpkin purée
- cup unsalted vegetable stock
- ½ cup low-fat evaporated milk
- ¾ teaspoon kosher or sea salt
- ½ teaspoon ground black pepper
- ½ teaspoon ground nutmeg
- ¼ teaspoon ground cayenne pepper
- ½ cup freshly grated Parmesan cheese, divided

Directions:

1. Cook the whole-grain linguine in a large pot of boiled water. Reserve ½ cup of pasta water and drain the rest. Set the pasta aside.

2. Warm-up olive oil over medium heat in a large skillet. Add the garlic and sage and sauté for 1 to 2 minutes, until soft and fragrant.

3. Whisk in the pumpkin purée, stock, milk, and reserved pasta water and simmer for 4 to 5 minutes, until thickened.

4. Whisk in the salt, black pepper, nutmeg, and cayenne pepper and half of the Parmesan cheese. Stir in the cooked whole-grain linguine. Evenly divide the pasta among 6 bowls and top with the remaining Parmesan cheese.

Nutrition:
Calories: 381 Fat: 8g Sodium: 175mg Carbohydrate: 63g Protein: 15g

Mexican-Style Potato Casserole

Preparation time: 15 minutes Cooking time: 60 minutes Servings: 8
Ingredients:

- Cooking spray
- tablespoons canola oil
- ½ yellow onion, peeled and diced 4 garlic cloves, peeled and minced 2 tablespoons all-purpose flour 1¼ cups milk
- 1 tablespoon chili powder
- ½ tablespoon ground cumin
- teaspoon kosher salt or sea salt
- ½ teaspoon ground black pepper
- ¼ teaspoon ground cayenne pepper
- 1½ cups shredded Mexican-style cheese, divided 1 (4-ounce) can green chilis, drained
- 1½ pounds baby Yukon Gold or red potatoes, thinly sliced 1 red bell pepper, thinly sliced

Directions:

1. Preheat the oven to 400°F. Oiled a 9-by-13-inch baking dish with cooking spray. In a large saucepan, warm canola oil on medium heat. Add the onion and sauté for 4 to 5 minutes, until soft. Mix in the garlic, then cook until fragrant, 30 to 60 seconds.

2. Mix in the flour, then put in the milk while whisking. Slow simmer for about 5 minutes, until thickened. Whisk in the chili powder, cumin, salt, black pepper, and cayenne pepper.

3. Remove from the heat and whisk in half of the shredded cheese and the green chilis. Taste and adjust the seasoning, if necessary. Line up one-third of the sliced potatoes and sliced bell pepper in the baking dish and top with a quarter of the remaining shredded cheese.

4. Repeat with 2 more layers. Pour the cheese sauce over the top and sprinkle with the remaining shredded cheese. Cover it with aluminum foil and bake within 45 to 50 minutes, until the potatoes are tender.

5. Remove the foil and bake again within 5 to 10 minutes, until the topping is slightly browned. Let cool within 20 minutes before slicing into 8 pieces. Serve.

Nutrition: Calories: 195 Fat: 10g Sodium: 487mg Carbohydrate: 19g Protein: 8g

Black Bean Stew with Cornbread

Preparation time: 15 minutes Cooking time: 55 minutes Servings: 6

Ingredients:
- For the black bean stew: tablespoons canola oil
- 1 yellow onion, peeled and diced 4 garlic cloves, peeled and minced 1 tablespoon chili powder
- tablespoon ground cumin
- ¼ teaspoon kosher or sea salt
- ½ teaspoon ground black pepper
- cans no-salt-added black beans, drained
- (10-ounce) can fire-roasted diced tomatoes
- ½ cup fresh cilantro leaves, chopped For the cornbread topping:
- 1¼ cups cornmeal
- ½ cup all-purpose flour
- ½ teaspoon baking powder
- ¼ teaspoon baking soda
- 1/8 teaspoon kosher or sea salt 1 cup low-fat buttermilk
- tablespoons honey
- 1 large egg

Directions:

1. Warm-up canola oil over medium heat in a large Dutch oven or stockpot. Add the onion and sauté for 4 to 6 minutes, until the onion is soft. Stir in the garlic, chili powder, cumin, salt, and black pepper.

2. Cook within 1 to 2 minutes, until fragrant. Add the black beans and diced tomatoes. Bring to a simmer and cook for 15 minutes. Remove, then stir in the fresh cilantro. Taste and adjust the seasoning, if necessary.

3. Preheat the oven to 375°F. While the stew simmers, prepare the cornbread topping. Mix the cornmeal, baking soda, flour, baking powder, plus salt in a bowl. In a measuring cup, whisk the buttermilk, honey, and egg until combined. Put the batter into the dry fixing until just combined.

4. In oven-safe bowls or dishes, spoon out the black bean soup. Distribute dollops of the cornbread batter on top and then spread it out evenly with a spatula. Bake within 30 minutes, until the cornbread is just set.

Nutrition: Calories: 359 Fat: 7g Sodium: 409mg Carbohydrate: 61g Protein: 14g

Vegetarian Lasagna

Preparation time: 15 minutes Cooking time: 30

minutes Servings: 6
Ingredients:

- 1 cup carrot, diced
- ½ cup bell pepper, diced 1 cup spinach, chopped 1 tablespoon olive oil
- 1 teaspoon chili powder 1 cup tomatoes, chopped
- 4 oz low-fat cottage cheese 1 eggplant, sliced
- 1 cup low-sodium vegetable broth

Directions:

1. Put carrot, bell pepper, and spinach in the saucepan. Add olive oil and chili powder and stir the vegetables well. Cook them for 5 minutes.

2. Make the sliced eggplant layer in the casserole mold and top it with vegetable mixture. Add tomatoes, vegetable stock, and cottage cheese. Bake the lasagna for 30 minutes at 375F.

Nutrition: Calories 77 Protein 4.1g
Carbohydrates 9.7g Fat 3g
Sodium 124mg

Carrot Cakes

Preparation time: 15 minutes Cooking time: 10 minutes Servings: 4
Ingredients:

- 1 cup carrot, grated
- 1 tablespoon semolina
- 1 egg, beaten
- 1 teaspoon Italian seasonings 1 tablespoon sesame oil

Directions:

1. In the mixing bowl, mix up grated carrot, semolina, egg, and Italian seasonings. Heat sesame oil in the skillet. Make the carrot cakes with the help of 2 spoons and put in the skillet. Roast the cakes for 4 minutes per side.

Nutrition: Calories 70 Protein 1.9g
Carbohydrates 4.8g Fat 4.9g
Sodium 35mg

Vegan Chili

Preparation time: 15 minutes Cooking time: 25 minutes Servings: 4
Ingredients:

- ½ cup bulgur
- 1 cup tomatoes, chopped 1 chili pepper, chopped

- cup red kidney beans, cooked
- cups low-sodium vegetable broth 1 teaspoon tomato paste
- ½ cup celery stalk, chopped

Directions:

1. Put all ingredients in the big saucepan and stir well. Close the lid and simmer the chili for 25 minutes over medium-low heat.

Nutrition: Calories 234 Protein 13.1g
Carbohydrates 44.9g Fat 0.9g
Sodium 92mg

Tuna Sandwich

Preparation time: 15 minutes Cooking time: 0 minutes Servings: 1
Ingredients:

- slices whole-grain bread
- 1 6-oz. can low sodium tuna in water, in its juice 2 tsp Yogurt (1.5% fat) or low-fat mayonnaise
- medium tomato, diced
- ½ small sweet onion, finely diced Lettuce leaves

Directions:

1. Toast whole grain bread slices. Mix tuna, yogurt, or mayonnaise, diced tomato, and onion. Cover a toasted bread with lettuce leaves and spread the tuna mixture on the sandwich. Spread tuna mixed on toasted bread with lettuce leaves. Place another disc as a cover on top. Enjoy the sandwich.

Nutrition: Calories 235 Fat 3g Protein 27.8g
Sodium 350mg Carbohydrate 25.9

Fruited Quinoa Salad

Preparation time: 15 minutes Cooking time: 0 minutes Servings: 2
Ingredients:

- cups cooked quinoa
- mango, sliced and peeled 1 cup strawberry, quartered
- ½ cup blueberries
- tablespoon pine nuts Chopped mint leave for garnish Lemon vinaigrette:
- ¼ cup olive oil
- ¼ cup apple cider vinegar Zest of lemon
- tablespoon lemon juice 1 teaspoon sugar

Directions:

1. For the Lemon Vinaigrette, whisk olive oil, apple cider vinegar, lemon zest and juice,

and sugar to a bowl; set aside. Combine quinoa, mango strawberries, blueberries, and pine nuts in a large bowl. Stir the lemon vinaigrette and garnish with mint. Serve and enjoy!

Nutrition: Calories 425
Carbohydrates 76.1g Proteins 11.3g
Fat 10.9
Sodium 16mg

Aromatic Whole Grain Spaghetti

Preparation time: 15 minutes Cooking time: 10 minutes Servings: 2
Ingredients:
- 1 teaspoon dried basil
- ¼ cup of soy milk
- 6 oz whole-grain spaghetti 2 cups of water
- teaspoon ground nutmeg

Directions:
1. Bring the water to boil, add spaghetti, and cook them for 8-10 minutes. Meanwhile, bring the soy milk to boil. Drain the cooked spaghetti and mix them up with soy milk, ground nutmeg, and dried basil. Stir the meal well.

Nutrition: Calories 128 Protein 5.6g
Carbohydrates 25g Fat 1.4g
Sodium 25mg

Chunky Tomatoes

Preparation time: 15 minutes Cooking time: 15 minutes Servings: 3
Ingredients:
- cups plum tomatoes, roughly chopped
- ½ cup onion, diced
- ½ teaspoon garlic, diced
- 1 teaspoon Italian seasonings 1 teaspoon canola oil
- chili pepper, chopped

Directions:
1. Heat canola oil in the saucepan. Add chili pepper and onion. Cook the vegetables for 5 minutes. Stir them from time to time. After this, add tomatoes, garlic, and Italian seasonings. Close the lid and sauté the dish for 10 minutes.

Nutrition: Calories 550 Protein 1.7g
Carbohydrates 8.4g
Fat 2.3g Sodium 17mg

Baked Falafel

Preparation time: 15 minutes Cooking time: 25 minutes Servings: 6
Ingredients:
- cups chickpeas, cooked 1 yellow onion, diced
- tablespoons olive oil
- cup fresh parsley, chopped 1 teaspoon ground cumin
- ½ teaspoon coriander
- garlic cloves, diced

Directions:
1. Blend all fixing in the food processor. Preheat the oven to 375F.

2. Then line the baking tray with the baking paper. Make the balls from the chickpeas mixture and press them gently in the shape of the falafel. Put the falafel in the tray and bake in the oven for 25 minutes.

Nutrition: Calories 316 Protein 13.5g
Carbohydrates 43.3g Fat 11.2g
Fiber 12.4g
Sodium 23mg

Paella

Preparation time: 15 minutes Cooking time: 25 minutes Servings: 6
Ingredients:
- 1 teaspoon dried saffron 1 cup short-grain rice
- tablespoon olive oil
- cups of water
- 1 teaspoon chili flakes
- 6 oz artichoke hearts, chopped
- ½ cup green peas 1 onion, sliced
- cup bell pepper, sliced

Directions:
1. Pour water into the saucepan. Add rice and cook it for 15 minutes. Meanwhile, heat olive oil in the skillet. Add dried saffron, chili flakes, onion, and bell pepper. Roast the vegetables for 5 minutes.

2. Add them to the cooked rice. Then add artichoke hearts and green

3. peas. Stir the paella well and cook it for 10 minutes over low heat.

Nutrition: Calories 170 Protein 4.2g

Carbohydrates 32.7g Fat 2.7g
Sodium 33mg

Mushroom Cakes

Preparation time: 15 minutes Cooking time: 10 minutes Servings: 4
Ingredients:

- cups mushrooms, chopped 3 garlic cloves, chopped
- 1 tablespoon dried dill
- 1 egg, beaten
- ¼ cup of rice, cooked
- 1 tablespoon sesame oil 1 teaspoon chili powder

Directions:

1. Grind the mushrooms in the food processor. Add garlic, dill, egg, rice, and chili powder. Blend the mixture for 10 seconds. After this, heat sesame oil for 1 minute.

2. Make the medium size mushroom cakes and put in the hot sesame oil. Cook the mushroom cakes for 5 minutes per side on medium heat.

Nutrition: Calories 103 Protein 3.7g
Carbohydrates 12g Fat 4.8g
Sodium 27mg

Glazed Eggplant Rings

Preparation time: 15 minutes Cooking time: 10 minutes Servings: 4
Ingredients:

- 3 eggplants, sliced
- 1 tablespoon liquid honey 1 teaspoon minced ginger 2 tablespoons lemon juice 3 tablespoons avocado oil
- ½ teaspoon ground coriander 3 tablespoons water

Directions:

1. Rub the eggplants with ground coriander. Then heat the avocado oil in the skillet for 1 minute. When the oil is hot, add the sliced eggplant and arrange it in one layer.

2. Cook the vegetables for 1 minute per side. Transfer the eggplant to the bowl. Then add minced ginger, liquid honey, lemon juice, and water in the skillet. Bring it to boil and add cooked eggplants. Coat the vegetables in the sweet liquid well and cook for 2 minutes more.

Nutrition: Calories 136 Protein 4.3g

Carbohydrates 29.6g Fat 2.2g
Sodium 11mg

Sweet Potato Balls

Preparation time: 15 minutes Cooking time: 10 minutes Servings: 4
Ingredients:

- 1 cup sweet potato, mashed, cooked 1 tablespoon fresh cilantro, chopped 1 egg, beaten
- 3 tablespoons ground oatmeal 1 teaspoon ground paprika
- ½ teaspoon ground turmeric
- 2 tablespoons coconut oil

Directions:

1. Mix mashed sweet potato, fresh cilantro, egg, ground oatmeal, paprika, and turmeric in a bowl. Stir the mixture until smooth and make the small balls. Heat the coconut oil in the saucepan. Put the sweet potato balls, then cook them until golden brown.

Nutrition: Calories 133 Protein 2.8g
Carbohydrates 13.1g Fat 8.2g
Sodium 44mg

Chickpea Curry

Preparation time: 15 minutes Cooking time: 10 minutes Servings: 4
Ingredients:

- 1 ½ cup chickpeas, boiled 1 teaspoon curry powder
- ½ teaspoon garam masala
- 1 cup spinach, chopped 1 teaspoon coconut oil
- ¼ cup of soy milk
- 1 tablespoon tomato paste
- ½ cup of water

Directions:

1. Heat coconut oil in the saucepan. Add curry powder, garam masala, tomato paste, and soy milk. Whisk the mixture until smooth and bring it to boil.

2. Add water, spinach, and chickpeas. Stir the meal and close the lid. Cook it within 5 minutes over medium heat.

Nutrition: Calories 298 Protein 15.4g
Carbohydrates 47.8g
Fat 6.1g Sodium 37mg

Pan-Fried Salmon with Salad

Preparation time: 15 minutes Cooking time: 20

minutes Servings: 4
Ingredients:

- Pinch of salt and pepper
- 1 tablespoon extra-virgin olive oil 2 tablespoon unsalted butter
- ½ teaspoon fresh dill
- 1 tablespoon fresh lemon juice
- 100g salad leaves, or bag of mixed leaves Salad Dressing:
- 3 tablespoons olive oil
- 2 tablespoons balsamic vinaigrette 1/2 teaspoon maple syrup (honey)

Directions:

1. Pat-dry the salmon fillets with a paper towel and season with a pinch of salt and pepper. In a skillet, warm-up oil over medium-high heat and add fillets. Cook each side within 5 to 7 minutes until golden brown.

2. Dissolve butter, dill, and lemon juice in a small saucepan. Put the butter mixture onto the cooked salmon. Lastly, combine all the salad dressing ingredients and drizzle to mixed salad leaves in a large bowl. Toss to coat. Serve with fresh salads on the side. Enjoy!

Nutrition: Calories 307 Fat 22g Protein 34.6g
Sodium 80mg
Carbohydrate 1.7g

Veggie Variety

Preparation time: 15 minutes Cooking time: 15 minutes Servings: 2
Ingredients:

- ½ onion, diced
- 1 teaspoon vegetable oil (corn or sunflower oil) 200 g Tofu/ bean curd
- 4 cherry tomatoes, halved
- 30ml vegetable milk (soy or oat milk)
- ½ tsp curry powder
- 0.25 tsp paprika
- Pinch of Salt & Pepper
- 2 slices of Vegan protein bread/ Whole grain bread Chives for garnish

Directions:

1. Dice the onion and fry in a frying pan with the oil. Break the tofu by hand into small pieces and put them in the pan. Sauté 7-8 min. Season with curry, paprika, salt, and pepper. The cherry tomatoes and milk and cook it all over roast a few minutes. Serve

with bread as desired and sprinkle with chopped chives.

Nutrition: Calories 216 Fat 8.4g Protein 14.1g
Sodium 140mg
Carbohydrate 24.8g

Vegetable Pasta

Preparation time: 15 minutes Cooking time: 15 minutes Servings: 4
Ingredients:

- 1 kg of thin zucchini 20 g of fresh ginger 350g smoked tofu
- lime
- cloves of garlic
- 2 tbsp sunflower oil
- 2 tablespoons of sesame seeds Pinch of salt and pepper
- 4 tablespoons fried onions

Directions:

1. Wash and clean the zucchini and, using a julienne cutter, cut the pulp around the kernel into long thin strips (noodles). Ginger peel and finely chop. Crumble tofu. Halve lime, squeeze juice. Peel and chop garlic.

2. Warm-up 1 tbsp of oil in a large pan and fry the tofu for about 5 minutes. After about 3 minutes, add ginger, garlic, and sesame. Season with soy sauce. Remove from the pan and keep warm.

3. Wipe out the pan, then warm 2 tablespoons of oil in it. Stir fry zucchini strips for about 4 minutes while turning. Season with salt, pepper, and lime juice. Arrange pasta and tofu. Sprinkle with fried onions.

Nutrition: Calories 262 Fat 17.7g Protein 15.4g
Sodium 62mg
Carbohydrate 17.1g

Vegetable Noodles with Bolognese

Preparation time: 15 minutes Cooking time: 15 minutes Servings: 4
Ingredients:

- 1.5 kg of small zucchini (e.g., green and yellow) 600g of carrots
- 1 onion
- tbsp olive oil 250g of beef steak
- Pinch of Salt and pepper
- tablespoons tomato paste 1 tbsp flour
- teaspoon vegetable broth (instant)
- 40g pecorino or parmesan 1 small potty of

basil

Directions:

1. Clean and peel zucchini and carrots and wash. Using a sharp, long knife, cut first into thin slices, then into long, fine strips. Clean or peel the soup greens, wash and cut into tiny cubes. Peel the onion and chop finely. Heat the Bolognese oil in a large pan. Fry hack in it crumbly. Season with salt and pepper.

2. Briefly sauté the prepared vegetable and onion cubes. Stir in tomato paste. Dust the flour, sweat briefly. Pour in 400 ml of water and stir in the vegetable stock. Boil everything, simmer for 7-8 minutes.

3. Meanwhile, cook the vegetable strips in plenty of salted water for 3-5 minutes. Drain, collecting some cooking water. Add the vegetable strips to the pan and mix well. If the sauce is not liquid enough, stir in some vegetable cooking water and season everything again.

4. Slicing cheese into fine shavings. Wash the basil, shake dry, peel off the leaves, and cut roughly. Arrange vegetable noodles, sprinkle with parmesan and basil

Nutrition: Calories 269 Fat 9.7g Protein 25.6g Sodium 253mg
Carbohydrate 21.7g

Harissa Bolognese with Vegetable Noodles

Preparation time: 15 minutes Cooking time: 30 minutes Servings: 4
Ingredients:
- onions
- 1 clove of garlic 3-4 tbsp oil
- 400g ground beef
- Pinch salt, pepper, cinnamon
- tsp Harissa (Arabic seasoning paste, tube) 1 tablespoon tomato paste
- sweet potatoes
- medium Zucchini
- stems/basil 100g of feta

Directions:

1. Peel onions and garlic, finely dice. Warm-up 1 tbsp of oil in a wide saucepan. Fry hack in it crumbly. Fry onions and garlic for a short time. Season with salt, pepper, and ½ teaspoon cinnamon. Stir in harissa

and tomato paste.

2. Add tomatoes and 200 ml of water, bring to the boil and simmer for about 15 minutes with occasional stirring. Peel sweet potatoes and zucchini or clean and wash. Cut vegetables into spaghetti with a spiral cutter.

3. Warm-up 2-3 tablespoons of oil in a large pan. Braise sweet potato spaghetti in it for about 3 minutes. Add the zucchini spaghetti and continue to simmer for 3-4 minutes while turning.

4. Season with salt and pepper. Wash the basil, shake dry and peel off the leaves. Garnish vegetable spaghetti and Bolognese on plates. Feta

5. crumbles over. Sprinkle with basil.

Nutrition: Calories 452 Fat 22.3g Protein 37.1g Sodium 253mg
Carbohydrate 27.6g

Curry Vegetable Noodles with Chicken

Preparation time: 15 minutes Cooking time: 15 minutes Servings: 2
Ingredients:
- 600g of zucchini 500g chicken fillet
- Pinch of salt and pepper
- 2 tbsp oil
- 150 g of red and yellow cherry tomatoes 1 teaspoon curry powder
- 150g fat-free cheese 200 ml vegetable broth 4 stalk (s) of fresh basil

Directions:

1. Wash the zucchini, clean, and cut into long thin strips with a spiral cutter. Wash meat, pat dry, and season with salt. Heat 1 tbsp oil in a pan. Roast chicken in it for about 10 minutes until golden brown.

2. Wash cherry tomatoes and cut in half. Approximately 3 minutes before the end of the cooking time to the chicken in the pan. Heat 1 tbsp oil in another pan. Sweat curry powder into it then stirs in cream cheese and broth. Flavor the sauce with salt plus pepper and simmer for about 4 minutes.

3. Wash the basil, shake it dry and pluck the leaves from the stems. Cut small leaves of 3 stems. Remove meat from the pan and cut it into strips. Add tomatoes, basil, and

zucchini to the sauce and heat for 2-3 minutes. Serve vegetable noodles and meat on plates and garnish with basil.

Nutrition: Calories 376
Fat 17.2g Protein 44.9g Sodium 352mg
Carbohydrate 9.5 Cholesterol 53mg

Sweet and Sour Vegetable Noodles

Preparation time: 15 minutes Cooking time: 30 minutes Servings: 4
Ingredients:

- 4 chicken fillets (75 g each) 300g of whole-wheat spaghetti 750g carrots
- ½ liter clear chicken broth (instant) 1 tablespoon sugar
- tbsp of green peppercorns
- 2-3 tbsp balsamic vinegar Capuchin flowers
- Pinch of salt

Directions:

1. Cook spaghetti in boiling water for about 8 minutes. Then drain. In the meantime, peel and wash carrots. Cut into long strips (best with a special grater). Blanch within 2 minutes in boiling salted water, drain. Wash chicken fillets. Add to the boiling chicken soup and cook for about 15 minutes.

2. Melt the sugar until golden brown. Measure 1/4 liter of chicken stock and deglaze the sugar with it. Add peppercorns, cook for 2 minutes. Season with salt and vinegar. Add the fillets, then cut into thin slices. Then turn the pasta and carrots in the sauce and serve garnished with capuchin blossoms. Serve and enjoy

Nutrition: Calories 374 Fat 21g Protein 44g Sodium 295mgCarbohydrate 23.1

Turkey Wrap

Preparation time: 15 minutes Cooking time: 0 minutes Servings: 2
Ingredients:

- 2 slices of low-fat Turkey breast (deli-style) 4 tablespoon non-fat cream cheese
- ½ cup lettuce leaves
- ½ cup carrots, slice into a stick
- 2 Homemade wraps or store-bought whole-wheat tortilla wrap

Directions:

1. Prepare all the ingredients. Spread 2 tablespoons of non-fat cream cheese on each wrap. Arrange lettuce leaves, then add

a slice of turkey breast; a slice of carrots stick on top. Roll and cut into half. Serve and enjoy!

Nutrition: Calories 224
Carbohydrates 35g Protein 10.3g
Fat 3.8g
Sodium 293mg

Chicken Wrap

Preparation time: 15 minutes Cooking time: 15 minutes Servings: 2
Ingredients:

- 1 tablespoon extra- virgin olive oil Lemon juice, divided into 3 parts 2 cloves garlic, minced
- lb. boneless skinless chicken breasts
- ½ cup non- fat plain Greek yogurt
- ½ teaspoon paprika Pinch of salt and pepper Hot sauce to taste
- Pita bread
-
- Tomato slice

Directions:

2. For the marinade, whisk 1 tablespoon olive oil, juice of 2 lemons, garlic, salt, and pepper in a bowl. Add chicken breasts to the marinade and place it into a large Ziploc. Let marinate for 30 mins. to 4 hours.

3. For the yogurt sauce, mix yogurt, hot sauce, and the remaining lemon juice season with paprika and a pinch of salt and pepper.

4. Warm skillet over medium heat and coat it with oil. Add chicken breast and cook until golden brown and cook about 8 minutes per side. Remove from pan and rest for few minutes, then slice.

5. To a piece of pita bread, add lettuce, tomato, and chicken slices. Drizzle with the prepared spicy yogurt sauce. Serve and enjoy!

Nutrition: Calories 348
Carbohydrates 8.7g
Proteins 56g Fat 10.2g Sodium 198mg

Mushroom Florentine

Preparation time: 15 minutes Cooking time: 20 minutes Servings: 4
Ingredients:

- 5 oz whole-grain pasta

- ¼ cup low-sodium vegetable broth 1 cup mushrooms, sliced
- ¼ cup of soy milk 1 teaspoon olive oil
- ½ teaspoon Italian seasonings

Directions:

1. Cook the pasta according to the direction of the manufacturer. Then pour olive oil into the saucepan and heat it. Add mushrooms and Italian seasonings. Stir the mushrooms well and cook for 10 minutes.

2. Then add soy milk and vegetable broth. Add cooked pasta and mix up the mixture well. Cook it for 5 minutes on low heat.

Nutrition: Calories 287 Protein 12.4g
Carbohydrates 50.4g Fat 4.2g
Sodium 26mg

Hassel back Eggplant

Preparation time: 15 minutes Cooking time: 25 minutes Servings: 2
Ingredients:
- 2 eggplants, trimmed
- 2 tomatoes, sliced
- 1 tablespoon low-fat yogurt 1 teaspoon curry powder
- teaspoon olive oil

Directions:

1. Make the cuts in the eggplants in the shape of the Hasselback. Then rub the vegetables with curry powder and fill with sliced tomatoes. Sprinkle the eggplants with olive oil and yogurt and wrap in the foil (each Hasselback eggplant wrap separately). Bake the vegetables at 375F for 25 minutes.

Nutrition: Calories 188 Protein 7g
Carbohydrates 38.1g Fat 3g
Sodium 23mg

Vegetarian Kebabs

Preparation time: 15 minutes Cooking time: 6 minutes Servings: 4
Ingredients:
- tablespoons balsamic vinegar 1 tablespoon olive oil
- teaspoon dried parsley
- tablespoons water
- 2 sweet peppers
- 2 red onions, peeled 2 zucchinis, trimmed

Directions:

1. Cut the sweet peppers and onions into medium size squares. Then slice the zucchini. String all vegetables into the skewers. After this, in the shallow bowl, mix up olive oil, dried parsley, water, and balsamic vinegar.

2. Sprinkle the vegetable skewers with olive oil mixture and transfer in the preheated to 390F grill. Cook the kebabs within 3 minutes per side or until the vegetables are light brown.

Nutrition: Calories 88 Protein 2.4g
Carbohydrates 13g Fat 3.9g
Sodium 14mg

White Beans Stew

Preparation time: 15 minutes Cooking time: 55 minutes Servings: 4
Ingredients:
- 1 cup white beans, soaked
- 1 cup low-sodium vegetable broth 1 cup zucchini, chopped
- 1 teaspoon tomato paste 1 tablespoon avocado oil 4 cups of water
- ½ teaspoon peppercorns
- ½ teaspoon ground black pepper
- ¼ teaspoon ground nutmeg

Directions:

1. Heat avocado oil in the saucepan, add zucchinis, and roast them for 5 minutes. After this, add white beans, vegetable broth, tomato paste, water, peppercorns, ground black pepper, and ground nutmeg. Simmer the stew within 50 minutes on low heat.

Nutrition: Calories 184 Protein 12.3g
Carbohydrates 32.6g
Fat 1g Sodium 55mg

Veggie Wrap

Preparation time: 15 minutes Cooking time: 0 minutes Servings: 2
Ingredients:
- Homemade wraps or any flour tortillas
- ½ cup spinach
- 1/2 cup alfalfa sprouts
- ½ cup avocado, sliced thinly
- medium tomato, sliced thinly
- ½ cup cucumber, sliced thinly Pinch of salt

and pepper

Directions:

1. Put 2 tablespoons of cream cheese on each tortilla. Layer each veggie according to your liking. Pinch of salt and pepper. Roll and cut into half. Serve and Enjoy!

Nutrition: Calories 249
Carbohydrates 12.3g
Protein 5.7g Fat 21.5g Sodium 169mg

Salmon Wrap

Preparation time: 15 minutes Cooking time: 0 minutes Servings: 1
Ingredients:

- oz. Smoke Salmon
- 2 teaspoon low-fat cream cheese
- ½ medium-size red onion, finely sliced
-
-
- ½ teaspoon fresh basil or dried basil Pinch of pepper
-
-
-
-
- Arugula leaves
- 1 Homemade wrap or any whole-meal tortilla

Directions:

1. Warm wraps or tortilla into a heated pan or oven. Combine cream cheese, basil, pepper, and spread into the tortilla. Top with salmon, arugula, and sliced onion. Roll up and slice. Serve and Enjoy!

Nutrition: Calories 151

Carbohydrates 19.2g
Protein 10.4g Fat 3.4g Sodium 316mg

Dill Chicken Salad

Preparation time: 15 minutes Cooking time: 15 minutes Servings: 3
Ingredients:

- tablespoon unsalted butter 1 small onion, diced
- cloves garlic, minced
- 500g boneless skinless chicken breasts Salad:
- 2/3 cup Fat-free yogurt
- ¼ cup mayonnaise light 2 large shallots, minced
- ½ cup fresh dill, finely chopped

Directions:

2. Dissolve the butter over medium heat in a wide pan. Sauté onion and garlic in the butter and chicken breasts. Put water to cover the chicken breasts by 1 inch. Bring to boil. Cover and reduce the heat to a bare simmer.

3. Cook within 8 to 10 minutes or until the chicken is cooked through. Cool thoroughly. The shred chicken finely using 2 forks. Set aside. Whisk yogurt and mayonnaise. Then toss with the chicken. Add shallots and dill. Mix again all. Serve and Enjoy!

Nutrition: Calories 253 Carbohydrates 9g Protein 33.1g
Fat 9.5g Sodium 236mg

CHAPTER 7:

Side Dishes

Turmeric Endives

Preparation time: 10 minutes Cooking time: 20 minutes Servings: 4

Ingredients:

- 2 endives, halved lengthwise 2 tablespoons olive oil
- 1 teaspoon rosemary, dried
- ½ teaspoon turmeric powder A pinch of black pepper

Directions:

1. Mix the endives with the oil and the other ingredients in a baking pan, toss gently, bake at 400 degrees F within 20 minutes. Serve as a side dish.

Nutrition: Calories 64 Protein 0.2g
Carbohydrates 0.8g Fat 7.1g
Fiber 0.6g Sodium 3mg Potassium 50mg

Parmesan Endives

Preparation time: 10 minutes Cooking time: 20 minutes Servings: 4

Ingredients:

- 4 endives, halved lengthwise 1 tablespoon lemon juice
- tablespoon lemon zest, grated
- tablespoons fat-free parmesan, grated 2 tablespoons olive oil
- A pinch of black pepper

Directions:

1. In a baking dish, combine the endives with the lemon juice and the other ingredients except for the parmesan and toss. Sprinkle the parmesan on top, bake the endives at 400 degrees F for 20 minutes, and serve.

Nutrition: Calories 71 Protein 0.9g
Carbohydrates 2.2g
Fat 7.1g Fiber 0.9g
Sodium 71mg
Potassium 88mg

Lemon Asparagus

Preparation time: 10 minutes Cooking time: 20 minutes Servings: 4

Ingredients:

- 1-pound asparagus, trimmed 2 tablespoons basil pesto
- tablespoon lemon juice
- A pinch of black pepper 3 tablespoons olive oil
- tablespoons cilantro, chopped

Directions:

1. Arrange the asparagus n a lined baking sheet, add the pesto and the other ingredients, toss, bake at 400 degrees F within 20 minutes. Serve as a side dish.

Nutrition: Calories 114 Protein 2.6g
Carbohydrates 4.5g
Fat 10.7g Fiber 2.4g Sodium 3mg
Potassium 240mg

Lime Carrots

Preparation time: 10 minutes Cooking time: 30 minutes Servings: 4

Ingredients:

- 1-pound baby carrots, trimmed 1 tablespoon sweet paprika
- 1 teaspoon lime juice
- 3 tablespoons olive oil A pinch of black pepper 1 teaspoon sesame seeds

Directions:

1. Arrange the carrots on a lined baking sheet, add the paprika and the other ingredients except for the sesame seeds, toss, bake at 400 degrees F within 30 minutes. Divide the carrots between plates, sprinkle sesame seeds on top and serve as a side dish.

Nutrition: Calories 139 Protein 1.1g
Carbohydrates 10.5g
Fat 11.2g 4g fiber
Sodium 89mg
Potassium 313mg

Creamy Cauliflower Mash

Preparation time: 10 minutes Cooking time: 25 minutes Servings: 4

Ingredients:

- pounds cauliflower florets

- ½ cup of coconut milk A pinch of black pepper
- ½ cup low-fat sour cream
- tablespoon cilantro, chopped 1 tablespoon chives, chopped

Directions:

1. Put the cauliflower in a pot, add water to cover, bring to a boil over medium heat, cook for 25 minutes and drain. Mash the cauliflower, add the milk, black pepper, and the cream, whisk well, divide between plates, sprinkle the rest of the ingredients on top, and serve.

Nutrition: Calories 188 Protein 6.1g
Carbohydrates 15g
Fat 13.4g Fiber 6.4g
Cholesterol 13mg
Sodium 88mg Potassium 811mg

Avocado, Tomato, and Olives Salad

Preparation time: 5 minutes Cooking time: 0 minutes Servings: 4
Ingredients:
- tablespoons olive oil
- 2 avocados, cut into wedges
- 1 cup kalamata olives, pitted and halved 1 cup tomatoes, cubed
- tablespoon ginger, grated A pinch of black pepper
- cups baby arugula
- tablespoon balsamic vinegar

Directions:

1. In a bowl, combine the avocados with the kalamata and the other ingredients, toss and serve as a side dish.

Nutrition: Calories 320 Protein 3g
Carbohydrates 13.9g Fat 30.4g
Fiber 8.7g Sodium 305mg Potassium 655mg

Radish and Olives Salad

Preparation time: 5 minutes Cooking time: 0 minutes Servings: 4
Ingredients:
- green onions, sliced
- 1-pound radishes, cubed
- 2 tablespoons balsamic vinegar 2 tablespoon olive oil
- 1 teaspoon chili powder
- cup black olives, pitted and halved A pinch of black pepper

Directions:

1. Mix radishes with the onions and the other ingredients in a large salad bowl, toss, and serve as a side dish.

Nutrition: Calories 123 Protein 1.3g
Carbohydrates 6.9g Fat 10.8g
Fiber 3.3g
Sodium 345mg Potassium 306mg

Spinach and Endives Salad

Preparation time: 5 minutes Cooking time: 0 minutes Servings: 4
Ingredients:
- endives, roughly shredded 1 tablespoon dill, chopped
- ¼ cup lemon juice
- ¼ cup olive oil
- 2 cups baby spinach 2 tomatoes, cubed
- cucumber, sliced
- ½ cups walnuts, chopped

Directions:

1. In a large bowl, combine the endives with the spinach and the other ingredients, toss and serve as a side dish.

Nutrition: Calories 238 Protein 5.7g
Carbohydrates 8.4g Fat 22.3g
Fiber 3.1g Sodium 24mg Potassium 506mg

Basil Olives Mix

Preparation time: 5 minutes Cooking time: 0 minutes Servings: 4
Ingredients:
- tablespoons olive oil
- 1 tablespoon balsamic vinegar A pinch of black pepper
- 4 cups corn
- 2 cups black olives, pitted and halved 1 red onion, chopped
- ½ cup cherry tomatoes halved 1 tablespoon basil, chopped
- tablespoon jalapeno, chopped
- cups romaine lettuce, shredded

Directions:

1. Mix the corn with the olives, lettuce, and the other ingredients in a large bowl, toss well, divide between plates and serve as a side dish.

Nutrition: Calories 290 Protein 6.2g
Carbohydrates 37.6g Fat 16.1g
Fiber 7.4g Sodium 613mg Potassium 562mg

Arugula Salad

Preparation time: 5 minutes Cooking time: 0 minutes Servings: 4

Ingredients:

- ¼ cup pomegranate seeds 5 cups baby arugula
- 6 tablespoons green onions, chopped
- 1 tablespoon balsamic vinegar 2 tablespoons olive oil
- 3 tablespoons pine nuts
- ½ shallot, chopped

Directions:

1. In a salad bowl, combine the arugula with the pomegranate and the other ingredients, toss and serve.

Nutrition: Calories 120 Protein 1.8g
Carbohydrates 4.2g Fat 11.6g
Fiber 0.9g
Sodium 9mg Potassium 163mg

Spanish Rice

Preparation time: 15 minutes Cooking time: 1 hour & 35 minutes Servings: 8

Ingredients:

- Brown rice – 2 cups
- Extra virgin olive oil – .25 cup Garlic, minced – 2 cloves Onion, diced – 1
- Tomatoes, diced – 2
- Jalapeno, seeded and diced – 1 Tomato paste – 1 tablespoon Cilantro, chopped - .5 cup
- Chicken broth, low-sodium – 2.5 cups

Directions:

1. Warm the oven to Fahrenheit 375 degrees. Puree the tomatoes, onion, plus garlic using a blender or food processor. Measure out two cups of this vegetable puree to use and discard the excess.

2. Into a large oven-safe Dutch pan, heat the extra virgin olive oil over medium heat until hot and shimmering. Add in the jalapeno and rice to toast, cooking while occasionally stirring for two to three minutes.

3. Slowly stir the chicken broth into the rice, followed by the vegetable puree and tomato paste. Stir until combine and increase the heat to medium-high until the broth reaches a boil.

4. Cover the Dutch pan with an oven-safe lid, transfer the pot to the preheated oven, and

bake within 1 hour and 15 minutes. Remove and stir the cilantro into the rice. Serve.

Nutrition: Calories: 265 Sodium: 32mg
Potassium: 322mg Carbs: 40g
Fat: 3g
Protein: 5g

Sweet Potatoes and Apples

Preparation time: 15 minutes Cooking time: 40 minutes Servings: 4

Ingredients:

- Sweet potatoes, sliced into 1" cubes – 2 Apples, cut into 1" cubes – 2
- Extra virgin olive oil, divided – 3 tablespoons
- Black pepper, ground - .25 teaspoon Cinnamon, ground – 1 teaspoon Maple syrup – 2 tablespoons

Directions:

1. Warm the oven to Fahrenheit 425 degrees and grease a large baking sheet with non-stick cooking spray. Toss the cubed sweet potatoes with two tablespoons of the olive oil and black pepper until coated. Roast the potatoes within twenty minutes, stirring them once halfway through the process.

2. Meanwhile, toss the apples with the remaining tablespoon of olive oil, cinnamon, and maple syrup until evenly coated. After the sweet potatoes have cooked for twenty minutes, add the apples to the baking sheet and toss the sweet potatoes and apples.

3. Return to the oven, then roast it for twenty more minutes, once again giving it a good stir halfway through. Once the potatoes and apples are caramelized from the maple syrup, remove them from the oven and serve hot.

Nutrition: Calories: 100 Carbs: 22g Fat: 0g Protein: 2g
Sodium: 38mg Potassium: 341mg

Roasted Turnips

Preparation time: 15 minutes Cooking time: 30 minutes Servings: 4

Ingredients:

- Turnips, peels, and cut into ½" cubes – 2 cups Black pepper, ground - .25 teaspoon
- Garlic powder - .5 teaspoon

- Onion powder - .5 teaspoon
- Extra virgin olive oil – 1 tablespoon

Directions:

1. Warm the oven to Fahrenheit 400 degrees and prepare a large baking sheet, setting it aside. Begin by trimming the top and bottom edges off of the turnips and peeling them if you wish. Slice them into 1/2-inch cubes.

2. Toss the turnips with the extra virgin olive oil and seasonings and then spread them out on the prepared baking sheet. Roast the turnips until tender, stirring them halfway through, about thirty minutes in total.

Nutrition: Calories: 50 Carbs: 5g Fat: 4g Protein: 1g Sodium: 44mg Potassium: 134mg

No-Mayo Potato Salad

Preparation time: 15 minutes Cooking time: 20 minutes Servings: 8
Ingredients:

- Red potatoes – 3 pounds Extra virgin olive oil - .5 cup
- White wine vinegar, divided – 5 tablespoons
- Dijon mustard – 2 teaspoons Red onion, sliced – 1 cup
- Black pepper, ground - .5 teaspoon
- Basil, fresh, chopped – 2 tablespoons
- Dill weed, fresh, chopped – 2 tablespoons Parsley, fresh, chopped – 2 tablespoons

Directions:

1. Add the red potatoes to a large pot and cover them with water until the water level is two inches above the potatoes. Put the pot on high heat, then boil potatoes until they are tender when poked with a fork, about fifteen to twenty minutes. Drain off the water.

2. Let the potatoes to cool until they can easily be handled but are still warm, then cut it in half and put them in a large bowl. Stir in three tablespoons of the white wine vinegar, giving the potatoes a good stir so that they can evenly absorb the vinegar.

3. Mix the rest of two tablespoons of vinegar, extra virgin olive oil, Dijon mustard, and black pepper in a small bowl. Add this mixture to the potatoes and give them a good toss to thoroughly coat the potatoes.

4. Toss in the red onion and minced herbs. Serve at room temperature or chilled. Serve immediately or store in the fridge for up to four days.

Nutrition: Calories: 144
Carbs: 19g Fat: 7g Protein: 2g Sodium: 46mg
Potassium: 814mg

Zucchini Tomato Bake

Preparation time: 15 minutes Cooking time: 30 minutes Servings: 4
Ingredients:

- Grape tomatoes, cut in half – 10 ounces Zucchini – 2
- Garlic, minced – 5 cloves
- Italian herb seasoning – 1 teaspoon Black pepper, ground - .25 teaspoon Parsley, fresh, chopped - .33 cup
- Parmesan cheese, low-sodium, grated - .5 cup

Directions:

1. Warm the oven to Fahrenheit 350 degrees and coat a large baking sheet with non-stick cooking spray. Mix the tomatoes, zucchini, garlic, Italian herb seasoning, Black pepper, and Parmesan cheese in a bowl.

2. Put the mixture out on the baking sheet and roast until the zucchini for thirty minutes. Remove, and garnish with parsley over the top before serving.

Nutrition: Calories: 35 Carbs: 4g Fat: 2g Protein: 2g Sodium: 30mg Potassium: 649mg

Creamy Broccoli Cheddar Rice

Preparation time: 15 minutes Cooking time: 40 minutes Servings: 6
Ingredients:

- Brown rice – 1 cup
- Chicken broth, low-sodium – 2 cups Onion, minced – 1
- Extra virgin olive oil, divided – 3 tablespoons Garlic, minced – 2 cloves
- Skim milk - .5 cup
- Black pepper, ground - .25 teaspoon Broccoli, chopped – 1.5 cups
- Cheddar cheese, low-sodium, shredded – 1 cup

Directions:

1. Put one tablespoon of the extra virgin olive oil in a large pot and sauté the onion plus garlic over medium heat within two

minutes.

2. Put the chicken broth in a pot and wait for it to come to a boil before adding in the rice. Simmer the rice over low heat for twenty-five minutes.

3. Stir the skim milk, black pepper, and remaining two tablespoons of olive oil into the rice. Simmer again within five more minutes. Stir in the broccoli and cook the rice for five more minutes, until the broccoli is tender. Stir in the rice and serve while warm.

Nutrition: Calories: 200 Carbs: 33g Fat: 3g Protein: 10g
Sodium: 50mg Potassium: 344mg

Smashed Brussels Sprouts

Preparation time: 15 minutes Cooking time: 40 minutes Servings: 6
Ingredients:

- Brussels sprouts – 2 pounds Garlic, minced – 3 cloves Balsamic vinegar – 3 tablespoons Extra virgin olive oil - .5 cup Black pepper, ground - .5 teaspoon Leek washed and thinly sliced – 1
- Parmesan cheese, low-sodium, grated - .5 cup

Directions:

1. Warm the oven to Fahrenheit 450 degrees and prepare two large baking sheets. Trim the yellow leaves and stems off of the Brussels sprouts and then steam them until tender, about twenty to twenty-five minutes.

2. Mix the garlic, black pepper, balsamic vinegar, and extra virgin olive oil in a large bowl. Add the steamed Brussels sprouts and leeks to the bowl and toss until evenly coated.

3. Spread the Brussels sprouts and leaks divided onto the prepared baking sheets.

4. Use a fork or a glass and press down on each of the Brussels sprouts to create flat patties. Put the Parmesan cheese on top and place the smashed sprouts in the oven for fifteen minutes until crispy. Enjoy hot and fresh from the oven.

Nutrition: Calories: 116 Carbs: 11g Fat: 5g Protein: 10g
Sodium: 49mg Potassium: 642mg

Cilantro Lime Rice

Preparation time: 15 minutes Cooking time: 40 minutes Servings: 6
Ingredients:

- Brown rice – 1.5 cups Lime juice – 2 tablespoons
- Lemon juice – 1.5 teaspoons
- Lime zest - .5 teaspoon Cilantro, chopped - .25 cup Bay leaf – 1
- Extra virgin olive oil – 1 tablespoon Water

Directions:

1. Cook rice and bay leaf in a pot with boiling water. Mix the mixture and allow it to boil for thirty minutes, reducing the heat slightly if need be.

2. Once the rice is tender, drain off the water and return the rice to the pot. Let it sit off of the heat within ten minutes. Remove the bay leaf and use a fork to fluff the rice. Stir the rest of the fixing into the rice and then serve immediately.

Nutrition: Calories: 94 Carbs: 15g Fat: 3g Protein: 2g
Sodium: 184mg Potassium: 245mg

Corn Salad with Lime Vinaigrette

Preparation time: 15 minutes Cooking time: 7 minutes Servings: 6
Ingredients:

- Corn kernels, fresh – 4.5 cups Lemon juice – 1 tablespoon Red bell pepper, diced – 1 Grape tomatoes halved – 1 cup Cilantro, chopped - .25 cup Green onion, chopped - .25 cup Jalapeno, diced – 1
- Red onion, thinly sliced - .25 Feta cheese - .5 cup
- Truvia baking blend – 2 tablespoons Extra virgin olive oil – 2 tablespoons Honey - .5 tablespoon
- Lime juice – 3 tablespoons
- Black pepper, ground - .125 teaspoon Cayenne pepper, ground - .125 teaspoon Garlic powder - .125 teaspoon
- Onion powder - .125 teaspoon

Directions:

1. To create your lime vinaigrette, add the lime juice, onion powder, garlic

2. powder, black pepper, cayenne pepper, and honey to a bowl. Mix, then slowly add in the extra virgin olive oil while whisking

vigorously.

3. Boil a pot of water and add in the lemon juice, Baking Truvia, and corn kernels. Allow the corn to boil for seven minutes until tender. Strain the boiling water and add the corn kernels to a bowl of ice water to stop the cooking process and cool the kernels. Drain off the ice water and reserve the corn.

4. Add the tomatoes, red pepper, jalapeno, green onion, red onion, cilantro, and cooked corn to a large bowl and toss it until the vegetables are well distributed. Add the feta cheese and vinaigrette to the vegetables and then toss until well combined and evenly coated. Serve immediately.

Nutrition: Calories: 88 Carbs: 23g Fat: 0g Protein: 3g
Sodium: 124mg Potassium: 508mg

Tex-Mex Cole Slaw

Preparation time: 15 minutes Cooking time: 0 minutes Servings: 12
Ingredients:
- Black beans, cooked – 2 cups
- Grape tomatoes, sliced in half – 1.5 cups Grilled corn kernels – 1.5 cups Jalapeno, seeded and minced – 1 Cilantro, chopped – .5 cup
- Bell pepper, diced – 1
- Coleslaw cabbage mix – 16 ounces Lime juice – 3 tablespoons
- Light sour cream - .66 cup
- Olive oil mayonnaise, reduced-fat – 1 cup Chili powder – 1 tablespoon
- Cumin, ground – 1 teaspoon
- Onion powder – 1 teaspoon Garlic powder – 1 teaspoon

Directions:

1. Mix the sour cream, mayonnaise, lime juice, garlic powder, onion powder, cumin, and chili powder in a bowl to create the dressing.

2. In a large bowl, toss the vegetables and then add in the prepared dressing and toss again until evenly coated. Chill the mixture in the fridge for thirty minutes to twelve hours before serving.

Nutrition: Calories: 50 Carbs: 10g
Fat: 1g Protein: 3g
Sodium: 194mg

Potassium: 345mg

Garlic Potato Pan

Preparation time: 10 minutes Cooking time: 1 hour
Servings: 8
Ingredients:
- 1-pound gold potatoes, peeled and cut into wedges 2 tablespoons olive oil
- red onion, chopped
- garlic cloves, minced 2 cups coconut cream
- 1 tablespoon thyme, chopped
- ¼ teaspoon nutmeg, ground
- ½ cup low-fat parmesan, grated

Directions:

1. Warm-up a pan with the oil over medium heat, put the onion plus the garlic, and sauté for 5 minutes. Add the potatoes and brown them for 5 minutes more.

2. Add the cream and the rest of the ingredients, toss gently, bring to a simmer and cook over medium heat within 40 minutes more. Divide the mix between plates and serve as a side dish.

Nutrition: Calories 230 Protein 3.6g
Carbohydrates 14.3g
Fat 19.1g Fiber 3.3g
Cholesterol 6mg Sodium 105mg Potassium 426mg

Balsamic Cabbage

Preparation time: 10 minutes Cooking time: 20 minutes Servings: 4
Ingredients:
- 1-pound green cabbage, roughly shredded 2 tablespoons olive oil
- A pinch of black pepper
- shallot, chopped
- garlic cloves, minced
- 2 tablespoons balsamic vinegar 2 teaspoons hot paprika
- teaspoon sesame seeds

Directions:

1. Heat-up a pan with the oil over medium heat, add the shallot and the garlic, and sauté for 5 minutes. Add the cabbage and the other ingredients, toss, cook over medium heat for 15 minutes, divide between plates and serve.

Nutrition: Calories 100 Protein 1.8g
Carbohydrates 8.2g Fat 7.5g
Fiber 3g Sodium 22mg
Potassium 225mg

Chili Broccoli

Preparation time: 10 minutes Cooking time: 30 minutes Servings: 4

Ingredients:

- tablespoons olive oil 1-pound broccoli florets 2 garlic cloves, minced
- 2 tablespoons chili sauce 1 tablespoon lemon juice A pinch of black pepper
- 2 tablespoons cilantro, chopped

Directions:

1. In a baking pan, combine the broccoli with the oil, garlic, and the other, toss a bit, and bake at 400 degrees F for 30 minutes. Divide the mix between plates and serve as a side dish.

Nutrition: Calories 103 Protein 3.4g
Carbohydrates 8.3gz 7.4g fat
3g fiber
Sodium 229mg Potassium 383mg

Sweet Butternut

Preparation time: 10 minutes Cooking time: 4 hours
Servings: 8

Ingredients:

- 1 cup carrots, chopped 1 tablespoon olive oil
- 1 yellow onion, chopped
- ½ teaspoon stevia
- garlic clove, minced
- ½ teaspoon curry powder 1 butternut squash, cubed
- and ½ cups low-sodium veggie stock
- ½ cup basmati rice
- ¾ cup of coconut milk
- ½ teaspoon cinnamon powder
- ¼ teaspoon ginger, grated

Directions:

1. Heat-up, a pan with the oil over medium-high heat, add the oil, onion, garlic, stevia, carrots, curry powder, cinnamon, ginger, stir, and cook 5 minutes and transfer to your slow cooker.

2. Add squash, stock, and coconut milk, stir, cover, and cook on Low for 4 hours. Divide the butternut mix between plates and serve as a side dish.

Nutrition: Calories 134 Fat 7.2g Sodium 59mg
Carbohydrate 16.5g
Fiber 1.7g Sugars 2.7g Protein 1.8g

Mushroom Sausages

Preparation time: 10 minutes Cooking time: 2 hours
Servings: 12

Ingredients:

- 6 celery ribs, chopped
- pound no-sugar, beef sausage, chopped 2 tablespoons olive oil
- ½ pound mushrooms, chopped
- ½ cup sunflower seeds, peeled 1 cup low-sodium veggie stock 1 cup cranberries, dried
- yellow onions, chopped 2 garlic cloves, minced
- 1 tablespoon sage, dried
- 1 whole-wheat bread loaf, cubed

Directions:

1. Heat-up a pan with the oil over medium-high heat, add beef, stir and brown for a few minutes. Add mushrooms, onion, celery, garlic, and sage, stir, cook for a few more minutes and transfer to your slow cooker.

2. Add stock, cranberries, sunflower seeds, and the bread cubes; cover and cook on High for 2 hours. Stir the whole mix, divide between plates and serve as a side dish.

Nutrition: Calories 188 Fat 13.8g Sodium 489mg
Carbohydrate 8.2g
Fiber 1.9g Protein 7.6g

Parsley Red Potatoes

Preparation time: 10 minutes Cooking time: 6 hours
Servings: 8

Ingredients:

- 16 baby red potatoes, halved
- 2 cups low-sodium chicken stock 1 carrot, sliced
- 1 celery rib, chopped
- ¼ cup yellow onion, chopped 1 tablespoon parsley, chopped 2 tablespoons olive oil
- A pinch of black pepper 1 garlic clove minced

Directions:

1. In your slow cooker, mix the potatoes with the carrot, celery, onion, stock, parsley, garlic, oil, and black pepper, toss, cover, and cook on Low for 6 hours. Serve.

Nutrition: Calories 257 Fat 9.5g Sodium 845mg
Carbohydrate 43.4g Protein 4.4g

Jalapeno Black-Eyed Peas Mix

Preparation time: 10 minutes Cooking time: 5 hours
Servings: 12
Ingredients:

- 17 ounces black-eyed peas 1 sweet red pepper, chopped
- ½ cup sausage, choppedyellow onion, chopped 1 jalapeno, chopped
- garlic cloves minced
- 6 cups of water
- ½ teaspoon cumin, ground A pinch of black pepper
- 2 tablespoons cilantro, chopped

Directions:

1. In your slow cooker, mix the peas with the sausage, onion, red pepper, jalapeno, garlic, cumin, black pepper, water, cilantro, cover, and cook low for 5 hours. Serve.

Nutrition: Calories 75 Fat 3.5g Sodium 94mg
Carbohydrate 7.2g Fiber 1.7g
Sugars 0.9g
Protein 4.3g

Sour Cream Green Beans

Preparation time: 10 minutes Cooking time: 4 hours
Servings: 8
Ingredients:

- 15 ounces green beans 14 ounces corn
- 4 ounces mushrooms, sliced
- 11 ounces cream of mushroom soup, low-fat and sodium-free
- ½ cup low-fat sour cream
- ½ cup almonds, chopped
- ½ cup low-fat cheddar cheese, shredded

Directions:

1. In your slow cooker, mix the green beans with the corn, mushrooms soup, mushrooms, almonds, cheese, sour cream, toss, cover, and cook on Low for 4 hours. Stir one more time, divide between plates andserve as a side dish.

Nutrition: Calories360 Fat 12.7g Sodium 220mg
Carbohydrate 58.3g Fiber 10g
Sugars 10.3g Protein 14g

Cumin Brussels Sprouts

Preparation time: 10 minutes Cooking time: 3 hours
Servings: 4
Ingredients:

- 1 cup low-sodium veggie stock

- 1-pound Brussels sprouts, trimmed and halved 1 teaspoon rosemary, dried
- teaspoon cumin, ground 1 tablespoon mint, chopped

Directions:

1. In your slow cooker, combine the sprouts with the stock and the other ingredients, cook on Low within 3 hours. Serve.

Nutrition: Calories 56 Fat 0.6g Sodium 65mg
Carbohydrate 11.4g Fiber 4.5g
Sugars 2.7g Protein 4g

Hot Brussels Sprouts

Preparation time: 10 minutes Cooking time: 25 minutes Servings: 4
Ingredients:

- tablespoon olive oil
- 1-pound Brussels sprouts, trimmed and halved 2 garlic cloves, minced
- ½ cup low-fat mozzarella, shredded A pinch of pepper flakes, crushed

Directions:

1. In a baking dish, combine the sprouts with the oil and the other ingredients except for the cheese and toss. Sprinkle the cheese on top, introduce in the oven and bake at 400 degrees F for 25 minutes. Divide between plates and serve as a side dish.

Nutrition: Calories 111 Protein 10g
Carbohydrates 11.6g Fat 3.9g
Fiber 5g Cholesterol 4mg Sodium 209mg
Potassium 447mg

Paprika Brussels Sprouts

Preparation time: 10 minutes Cooking time: 25 minutes Servings: 4
Ingredients:

- tablespoons olive oil
- 1-pound Brussels sprouts, trimmed and halved 3 green onions, chopped
- 2 garlic cloves, minced
- tablespoon balsamic vinegar 1 tablespoon sweet paprika
- A pinch of black pepper

Directions:

1. In a baking pan, combine the Brussels sprouts with the oil and the other ingredients, toss and bake at 400 degrees F within 25 minutes. Divide the mix between plates and serve.

Nutrition: Calories 121 Protein 4.4g

Carbohydrates 12.6g Fat 7.6g
Fiber 5.2g
Sodium 31mg Potassium 521mg

Roasted Okra

Preparation time: 15 minutes Cooking time: 20 minutes Servings: 4
Ingredients:

- Okra, fresh – 1 pound
- Extra virgin olive oil – 2 tablespoons Cayenne pepper, ground - .125 teaspoon Paprika – 1 teaspoon
- Garlic powder - .25 teaspoon

Directions:

1. Warm the oven to Fahrenheit 450 degrees and prepare a large baking sheet. Cut the okra into pieces appropriate 1/2-inch in size.

2. Place the okra on the baking pan and top it with the olive oil and seasonings, giving it a good toss until evenly coated. Roast the okra in the heated oven until it is tender and lightly browned and seared. Serve immediately while hot.

Nutrition: Calories: 65 Carbs: 6g Fat: 5g Protein: 2g
Sodium: 9mg
Potassium: 356mg

Brown Sugar Glazed Carrots

Preparation time: 15 minutes Cooking time: 25 minutes Servings: 6
Ingredients:

- Carrots, sliced into 1-inch pieces – 2 pounds Light olive oil - .33 cup
- Truvia Brown Sugar Blend - .25 cup
- Black pepper, ground - .25 teaspoon

Directions:

1. Warm the oven to Fahrenheit 400 degrees and prepare a large baking sheet. Toss the carrots with the oil, Truvia, and black pepper until evenly coated and then spread them out on the prepared baking sheet.

2. Place the carrots in the oven and allow them to roast until tender, about twenty to twenty-five minutes. Halfway through the cooking time, give the carrots a good serve. Remove the carrots from the oven and serve them alone or topped with fresh parsley.

Nutrition: Calories: 110 Carbs: 16g Fat: 4g Protein: 1g

Sodium: 105mg Potassium: 486mg

Oven-Roasted Beets with Honey Ricotta

Preparation time: 15 minutes Cooking time: 40 minutes Servings: 6
Ingredients:

- Purple beets – 1 pound Golden beets – 1 pound
- Ricotta cheese, low-fat - .5 cup
- Extra virgin olive oil – 3 tablespoons Honey – 1 tablespoon
- Rosemary, fresh, chopped – 1 teaspoon
- Black pepper, ground - .25 teaspoon

Directions:

1. Warm the oven to Fahrenheit 375 degrees and prepare a large baking sheet by lining it with kitchen parchment. Slice the beets into 1/2-inch cubes before tossing them with the extra virgin olive oil and black pepper.

2. Put the beets on the prepared baking sheet and allow them to roast until tender, about thirty-five to forty minutes. Halfway through the cooking process, flip the beets over.

3. Meanwhile, in a small bowl, whisk the ricotta with the rosemary and honey. Fridge until ready to serve. Once the beets are done cooking, serve them topped with the ricotta mixture, and enjoy.

Nutrition: Calories: 195 Carbs: 24g Fat: 8g Protein: 8g
Sodium: 139mg
Potassium: 521mg

Easy Carrots Mix

Preparation time: 10 minutes Cooking time: 40 minutes Servings: 6
Ingredients:

- 15 carrots, halved lengthwise 2 tablespoons coconut sugar
- ¼ cup olive oil
- ½ teaspoon rosemary, dried
- ½ teaspoon garlic powder A pinch of black pepper

Directions:

1. In a bowl, combine the carrots with the sugar, oil, rosemary, garlic powder, and

black pepper, toss well, spread on a lined baking sheet, introduce in the oven and bake at 400 degrees F for 40 minutes. Serve.

Nutrition: Calories: 60 Carbs: 9g Fat: 0g Protein: 2g Sodium: 0 mg

Tasty Grilled Asparagus

Preparation time: 10 minutes Cooking time: 6 minutes Servings: 4

Ingredients:

- 2 pounds asparagus, trimmed 2 tablespoons olive oil
- A pinch of salt and black pepper

Directions:

1. In a bowl, combine the asparagus with salt, pepper, and oil and toss well. Place the asparagus on a preheated grill over medium-high heat, cook for 3 minutes on each side, then serve.

Nutrition: Calories: 50 Carbs: 8g Fat: 1g Protein: 5g Sodium: 420 mg

Roasted Carrots

Preparation time: 10 minutes Cooking time: 30 minutes Servings: 4

Ingredients:

- pounds carrots, quartered A pinch of black pepper
- tablespoons olive oil
- 2 tablespoons parsley, chopped

Directions:

1. Arrange the carrots on a lined baking sheet, add black pepper and oil, toss, introduce in the oven, and cook within 30 minutes at 400 degrees

2. F. Add parsley, toss, divide between plates and serve as a side dish.

Nutrition:
Calories: 89
Carbs: 10g Fat: 6g Protein: 1g Sodium: 0 mg

Oven Roasted Asparagus

Preparation time: 10 minutes Cooking time: 25 minutes Servings: 4

Ingredients:

- 2 pounds asparagus spears, trimmed 3 tablespoons olive oil
- A pinch of black pepper
- 2 teaspoons sweet paprika 1 teaspoon

sesame seeds

Directions:

1. Arrange the asparagus on a lined baking sheet, add oil, black pepper, and paprika, toss, introduce in the oven and bake within 25 minutes at 400 degrees F. Divide the asparagus between plates, sprinkle sesame seeds on top, and serve as a side dish.

Nutrition: Calories: 45 Carbs: 5g Fat: 2g Protein: 2g Sodium: 0 mg

Baked Potato with Thyme

Preparation time: 10 minutes Cooking time: 1 hour and 15 minutes Servings: 8

Ingredients:

- 6 potatoes, peeled and sliced 2 garlic cloves, minced
- 2 tablespoons olive oil
- 1 and ½ cups of coconut cream
- ¼ cup of coconut milk
- 1 tablespoon thyme, chopped
- ¼ teaspoon nutmeg, ground A pinch of red pepper flakes
- and ½ cups low-fat cheddar, shredded
- ½ cup low-fat parmesan, grated

Directions:

1. Heat-up a pan with the oil over medium heat, add garlic, stir and cook for 1 minute. Add coconut cream, coconut milk, thyme, nutmeg, and pepper flakes, stir, bring to a simmer, adjust to low and cook within 10 minutes.

2. Put one-third of the potatoes in a baking dish, add 1/3 of the cream, repeat the process with the remaining potatoes and the cream, sprinkle the cheddar on top, cover with tin foil, introduce in the oven and cook at 375 degrees F for 45 minutes. Uncover the dish, sprinkle the parmesan, bake everything for 20 minutes, divide between plates, and serve as a side dish.

Nutrition: Calories: 132 Carbs: 21g Fat: 4g Protein: 2g Sodium: 56 mg

Spicy Brussels Sprouts

Preparation time: 10 minutes Cooking time: 20 minutes Servings: 6

Ingredients:

- pounds Brussels sprouts, halved 2 tablespoons olive oil
- A pinch of black pepper

- tablespoon sesame oil 2 garlic cloves, minced
- ½ cup coconut aminos
- teaspoons apple cider vinegar 1 tablespoon coconut sugar
- teaspoons chili sauce
- A pinch of red pepper flakes Sesame seeds for serving

Directions:

1. Spread the sprouts on a lined baking dish, add the olive oil, the sesame oil, black pepper, garlic, aminos, vinegar, coconut sugar, chili sauce, and pepper flakes, toss well, introduce in the oven and bake within 20 minutes at 425 degrees F. Divide the sprouts between plates, sprinkle sesame seeds on top and serve as a side dish.

Nutrition: Calories: 64 Carbs: 13g Fat: 0g Protein: 4g
Sodium: 314 mg

Baked Cauliflower with Chili

Preparation time: 10 minutes Cooking time: 30 minutes Servings: 4
Ingredients:
- tablespoons olive oil
- tablespoons chili sauce Juice of 1 lime
- garlic cloves, minced
- 1 cauliflower head, florets separated A pinch of black pepper
- 1 teaspoon cilantro, chopped

Directions:

1. In a bowl, combine the oil with the chili sauce, lime juice, garlic, and black pepper and whisk. Add cauliflower florets, toss, spread on a lined baking sheet, introduce in the oven and bake at 425 degrees F for 30 minutes. Divide the cauliflower between plates, sprinkle cilantro on top, and serve as a side dish.

Nutrition: Calories: 31 Carbs: 3g Fat: 0g Protein: 3g
Sodium: 4 mg

Baked Broccoli

Preparation time: 10 minutes Cooking time: 15 minutes Servings: 4
Ingredients:
- 1 tablespoon olive oil
- broccoli head, florets separated 2 garlic cloves, minced
- ½ cup coconut cream

- ½ cup low-fat mozzarella, shredded
- ¼ cup low-fat parmesan, grated A pinch of pepper flakes, crushed

Directions:

1. In a baking dish, combine the broccoli with oil, garlic, cream,

2. pepper flakes, mozzarella, and toss. Sprinkle the parmesan on top,

3. introduce in the oven and bake at 375 degrees F for 15 minutes. Serve.

Nutrition: Calories: 90 Carbs: 6g Fat: 7g Protein: 3g
Sodium: 30 mg

Slow Cooked Potatoes with Cheddar

Preparation time: 10 minutes Cooking time: 6 hours
Servings: 6
Ingredients:
- Cooking spray
- pounds baby potatoes, quartered
- cups low-fat cheddar cheese, shredded 2 garlic cloves, minced
- 8 bacon slices, cooked and chopped
- ¼ cup green onions, chopped 1 tablespoon sweet paprika A pinch of black pepper

Directions:

1. Spray a slow cooker with the cooking spray, add baby potatoes, cheddar, garlic, bacon, green onions, paprika, and black pepper, toss, cover, and cook on High for 6 hours. Serve.

Nutrition: Calories: 112 Carbs: 26g Fat: 4g Protein: 8g
Sodium: 234 mg

Squash Salad with Orange

Preparation time: 10 minutes Cooking time: 30 minutes Servings: 6
Ingredients:
- 1 cup of orange juice
- 3 tablespoons coconut sugar 1 and ½ tablespoons mustard 1 tablespoon ginger, grated
- 1 and ½ pounds butternut squash, peeled and roughly cubed Cooking spray
- A pinch of black pepper 1/3 cup olive oil
- 6 cups salad greens
- 1 radicchio, sliced
- ½ cup pistachios, roasted

Directions:

1. Mix the orange juice with the sugar,

mustard, ginger, black pepper, squash in a bowl, toss well, spread on a lined baking sheet, spray everything with cooking oil, and bake for 30 minutes 400 degrees F.

2. In a salad bowl, combine the squash with salad greens, radicchio,

3.

4. pistachios, and oil, toss well, then serve.

Nutrition: Calories: 17 Carbs: 2g Fat: 0g Protein: 0g Sodium: 0 mg

Colored Iceberg Salad

Preparation time: 10 minutes Cooking time: 0 minutes Servings: 4
Ingredients:
- 1 iceberg lettuce head, leaves torn 6 bacon slices, cooked and halved 2 green onions, sliced
- 3 carrots, shredded
- 6 radishes, sliced
- ¼ cup red vinegar
- ¼ cup olive oil
- 3 garlic cloves, minced A pinch of black pepper

Directions:
1. Mix the lettuce leaves with the bacon, green onions, carrots, radishes, vinegar, oil, garlic, and black pepper in a large salad bowl, toss, divide between plates and serve as a side dish.

Nutrition: Calories: 15 Carbs: 3g Fat: 0g Protein: 1g Sodium: 15 mg

Fennel Salad with Arugula

Preparation time: 10 minutes Cooking time: 0 minutes Servings: 4
Ingredients:
- 2 fennel bulbs, trimmed and shaved 1 and ¼ cups zucchini, sliced
- 2/3 cup dill, chopped
- ¼ cup lemon juice
- ¼ cup olive oil 6 cups arugula
- ½ cups walnuts, chopped
- 1/3 cup low-fat feta cheese, crumbled

Directions:
1. Mix the fennel with the zucchini, dill, lemon juice, arugula, oil, walnuts, and cheese in a large bowl, toss, then serve.

Nutrition: Calories: 65 Carbs: 6g Fat: 5g Protein: 1g

Sodium: 140 mg

Corn Mix

Preparation time: 10 minutes Cooking time: 0 minutes Servings: 4
Ingredients:
- ½ cup cider vinegar
- ¼ cup of coconut sugar A pinch of black pepper 4 cups corn
- ½ cup red onion, chopped
- ½ cup cucumber, sliced
- ½ cup red bell pepper, chopped
- ½ cup cherry tomatoes halved 3 tablespoons parsley, chopped 1 tablespoon basil, chopped
- tablespoon jalapeno, chopped 2 cups baby arugula leaves

Directions:
1. Mix the corn with onion, cucumber, bell pepper, cherry tomatoes, parsley, basil, jalapeno, and arugula in a large bowl. Add vinegar, sugar, and black pepper, toss well, divide between plates and serve as a side dish.

Nutrition: Calories: 110 Carbs: 25g Fat: 0g Protein: 2g
Sodium: 120 mg

Persimmon Salad

Preparation time: 10 minutes Cooking time: 0 minutes Servings: 4
Ingredients:
- Seeds from 1 pomegranate
- persimmons, cored and sliced 5 cups baby arugula
- 6 tablespoons green onions, chopped 4 navel oranges, cut into segments
- ¼ cup white vinegar
- 1/3 cup olive oil
- 3 tablespoons pine nuts
- 1 and ½ teaspoons orange zest, grated 2 tablespoons orange juice
- 1 tablespoon coconut sugar
- ½ shallot, chopped
- A pinch of cinnamon powder

Directions:
1. In a salad bowl, combine the pomegranate seeds with persimmons, arugula, green onions, and oranges and toss. In another bowl, combine the vinegar with the oil, pine nuts, orange zest, orange

2.

3. juice, sugar, shallot, and cinnamon, whisk well, add to the salad, toss and serve as a side dish.

Nutrition: Calories: 310 Carbs: 33g Fat: 16g
Protein: 7g
Sodium: 320 mg

Avocado Side Salad

Preparation time: 10 minutes Cooking time: 0 minutes Servings: 4
Ingredients:
- 4 blood oranges, slice into segments 2 tablespoons olive oil
- A pinch of red pepper, crushed
- 2 avocados, peeled, cut into wedges 1 and ½ cups baby arugula
- ¼ cup almonds, toasted and chopped
- 1 tablespoon lemon juice

Directions:

1. Mix the oranges with the oil, red pepper, avocados, arugula, almonds, and lemon juice in a bowl, then serve.

Nutrition: Calories: 146 Carbs: 8g Fat: 7g Protein: 15g
Sodium: 320 mg

Spiced Broccoli Florets

Preparation time: 10 minutes Cooking time: 3 hours
Servings: 10
Ingredients:
- 6 cups broccoli florets
- 1 and ½ cups low-fat cheddar cheese, shredded
- ½ teaspoon cider vinegar
- ¼ cup yellow onion, chopped
- 10 ounces tomato sauce, sodium-free 2 tablespoons olive oil
- A pinch of black pepper

Directions:

1. Grease your slow cooker with the oil, add broccoli, tomato sauce, cider vinegar, onion, and black pepper, cook on High within 2 hours, and 30 minutes. Sprinkle the cheese all over, cover, cook on High for 30 minutes more, divide between plates, and serve as a side dish.

Nutrition: Calories 119 Fat 8.7g Sodium 272mg
Carbohydrate 5.7g Fiber 1.9g
Sugars 2.3g Protein 6.2g

Lima Beans Dish

Preparation time: 10 minutes Cooking time: 5 hours
Servings: 10
Ingredients:
- 1 green bell pepper, chopped 1 sweet red pepper, chopped
- 1 and ½ cups tomato sauce, salt-free
- 1 yellow onion, chopped
- ½ cup of water
- 16 ounces canned kidney beans, no-salt-added, drained and rinsed 16 ounces canned black-eyed peas, no-salt-added, drained and rinsed 15 ounces corn
- 15 ounces canned lima beans, no-salt-added, drained and rinsed
- 15 oz canned black beans, no-salt-added, drained 2 celery ribs, chopped
- 2 bay leaves
- 1 teaspoon ground mustard 1 tablespoon cider vinegar

Directions:

1. In your slow cooker, mix the tomato sauce with the onion, celery, red pepper, green bell pepper, water, bay leaves, mustard, vinegar, kidney beans, black-eyed peas, corn, lima beans, and black beans, cook on Low within 5 hours. Discard bay leaves, divide the whole mix between plates, and serve.

Nutrition: Calories 602 Fat 4.8g Sodium 255mg
Carbohydrate 117.7g Fiber 24.6g
Sugars 13.4g
Protein 33g

Mediterranean Chickpea Salad

Preparation time: 15 minutes Cooking time: 0 minutes Servings: 6
Ingredients:
- Chickpeas, cooked – 4 cups Bell pepper, diced – 2 cups Cucumber, chopped – 1 cup Tomato, chopped – 1 cup Avocado, diced – 1
- Red wine vinegar – 2.5 tablespoons
- Lemon juice – 1 tablespoon
- Extra virgin olive oil – 3 tablespoons Parsley, fresh, chopped – 1 teaspoon Oregano, dried - .5 teaspoon
- Garlic, minced – 1 teaspoon Dill weed, dried - .25 teaspoon
- Black pepper, ground - .25 teaspoon

Directions:

1. Add the diced vegetables except for the avocado and the chickpeas to a large bowl and toss them. In a separate bowl, whisk the seasonings, lemon juice, red wine vinegar, and extra virgin olive oil to create a vinaigrette. Once combined, pour the mixture over the salad and toss to combine.

2. Place the salad in the fridge and allow it to marinate for at least a couple of hours before serving or up to two days. Immediately before serving the salad, dice the avocado and toss it in.

Nutrition: Calories: 120
Carbs: 14g Fat: 5g Protein: 4g Sodium: 15mg
Potassium: 696mg

Italian Roasted Cabbage

Preparation time: 15 minutes Cooking time: 15 minutes Servings: 8
Ingredients:
- Cabbage, sliced into 8 wedges – 1 Black pepper, ground – 1.5 teaspoons Extra virgin olive oil - .66 cup
- Italian herb seasoning – 2 teaspoons
-
  Parmesan cheese, low-sodium, grated - .66 cup

Directions:

1. Warm the oven to Fahrenheit 425 degrees. Prepare a large lined baking sheet with aluminum foil and then spray it with non-stick cooking spray.

2. Slice your cabbage in half, remove the stem, and then cut each half into four wedges so that you are left with eight wedges in total.

3. Arrange the cabbage wedges on the baking sheet and then drizzle half of the extra virgin olive oil over them. Sprinkle half of the seasonings and Parmesan cheese over the top.

4. Place the baking sheet in the hot oven, allow the cabbage to roast for fifteen minutes, and then flip the wedges. Put the rest of the olive oil over the top and then sprinkle the remaining seasonings and cheese over the top as well.

5. Return the cabbage to the oven and allow it to roast for fifteen more minutes, until tender. Serve fresh and hot.

Nutrition: Calories: 17 Carbs: 4g Fat: 0g Protein: 1g
Sodium: 27mg Potassium: 213mg

Soy Sauce Green Beans

Preparation time: 10 minutes Cooking time: 2 hours
Servings: 12
Ingredients:
- 3 tablespoons olive oil 16 ounces green beans
- ½ teaspoon garlic powder
- ½ cup of coconut sugar
-
- 1 teaspoon low-sodium soy sauce

Directions:

1. In your slow cooker, mix the green beans with the oil, sugar, soy sauce, and garlic powder, cover, and cook on Low for 2 hours. Toss the beans, divide them between plates, and serve as a side dish.

Nutrition: Calories 46 Fat 3.6g Sodium 29mg
Carbohydrate 3.6g Fiber 1.3g
Sugars 0.6g Protein 0.8g

Butter Corn

Preparation time: 10 minutes Cooking time: 4 hours
Servings: 12
Ingredients:
- 20 ounces fat-free cream cheese 10 cups corn
- ½ cup low-fat butter
- ½ cup fat-free milk
- A pinch of black pepper
-
- 2 tablespoons green onions, chopped

Directions:

2. In your slow cooker, mix the corn with cream cheese, milk, butter, black pepper, and onions, cook on Low within 4 hours. Toss one more time, divide between plates and serve as a side dish.

Nutrition: Calories 279 Fat 18g
Cholesterol 52mg
Sodium 165mg Carbohydrate 26g Fiber 3.5g
Sugars 4.8g Protein 8.1g

Stevia Peas with Marjoram

Preparation time: 10 minutes Cooking time: 5 hours
Servings: 12
Ingredients:

- 1-pound carrots, sliced
- yellow onion, chopped 16 ounces peas
- tablespoons stevia
- 2 tablespoons olive oil 4 garlic cloves, minced
- ¼ cup of water
- 1 teaspoon marjoram, dried A pinch of white pepper

Directions:

1. In your slow cooker, mix the carrots with water, onion, oil, stevia, garlic, marjoram, white pepper, peas, toss, cover, and cook on High for 5 hours. Divide between plates and serve as a side dish.

Nutrition: Calories 71 Fat 2.5g Sodium 29mg
Carbohydrate 12.1g Fiber 3.1g
Sugars 4.4g Protein 2.5g Potassium 231mg

Pilaf with Bella Mushrooms

Preparation time: 10 minutes Cooking time: 3 hours
Servings: 6
Ingredients:
- 1 cup wild rice
- 6 green onions, chopped
- ½ pound baby Bella mushrooms 2 cups of water
- 2 tablespoons olive oil 2 garlic cloves, minced

Directions:

1. In your slow cooker, mix the rice with garlic, onions, oil, mushrooms, water, toss, cover, and cook on Low for 3 hours. Stir the pilaf one more time, divide between plates and serve.

Nutrition: Calories 151 Fat 5.1g Sodium 9mg
Carbohydrate 23.3g Fiber 2.6g
Sugars 1.7g
Protein 5.2g

Parsley Fennel

Preparation time: 10 minutes
Cooking time: 2 hours and 30 minutes Servings: 4
Ingredients:
- 2 fennel bulbs, sliced Juice and zest of 1 lime 2 teaspoons avocado oil
- ½ teaspoon turmeric powder 1 tablespoon parsley, chopped
- ¼ cup veggie stock, low-sodium

Directions:

1. In a slow cooker, combine the fennel with the lime juice, zest, and the other ingredients, cook on Low within 2 hours and 30 minutes. Serve.

Nutrition: Calories 47 Fat 0.6g Sodium 71mg
Carbohydrate 10.8g Protein 1.7g

Peach and Carrots

Preparation time: 10 minutes Cooking time: 6 hours
Servings: 6
Ingredients:
- pounds small carrots, peeled
- ½ cup low-fat butter, melted
- ½ cup canned peach, unsweetened 2 tablespoons cornstarch
- tablespoons stevia
- 2 tablespoons water
- ½ teaspoon cinnamon powder 1 teaspoon vanilla extract
- A pinch of nutmeg, ground

Directions:

1. In your slow cooker, mix the carrots with the butter, peach, stevia, cinnamon, vanilla, nutmeg, and cornstarch mixed with water, toss, cover, and cook on Low for 6 hours. Toss the carrots one more time, divide between plates and serve as a side dish.

Nutrition: Calories139 Fat 10.7g Sodium 199mg
Carbohydrate 35.4g Fiber 4.2g
Sugars 6.9g Protein 3.8g

Tasty Cauliflower

Preparation time: 15 minutes Cooking time: 6 hours & 15 minutes Servings: 4
Ingredients:
- minced cloves Garlic
- 2 cups Cauliflower florets 2 tbsp. Olive Oil
- Pinch of Sea Salt
- ¼ tsp. Pepper Flakes (chili) Pinch of Black Pepper (cracked) 4 tbsp. Water
- Zest of ½ lemon

Directions:

1. In a slow cooker, place cauliflower and oil. Add vinegar. Toss well to coat thoroughly. Put in the rest of the ingredients and toss again. Cook on "low" for 2 hrs. Serve immediately.

Nutrition: Calories 150
Fats 14 g
Sodium 69 mg
Carbohydrates 6 g

Protein 2.2 g

Artichoke and Spinach Dip

Preparation time: 15 minutes Cooking time: 2 hours & 10 minutes Servings: 2

Ingredients:

- 1/8 tsp. Basil (dried)
- 14 oz. chopped Artichoke Hearts 1 ½ cups spinach
- ½ minced clove Garlic
- ¼ cup Sour Cream (low fat)
- ¼ cup shredded Cheese (Parmesan)
- ¼ cup Mozzarella Cheese (shredded) 1/8 tsp. Parsley (dried)
- ½ cup Yogurt (Greek)
- Pinch of Black Pepper Pinch of Kosher Salt

Directions:

1. Boil spinach in water for 1 min. Drain the water. Set the spinach aside to cool and then chop. Puree all the ingredients, including spinach, in a blender.

2. Transfer the mixture to the slow cooker. Add cheeses and cook for 1 hour on "low." Serve with sliced vegetables.

Nutrition: Calories 263

Fats 14 g

Sodium 537 mg

Carbohydrates 18 g

Protein 20 g

Baby Spinach and Grains Mix

Preparation time: 10 minutes Cooking time: 4 hours

Servings: 12

Ingredients:

- 1 butternut squash, peeled and cubed 1 cup whole-grain blend, uncooked 12 ounces low-sodium veggie stock 6 ounces baby spinach
- yellow onion, chopped 3 garlic cloves, minced
- ½ cup of water
- teaspoons thyme, chopped A pinch of black pepper

Directions:

1. In your slow cooker, mix the squash with whole grain, onion, garlic, water, thyme, black pepper, stock, spinach, cover, and cook on Low for 4 hours. Serve.

Nutrition: Calories78 Fat 0.6g

Sodium 259mg

Carbohydrate 16.4g Fiber 1.8g

Sugars 2g Protein 2.5g

Quinoa Curry

Preparation time: 15 minutes Cooking time: 4 hours

Servings: 8

Ingredients:

- 1 chopped Sweet Potato 2 cups Green Beans
- ½ diced onion (white)
- 1 diced Carrot
- 15 oz Chick Peas (organic and drained) 28 oz. Tomatoes (diced)
- 29 oz Coconut Milk
- 2 minced cloves of garlic
- ¼ cup Quinoa
- 1 tbs. Turmeric (ground) 1 tbsp. Ginger (grated)
- 1 ½ cups Water
- 1 tsp. of Chili Flakes 2 tsp. of Tamari Sauce

Directions:

1. Put all the listed fixing in the slow cooker. Add 1 cup of water. Stir well. Cook on "high" for 4 hrs. Serve with rice.

Nutrition: Calories 297

Fat 18 g

Sodium 364 mg

Carbohydrates 9 mg

Protein 28 g

Lemon and Cilantro Rice

Preparation time: 15 minutes Cooking time: 6 hours

Servings: 4

Ingredients:

- 3 cups Vegetable Broth (low sodium) 1 ½ cups Brown Rice (uncooked) Juice of2 lemons
- 2 tbsp. chopped cilantro

Directions:

1. In a slow cooker, place broth and rice. Cook on "low" for 5 hrs. Check the rice for doneness with a fork. Add the lemon juice and cilantro before serving.

Nutrition: Calories 56

Fats 0.3 g

Sodium 174 mg

Carbohydrates 12 g

Protein 1 g

Chili Beans

Preparation time: 15 minutes Cooking time: 4 hours
Servings: 5
Ingredients:

- 1 ½ cup chopped Bell Pepper
- 1 ½ cup sliced Mushrooms (white) 1 cup chopped Onion
- 1 tbsp. Olive Oil
- tbsp. Chili Powder
- chopped cloves Garlic
- 1 tsp. chopped Chipotle Chili
- ½ ts. Cumin
-
- 15.5 oz drained Black Beans 1 cup diced tomatoes (no salt) 2 tbsp. chopped cilantro

Directions:

1. Put all the fixing above in the slow cooker. Cook on "high" for 4 hrs. Serve

Nutrition: Calories 343
Fat 11 g
Sodium 308 mg
Carbohydrates 9 mg
Protein 29 g

Bean Spread

Preparation time: 15 minutes Cooking time: 4 hours
Servings: 20
Ingredients:

- 30 ounces Cannellini Beans
- ½ cup Broth (chicken or veg) 1 tbsp. Olive Oil
- 3 minced cloves Garlic
- ½ tsp. Marjoram
- ½ tsp. Rosemary 1/8 tsp. Pepper Pita Chips
- 1 tbsp Olive Oil

Directions:

1. Place olive oil, beans, broth, marjoram, garlic, rosemary, and pepper in the slow cooker. Cook on "low" for 4 hrs. Mash the mixture and transfer to a bowl. Serve with Pita.

Nutrition: Calories 298
Fat 18 g
Sodium 298 mg
Carbohydrates 30 mg
Protein 19 g

Stir-Fried Steak, Shiitake, and Asparagus

Preparation time: 15 minutes Cooking time: 2 hours
& 20 minutes Servings: 4
Ingredients:

- 1 tbsp. Sherry (dry) 1 tbsp. Vinegar (rice)
- ½ tbsp. Soy Sauce (low sodium)
- ½ tbsp. Cornstarch 2 tsp. Canola Oil
- ¼ tsp. Black Pepper (ground)
- minced clove Garlic
- ½ lb. sliced Sirloin Steak 3 oz. Shiitake Mushrooms
- ½ tbsp. minced Ginger 6 oz. sliced Asparagus 3 oz. Peas (sugar snap) 2 sliced scallions
- ¼ cup Water

Directions:

1. Combine cornstarch, soy sauce, sherry vinegar, broth, and pepper. Place the steaks in 1 tsp hot oil in the slow cooker for 2 mins. Transfer the steaks to a plate. Sauté ginger and garlic in the remaining oil. Add in the mushrooms, peas, and asparagus.

2. Add water and cook on "low" for 1 hr. Add the scallions and cook again for 30 mins on low. Change the heat to "high" and add the vinegar. When the sauce has thickened, transfer the steaks to the slow cooker. Stir well and serve immediately.

Nutrition:
Calories 182
Fats 7 g
Sodium 157 mg
Carbohydrates 10 mg
Protein 20 g

Chickpeas and Curried Veggies

Preparation time: 15 minutes Cooking time: 4 hours
Servings: 2
Ingredients:

- ½ tbsp. Canola Oil 2 sliced Celery Ribs
- 1/8 tsp. Cayenne Pepper
- ¼ cup Water
- sliced Carrots
- 2 sliced red Potatoes (sliced)
- ½ tbsp. Curry Powder
- ½ cup of Coconut Milk (light)
- ¼ cup drained Chickpeas (low sodium) Chopped Cilantro
- ¼ cup Yogurt (low fat)

Directions:

1. Sauté potatoes for 5 mins in oil. Add the carrots, celery, and onion. Sauté for 5 more mins. Sprinkle on the curry powder and cayenne pepper. Stir well to combine.

2. In a slow cooker, pour water and coconut milk. Add in the potatoes. Cook on "low" for 3 hrs. Add chickpeas and cook for 30 more mins. Serve in bowls along with the yogurt and cilantro garnish.

Nutrition: Calories 271
Fats 11 g
Sodium 207 mg
Carbohydrates 39 g
Protein 7 g

Brussels Sprouts Casserole

Preparation time: 15 minutes Cooking time: 4 hours & 15 minutes Servings: 3
Ingredients:

- ¾ lb. Brussels Sprouts 1 diced slice Pancetta 1 minced clove Garlic
- tbsp. chopped Shallot
- ¼ cup pine nuts (toasted)
- ¼ tsp. Black Pepper (cracked) 4 tbsp. Water

Directions:

1. Slice sprouts and place them in the slow cooker along with the water. Cook on "high" for 1 hr. Drain well. Remove the fat from the pancetta. Sauté the pancetta for 4 mins. Add the shallots, garlic, and 1/8 cup of Pine Nuts to the sauté.

2. Now, add the sprouts. Cook for 3 mins. Transfer the prepared mixture to the slow cooker. Add black pepper. 4 tbsp of water, and cook again on "low" for 2 hrs. Serve

immediately.

Nutrition: Calories 128
Fats 9 g
Sodium 56 mg
Carbohydrates 5 g
Protein 5 g

Apple Salsa

Preparation time: 15 minutes Cooking time: 2 hours
Servings: 3
Ingredients:

- 7 ½ oz. drained Black Beans
- ¼ cubed Apples (Granny Smith)
- ¼ chopped Chili Pepper (Serrano) 1/8 cup chopped onion (red)
- 1 ½ tbsp. chopped cilantro
- ¼ Lemon
- ¼ Orange
- Pinch of Sea Salt
- Pinch of Black Pepper (cracked)

Directions:

1. Mix all the ingredients in the cooker (slow cooker). Cook on "low" for an hour. Transfer to a covered container and allow to cool for 1 hr. Serve.

Nutrition: Calories 100
Fats 0.4 g
Sodium 50 mg
Carbohydrates 20 g
Protein 5 g

CHAPTER 8:

Fish and Seafood

Cod and Cauliflower Chowder

Preparation time: 15 minutes Cooking time: 40 minutes Servings: 4
Ingredients:
- 2 tablespoons extra-virgin olive oil 1 leek, sliced thinly
- 4 garlic cloves, sliced
- medium head cauliflower, coarsely chopped 1 teaspoon kosher salt
- ¼ teaspoon freshly ground black pepper
- pints cherry tomatoes
- 2 cups no-salt-added vegetable stock
- ¼ cup green olives, pitted and chopped 1 to 1½ pounds cod
-
- ¼ cup fresh parsley, minced

Directions:
1. Heat-up the olive oil in a Dutch oven or large pot over medium heat. Add the leek and sauté until lightly golden brown, about 5 minutes.

2. Add the garlic and sauté within 30 seconds. Add the cauliflower, salt, and black pepper and sauté 2 to 3 minutes.

3. Add the tomatoes and vegetable stock, increase the heat to high and boil, then turn the heat to low and simmer within 10 minutes.

4. Add the olives and mix. Add the fish, cover, and simmer 20 minutes or until fish is opaque and flakes easily. Gently mix in the parsley.

Nutrition: Calories: 270 Fat: 9g Sodium: 545mg Potassium: 1475mg Carbohydrates: 19g Protein: 30g

Sardine Bruschetta with Fennel and Lemon Crema

Preparation time: 15 minutes Cooking time: 0 minutes Servings: 4
Ingredients:
- 1/3 cup plain Greek yogurt 2 tablespoons mayonnaise
- 2 tablespoons lemon juice, divided
- 2 teaspoons lemon zest
- ¾ teaspoon kosher salt, divided
- 1 fennel bulb, cored and thinly sliced
- ¼ cup parsley, chopped, plus more for garnish
- ¼ cup fresh mint, chopped2 teaspoons extra-virgin olive oil 1/8 teaspoon freshly ground black pepper
- 8 slices multigrain bread, toasted
- 2 (4.4-ounce) cans of smoked sardines

Directions:
1. Mix the yogurt, mayonnaise, 1 tablespoon of the lemon juice, the lemon zest, and ¼ teaspoon of the salt in a small bowl.

2. Mix the remaining ½ teaspoon salt, the remaining 1 tablespoon lemon juice, the fennel, parsley, mint, olive oil, and black pepper in a separate small bowl.

3. Spoon 1 tablespoons of the yogurt mixture on each piece of toast. Divide the fennel mixture evenly on top of the yogurt mixture. Divide the sardines among the toasts, placing them on top of the fennel mixture. Garnish with more herbs, if desired.

Nutrition: Calories: 400 Fat: 16g Sodium: 565mg Carbohydrates: 51g Protein: 16g

Chopped Tuna Salad

Preparation time: 15 minutes Cooking time: 0 minutes Servings: 4
Ingredients:
- 2 tablespoons extra-virgin olive oil 2 tablespoons lemon juice
- 2 teaspoons Dijon mustard
- ½ teaspoon kosher salt
- ¼ teaspoon freshly ground black pepper 12 olives, pitted and chopped
- ½ cup celery, diced
- ½ cup red onion, diced
- ½ cup red bell pepper, diced

- ½ cup fresh parsley, chopped
- 2 (6-ounce) cans no-salt-added tuna packed in water, drained 6 cups baby spinach

Directions:

1. Mix the olive oil, lemon juice, mustard, salt, and black pepper in a medium bowl. Add in the olives, celery, onion, bell pepper, and parsley and mix well. Add the tuna and gently incorporate. Divide the spinach evenly among 4 plates or bowls. Spoon the tuna salad evenly on top of the spinach.

Nutrition: Calories: 220 Fat: 11g Sodium: 396mg
Carbohydrates: 7g
Protein: 25g

Citrus-Glazed Salmon with Zucchini Noodles

Preparation time: 15 minutes Cooking time: 20 minutes Servings: 4
Ingredients:

- 4 (5- to 6-ounce) pieces salmon
- ½ teaspoon kosher salt
- ¼ teaspoon freshly ground black pepper 1 tablespoon extra-virgin olive oil
- cup freshly squeezed orange juice 1 teaspoon low-sodium soy sauce
- zucchinis (about 16 ounces), spiralized 1 tablespoon fresh chives, chopped
- 1 tablespoon fresh parsley, chopped

Directions:

1. Preheat the oven to 350°F. Flavor the salmon with salt plus black pepper. Heat-up the olive oil in a large oven-safe skillet or sauté pan over medium-high heat. Add the salmon, skin-side down, and sear for 5 minutes, or until the skin is golden brown and crispy.

2. Flip the salmon over, then transfer to the oven until your desired doneness is reached—about 5 minutes. Place the salmon on a cutting board to rest.Place the same pan on the stove over medium-high heat.

3. Add , scraping up any brown bits, and simmering 5 to 7 minutes.

4. Split or divide the zucchini noodles into 4 plates and place 1 piece of salmon on each.

Pour the orange glaze over the salmon and zucchini noodles. Garnish with the chives and parsley.
Nutrition: Calories: 280
Fat: 13g Sodium: 255mg
Carbohydrates: 11g
Protein: 30g

Salmon Cakes with Bell Pepper Plus Lemon Yogurt

Preparation time: 15 minutes Cooking time: 15 minutes Servings: 4
Ingredients:

- ¼ cup whole-wheat bread crumbs
- ¼ cup mayonnaise 1 large egg, beaten
- 1 tablespoon chives, chopped
- tablespoon fresh parsley, chopped Zest of 1 lemon
- ¾ teaspoon kosher salt, divided
- ¼ teaspoon freshly ground black pepper
- (5- to 6-ounce) cans no-salt boneless/skinless salmon, drained and finely flaked
- ½ bell pepper, diced small
- 2 tablespoons extra-virgin olive oil, divided 1 cup plain Greek yogurt
-
- Juice of 1 lemon

Directions:

1. Mix the bread crumbs, mayonnaise, egg, chives, parsley, lemon zest, ½ teaspoon of salt, and black pepper in a large bowl. Add the salmon and the bell pepper and stir gently until well combined. Shape the mixture into 8 patties.

2. Heat-up 1 tablespoon of the olive oil in a large skillet over medium-high heat. Cook half the cakes until the bottoms are golden brown, 4 to 5 minutes. Adjust the heat to medium if the bottoms start to burn.

3. Flip the cakes and cook until golden brown, an additional 4 to 5 minutes. Repeat process with the rest of the 1 tablespoon olive oil and the rest of the cakes.

4. Mix the yogurt, lemon juice, and the remaining ¼ teaspoon salt in a small bowl. Serve with the salmon cakes.

Nutrition: Calories: 330 Fat: 23g Sodium: 385mg
Carbohydrates: 9g Protein: 21g

Halibut in Parchment with Zucchini, Shallots, and Herbs

Preparation time: 15 minutes Cooking time: 15 minutes Servings: 4

Ingredients:

- ½ cup zucchini, diced small 1 shallot, minced
- 4 (5-ounce) halibut fillets (about 1 inch thick)
- 4 teaspoons extra-virgin olive oil
- ¼ teaspoon kosher salt
- 1/8 teaspoon freshly ground black pepper 1 lemon, sliced into 1/8 -inch-thick rounds 8 sprigs of thyme

Directions:

1. Preheat the oven to 450°F. Combine the zucchini and shallots in a medium bowl. Cut 4 (15-by-24-inch) pieces of parchment paper. Fold each sheet in half horizontally.

2. Draw a large half heart on one side of each folded sheet, with the fold along the heart center. Cut out the heart, open the parchment, and lay it flat.

3. Place a fillet near the center of each parchment heart. Drizzle 1 teaspoon olive oil on each fillet. Sprinkle with salt and pepper. Top each fillet with lemon slices and 2 sprigs of thyme. Sprinkle each fillet with one- quarter of the zucchini and shallot mixture. Fold the parchment over.

4. Starting at the top, fold the parchment edges over, and continue all the way around to make a packet. Twist the end tightly to secure. Arrange the 4 packets on a baking sheet. Bake for about 15 minutes. Place on plates; cut open. Serve immediately.

Nutrition: Calories: 190
Fat: 7g Sodium: 170mg
Carbohydrates: 5g
Protein: 27g

Flounder with Tomatoes and Basil

Preparation time: 15 minutes Cooking time: 20 minutes Servings: 4

Ingredients:

- 1-pound cherry tomatoes 4 garlic cloves, sliced
- 2 tablespoons extra-virgin olive oil
- 2 tablespoons lemon juice
- 2 tablespoons basil, cut into ribbons
- ½ teaspoon kosher salt
- ¼ teaspoon freshly ground black pepper 4 (5- to 6-ounce) flounder fillets

Directions:

1. Preheat the oven to 425°F.

2. Mix the tomatoes, garlic, olive oil, lemon juice, basil, salt, and black pepper in a baking dish. Bake for 5 minutes.

3. Remove, then arrange the flounder on top of the tomato mixture. Bake until the fish is opaque and begins to flake, about 10 to 15 minutes, depending on thickness.

Nutrition: Calories: 215 Fat: 9g Sodium: 261mg
Carbohydrates: 6g Protein: 28g

Grilled Mahi-Mahi with Artichoke Caponata

Preparation time: 15 minutes Cooking time: 30 minutes Servings: 4

Ingredients:

- 2 tablespoons extra-virgin olive oil 2 celery stalks, diced
- onion, diced
- garlic cloves, minced
- ½ cup cherry tomatoes, chopped
- ¼ cup white wine
- 2 tablespoons white wine vinegar
- can artichoke hearts, drained and chopped
- ¼ cup green olives, pitted and chopped 1 tablespoon capers, chopped
- ¼ teaspoon red pepper flakes
- tablespoons fresh basil, chopped
- 4 (5- to 6-ounces each) skinless mahi-mahi fillets
- ½ teaspoon kosher salt
- ¼ teaspoon freshly ground black pepper Olive oil cooking spray

Directions:

1. Warm-up olive oil in a skillet over medium heat, then put the celery and onion, and sauté 4 to 5 minutes. Add the garlic and sauté 30 seconds. Add the tomatoes and cook within 2 to 3 minutes. Add the wine and vinegar to deglaze the pan, increasing the heat to medium-high.

2. Add the artichokes, olives, capers, and red pepper flakes and simmer, reducing the liquid by half, about 10 minutes. Mix in the basil.

3. Season the mahi-mahi with salt and pepper. Heat a grill skillet or grill pan over medium-high heat and coat with olive oil cooking spray. Add the fish and cook within 4 to 5 minutes per side. Serve topped with the artichoke caponata.

Nutrition: Calories: 245 Fat: 9g Sodium: 570mg Carbohydrates: 10g Protein: 28g

Monkfish with Sautéed Leeks, Fennel, and Tomatoes

Preparation time: 15 minutes Cooking time: 35 minutes Servings: 4
Ingredients:

- 1 to 1½ pounds monkfish
- 3 tablespoons lemon juice, divided 1 teaspoon kosher salt, divided
- 1/8 teaspoon freshly ground black pepper 2 tablespoons extra-virgin olive oil
- 1 leek, sliced in half lengthwise and thinly sliced
- ½ onion, julienned
- 3 garlic cloves, minced
- 2 bulbs fennel, cored and thinly sliced, plus ¼ cup fronds for garnish 1 (14.5-ounce) can no-salt-added diced tomatoes
- 2 tablespoons fresh parsley, chopped 2 tablespoons fresh oregano, chopped
- ¼ teaspoon red pepper flakes

Directions:

2. Place the fish in a medium baking dish and add 2 tablespoons of the lemon juice, ¼ teaspoon of the salt, plus the black pepper. Place in the refrigerator.

3. Warm-up olive oil in a large skillet over medium heat, then put the leek and onion and sauté until translucent, about 3 minutes. Add the garlic and sauté within 30 seconds. Add the fennel and sauté 4 to 5 minutes. Add the tomatoes and simmer for 2 to 3 minutes.

4. Stir in the parsley, oregano, red pepper flakes, the remaining ¾ teaspoon salt, and the remaining 1 tablespoon lemon juice. Put the fish over the leek mixture, cover, and simmer for 20 to 25 minutes. Garnish with the fennel fronds.

Nutrition: Calories: 220 Fat: 9g Sodium: 345mg Carbohydrates: 11g Protein: 22g

Caramelized Fennel and Sardines with Penne

Preparation time: 15 minutes Cooking time: 30 minutes Servings: 4
Ingredients:

- 8 ounces whole-wheat penne
- 2 tablespoons extra-virgin olive oil
- 1 bulb fennel, cored and thinly sliced, plus ¼ cup fronds 2 celery stalks, thinly sliced, plus ½ cup leaves
- 4 garlic cloves, sliced
- ¾ teaspoon kosher salt
- ¼ teaspoon freshly ground black pepper Zest of 1 lemon
- Juice of 1 lemon
- 2 (4.4-ounce) cans boneless/skinless sardines packed in olive oil, undrained

Directions:

1. Cook the penne, as stated in the package directions. Drain, reserving 1 cup of pasta water. Warm-up olive oil in a large skillet over medium heat, then put the fennel and celery and cook within 10 to 12 minutes. Add the garlic and cook within 1 minute.

2. Add the penne, reserved pasta water, salt, and black pepper. Adjust the heat to medium-high and cook for 1 to 2 minutes.

3. Remove, then stir in the lemon zest, lemon juice, fennel fronds, and celery leaves. Break the sardines into bite-size pieces and gently mix in, along with the oil they were packed in.

Nutrition: Calories: 400 Fat: 15g Sodium: 530mg Carbohydrates: 46g Protein: 22g

Cioppino

Preparation time: 15 minutes Cooking time: 35 minutes Servings: 4
Ingredients:

- 2 tablespoons extra-virgin olive oil 1 onion, diced
- 1 bulb fennel, chopped, plus ½ cup fronds for garnish
- 1-quart no-salt-added vegetable stock 4 garlic cloves, smashed
- 8 thyme sprigs
- 1 teaspoon kosher salt
- ¼ teaspoon red pepper flakes 1 dried bay leaf
- 1 bunch kale, stemmed and chopped

- 1 dozen littleneck clams tightly closed, scrubbed
- 1-pound fish (cod, halibut, and bass are all good choices)
- ¼ cup fresh parsley, chopped

Directions:

1. Heat-up the olive oil in a large stockpot over medium heat. Add the onion and fennel and sauté for about 5 minutes. Add the vegetable stock, garlic, thyme, salt, red pepper flakes, and bay leaf. Adjust the heat to medium-high, and simmer. Add the kale, cover, and simmer within 5 minutes.

2. Carefully add the clams, cover, and simmer about 15 minutes until they open. Remove the clams and set aside. Discard any clams that do not open.

3. Add the fish, cover, and simmer within 5 to 10 minutes, depending on the fish's thickness, until opaque and easily separated. Gently mix in the parsley. Divide the cioppino among 4 bowls. Place 3 clams in each bowl and garnish with the fennel fronds.

Nutrition: Calories: 285 Fat: 9g Sodium: 570mg
Carbohydrates: 19g Protein: 32g

Green Goddess Crab Salad with Endive

Preparation time: 15 minutes Cooking time: 10 minutes Servings: 4
Ingredients:
- 1-pound lump crabmeat 2/3 cup plain Greek yogurt 3 tablespoons mayonnaise
- 3 tablespoons fresh chives, chopped, plus additional for garnish 3 tablespoons fresh parsley, chopped, plus extra for garnish
- tablespoons fresh basil, chopped, plus extra for garnish
- Zest of 1 lemon Juice of 1 lemon
- ½ teaspoon kosher salt
- ¼ teaspoon freshly ground black pepper
- endives, ends cut off and leaves separated

Directions:

1. In a medium bowl, combine the crab, yogurt, mayonnaise, chives, parsley, basil, lemon zest, lemon juice, salt, plus black pepper and mix until well combined.

2. Place the endive leaves on 4 salad plates. Divide the crab mixture evenly on top of the endive. Garnish with additional herbs, if

desired.

Nutrition: Calories: 200 Fat: 9g Sodium: 570mg
Carbohydrates: 44g
Protein: 25g

Seared Scallops with Blood Orange Glaze

Preparation time: 15 minutes Cooking time: 20 minutes Servings: 4
Ingredients:
- tablespoons extra-virgin olive oil, divided 3 garlic cloves, minced
- ½ teaspoon kosher salt, divided
- blood oranges, juiced
- teaspoon blood orange zest
- ½ teaspoon red pepper flakes
- 1-pound scallops, small side muscle removed
- ¼ teaspoon freshly ground black pepper
- ¼ cup fresh chives, chopped

Directions:

1. Heat-up 1 tablespoon of the olive oil in a small saucepan over medium- high heat. Add the garlic and ¼ teaspoon of the salt and sauté for 30 seconds.

2. Add the orange juice and zest, bring to a boil, reduce the heat to medium-low, and cook within 20 minutes, or until the liquid reduces by half and becomes a thicker syrup consistency. Remove and mix in the red pepper flakes.

3. Pat the scallops dry with a paper towel and season with the remaining ¼ teaspoon salt and the black pepper. Heat-up the remaining 2 tablespoons of olive oil in a large skillet on medium-high heat. Add the scallops gently and sear.

4. Cook on each side within 2 minutes. If cooking in 2 batches, use 1 tablespoon of oil per batch. Serve the scallops with the blood orange glaze and garnish with the chives.

Nutrition:
Calories: 140 Fat: 4g Sodium: 570mg
Carbohydrates: 12g Protein: 15g

Air-Fryer Fish Cakes

Preparation time: 15 minutes Cooking time: 10 minutes Servings: 2
Ingredients:

- Cooking spray
- 10 oz finely chopped white fish
- 2/3 cup whole-wheat panko breadcrumbs
- 3 tablespoons finely chopped fresh Cilantro
  2 tablespoons Thai sweet chili sauce
- 2 tablespoons canola mayonnaise
- 1 large egg
- 1/8 teaspoon salt
- ¼ teaspoon ground pepper 2 lime wedges

Directions:

1. Oiled the basket of an air fryer with cooking spray. Put fish, cilantro, panko, chili sauce, egg, mayonnaise, pepper, and salt in a medium bowl; stir until well mixed. Shape the mixture into four 3-inch-diameter cakes.

2. Oiled the cakes with cooking spray; place in the basket. Cook at 400oF until the cakes are browned for 9 to 10 minutes. Serve with lime wedges.

Nutrition: Calories 399
Fat 15.5 g
Sodium 537 mg
Carbohydrates 27.9 g
Protein 34.6 g

Pesto Shrimp Pasta

Preparation time: 15 minutes Cooking time: 12 minutes Servings: 4
Ingredients:

- 1/8 teaspoon freshly cracked pepper 1 cup dried orzo
- 4 tsp packaged pesto sauce mix
- 1 lemon, halved
- 1/8 teaspoon coarse salt
- 1-pound medium shrimp, thawed
- medium zucchini, halved lengthwise and sliced 2 tablespoons olive oil, divided
- 1-ounce shaved Parmesan cheese

Directions:

1. Prepare orzo pasta concerning package directions. Drain; reserving ¼ cup of the pasta cooking water. Mix 1 teaspoon of the pesto mix into the kept cooking water and set aside.

2. Mix 3 teaspoons of the pesto mix plus 1 tablespoon of the olive oil in a large plastic bag. Seal and shake to mix. Put the shrimp in the bag; seal and turn to coat. Set aside.

3. Sauté zucchini in a big skillet over moderate heat for 1 to 2 minutes, stirring repeatedly. Put the pesto-marinated shrimp in the skillet and cook for 5 minutes or until shrimp is dense.

4. Put the cooked pasta in the skillet with the zucchini and shrimp combination. Stir in the kept pasta water until absorbed, grating up any seasoning in the bottom of the pan. Season with pepper and salt. Squeeze the lemon over the pasta. Top with Parmesan, then serve.

Nutrition: Calories 361
Fat 10.1 g
Sodium 502 mg
Carbohydrates 35.8 g
Protein 31.6 g

Quick Shrimp Scampi

Preparation time: 5 minutes Cooking time: 10 minutes Servings: 4
Ingredients:

- tablespoons olive oil
- ½ cup (120 ml) dry white wine 3 garlic cloves, minced
- 1 1/2 pound (680 g) large shrimp, peeled and stroked dry Large pinch of crushed red pepper flakes
- 1 lemon, zested, one half cut into slices
- 1/8 Salt 1/8 pepper
- 4 tbsp unsalted butter, slice into 4 pieces
- Large handful of fresh chopped flat-leaf parsley.

Directions:

1. In a large skillet, warm up the oil over moderate heat. Flavor the shrimp with salt plus pepper, then put them in the skillet in a single coating. Cook, without interruption, until the shrimp's bottoms begin to turn pink, about 1 minute after.

2. Turnover the shrimp and cook until almost cooked through, about 1 minute more. Keep the shrimp on a plate and set aside.

3. Adjust to medium, add the pepper flakes, garlic, and a little more oil if the pan seems dry; cook, repeatedly stirring until the garlic just begins to turn golden, about 1 minute. Add the wine, scraping up any burnt bits from the bottom of the pan, and simmer until most of the wine has vanished.

4. Mix in the butter, then season the sauce

with lemon juice and salt from one lemon half. Add the cooked shrimp, the lemon zest, any juices accrued on the plate, and parsley and heave until the shrimp is warmed

5. through, about 1 minute. Serve with lemon wedges, if you wish.

Nutrition: Calories 316
Fat 20.3 g
Sodium 1039 mg
Carbohydrates 4 g
Protein 23.5 g

Poached Salmon with Creamy Piccata Sauce

Preparation time: 5 minutes Cooking time: 15 minutes Servings: 4
Ingredients:

- 1-pound center-cut salmon fillet skinned and cut into 4 portions 2 tablespoons lemon juice
- 2 teaspoons extra-virgin olive oil
- ¼ cup reduced-fat sour cream 1 large shallot, minced
- 1 cup dry white wine, divided
- tablespoon chopped fresh dill 4 teaspoons capers, rinsed
- ¼ teaspoon salt

Directions:

1. Place salmon in a wide skillet and add ½ cup wine and sufficient water to cover the salmon. Bring it to boil over high-temperature heat. Simmer, turn the salmon over, cook within 5 minutes and then remove from the heat.

2. In the meantime, heat-up oil in a medium skillet over moderate heat. Add shallot and cook, stirring, until scented, about 30 seconds. Add the remaining ½ cup wine; boil until slightly condensed, about 1 minute.

3. Stir in lemon juice plus capers; cook 1 minute more. Remove, stir in sour cream and salt. Top the salmon with the sauce and relish it with dill before serving.

Nutrition: Calories 229
Fat 8.3 g
Sodium 286 mg
Carbohydrates 3.7 g
Protein 23.3 g

Tuscan-Style Tuna Salad

Preparation time: 15 minutes Cooking time: 0 minutes Servings: 4
Ingredients:

- 6-ounce cans chunk light tuna, drained.
- ¼ teaspoon salt
- 10 cherry tomatoes
- 2 tablespoons lemon juice
- 4 scallions, trimmed and sliced
- 2 tablespoons extra-virgin olive oil 1 15-ounce can small white beans Freshly ground pepper

Directions:

1. Mix tuna, beans, scallions, tomatoes, juice, oil, lemon, pepper, and salt in a medium bowl. Stir gently. Refrigerate until ready to serve.

Nutrition: Calories 199
Fat 8.8 g
Sodium 555 mg
Carbohydrates 19.8 g
Protein 16.5 g

Tuna Salad-Stuffed Tomatoes with Arugula

Preparation time: 5 minutes Cooking time: 15 minutes Servings: 4
Ingredients:

- 1 teaspoon dried thyme
- 3 tablespoons sherry vinegar
- 3 tablespoons extra-virgin olive oil 1/3 cup chopped celery
- ¼ teaspoon freshly ground pepper 4 large tomatoes
- 8 cups baby arugula
- ¼ cup finely chopped red onion
- ¼ teaspoon salt
- ¼ cup chopped Kalamata olives
- 2 5-oz cans chunk light tuna in olive oil, drained 1 can great northern beans, rinsed

Directions:

1. Whisk oil, salt, vinegar, and pepper in an average-sized bowl. Put 3 tablespoons of the dressing in a big bowl and set aside.

2. Slice enough off the top of each tomato to remove the core, chop enough of the tops to equal ½ cup and add to the average-sized bowl. Scoop out the soft tomato tissue using a teaspoon or melon baller and discard the pulp

3. Add tuna, onion, thyme, olives, and celery to the average-sized bowl; gently toss to mix. Fill the scooped tomatoes with the tuna mixture. Add beans and arugula to the gauze in the large bowl and toss to combine. Divide the salad into four plates and top each with a stuffed tomato.

Nutrition:
Calories 353
Fat 17.6 g
Sodium 501 mg
Carbohydrates 29.9 g
Protein 19.7 g

Herbed Seafood Casserole

Preparation time: 15 minutes Cooking time: 50 minutes Servings: 12
Ingredients:
- ½ cups uncooked long grain rice 2 tablespoons butter
- ¼ teaspoon pepper
- tablespoons minced fresh parsley 1 medium onion, finely chopped
- garlic cloves, minced
- 1 medium carrot, shredded
- ½ teaspoon salt
- 3 celery ribs, thinly sliced
- 1 ½ teaspoon snipped fresh dill or ½ teaspoon dill weed Seafood:
- 1-pound
- uncooked medium shrimp, peeled and deveined 1 can
  crab meat, drained, flaked, and cartilage removed
  ¼ cup all-purpose flour 1-pound bay scallops
- ½ teaspoon salt
- 1 package (8 ounces) cream cheese, cubed 5 tablespoons butter, cubed
- 1 ½ cups half-and-half cream
- ½ teaspoon snipped fresh dill or ½ teaspoon dill weed
- ¼ teaspoon dried thyme
- ¼ teaspoon pepper Topping:
- Tablepoons butter, melted 1 ½ cups soft bread crumbs

Directions:
1. Preheat oven to 325°F. Cook rice according to package directions. In the meantime, in a big skillet, heat butter over moderate heat. Add onion, celery, and carrot; cook and stir until crisp-tender. Add garlic, pepper, and salt; cook 1 minute longer. Add to the cooked rice. Stir in parsley and dill. Transfer to a greased baking dish.

2. Fill a large saucepan with 2/3 full with water and bring to a boil. Reduce heat to medium. Add shrimp; simmer, uncovered, for 30 seconds. Add scallops; simmer for 3 minutes or just until shrimp turn pink and scallops are firm and dense. Reserve 1 cup of cooking liquid. Put the seafood in a large bowl; stir in crab.

3. Dissolve the butter over medium heat in a small saucepan. Stir in flour until mixed; slowly stir in cream and kept cooking liquid. Boil within 2 minutes or until condensed and foamy. Reduce heat. Stir in cream cheese, dill and season until smooth. Stir into the seafood blend.

4. Pour over rice mixture. Mix the bread crumbs with melted butter; sprinkle over the top. Bake, uncovered, 50 minutes or until it turns golden brown. Stand 10 minutes before dishing.

Nutrition:
Calories 404 Fat 20g Sodium 616mg
Carbohydrate 29g Protein 26g

Lemon Herb Baked Salmon

Preparation time: 15 minutes Cooking time: 20 minutes Servings: 8
Ingredients:
- 1 salmon fillet 3-4lbs salt & pepper
- lemon divided
- tablespoons butter melted Topping:
- ¾ cup Panko bread crumbs
- tablespoons butter melted
- 2 tablespoons parmesan cheese shredded 1 tablespoon fresh dill minced
- zest from one lemon
- 2 tablespoons fresh parsley minced 3 cloves garlic minced

Directions:
1. Preheat the oven to 400oF. Put all ingredients in a small bowl. Streak a pan with foil and spray with cooking spray. Put salmon on the pan and brush with melted butter.

2. Season with salt and pepper and crush ½ of the lemon over the top. Sprinkle crumb mixture over salmon. Bake exposed for 15 minutes or until salmon flakes easily and is cooked.

Nutrition: Calories: 377 Carbohydrates: 5g Protein: 40g
Fat: 20g
Sodium: 212mg

Baked Salmon Foil Packets with Vegetables

Preparation time: 15 minutes Cooking time: 15 minutes Servings: 4
Ingredients:

- 1 lb. Salmon (cut into 4 6-oz fillets)
- 1/2 lb. Asparagus (trimmed, then cut in half) 1/2 tsp Sea salt
- tbsp Fresh dill (chopped) 1/4 cup Olive oil
- cloves Garlic (minced)
- 10 oz Grape tomatoes 1/4 tsp Black pepper
- 1 tbsp lemon juice and ½ tbsp zest
- 10 oz Zucchini (sliced into half-moons) 1 tbsp Fresh parsley (chopped)

Directions:

1. Preheat the oven to 400oF or preheat the grill to medium. Layout 4 large squares of foil [at least 12x12 inches (30x30 cm)]. Put a salmon fillet in the center of each piece of foil. Divide the veggies squarely among the foil around the salmon.

2. Mix the olive oil, black pepper, parsley, sea salt, lemon juice, minced garlic, lemon zest, and dill in a small bowl. Put half of the oil mixture to skirmish the salmon, getting most of the garlic onto the salmon.

3. Pour the residual oil mixture on the veggies. Put more salt plus pepper on the salmon and veggies. Fold the foil and seal to form packets. Place onto a baking sheet. Bake within 15-20 minutes, or grill (enclosed) within 13-18 minutes.

Nutrition: Calories 400
Fat 24g Protein 36g
Sodium: 212mg
Carbs 8g

Lemon Garlic Shrimp

Preparation time: 15 minutes Cooking time: 10 minutes Servings: 4
Ingredients:

- tablespoons extra-virgin olive oil 3 garlic cloves, sliced
- ½ teaspoon kosher salt
- ¼ teaspoon red pepper flakes
- 1-pound large shrimp, peeled and deveined
- ½ cup white wine
- tablespoons fresh parsley, minced Zest of ½ lemon
- Juiceof ½ lemon

Directions:

1. Heat-up the olive oil in a wok or large skillet over medium-high heat. Add the garlic, salt, and red pepper flakes and sauté until the garlic starts to brown, 30 seconds to 1 minute.

2. Add the shrimp and cook within 2 to 3 minutes on each side. Pour in the wine and deglaze the wok, scraping up any flavorful brown bits, for 1 to 2 minutes. Turn off the heat; mix in the parsley, lemon zest, and lemon juice.

Nutrition: Calories: 200 Fat: 9g Sodium: 310mg
Carbohydrates: 3g Protein: 23g

Shrimp Fra Diavolo

Preparation time: 15 minutes Cooking time: 10 minutes Servings: 4
Ingredients:

- 2 tablespoons extra-virgin olive oil 1 onion, diced small
- 1 fennel bulb, cored and diced small, plus ¼ cup fronds for garnish
- 1 bell pepper, diced small
- ½ teaspoon dried oregano
- ½ teaspoon dried thyme
- ½ teaspoon kosher salt
- ¼ teaspoon red pepper flakes
- (14.5-ounce) can no-salt-added diced tomatoes 1-pound shrimp, peeled and deveined
- Juice of 1 lemon Zest of 1 lemon
- tablespoons fresh parsley, chopped, for garnish

Directions:

1. Heat-up the olive oil in a large skillet or sauté pan over medium heat.

2. Add the onion, fennel, bell pepper, oregano, thyme, salt, and red pepper flakes and sauté until translucent, about 5 minutes.

3. Drizzle the pan using the canned tomatoes' juice, scraping up any brown bits, and bringing to a boil. Add the diced tomatoes and the shrimp. Lower heat to a simmer within 3 minutes.

4. Turn off the heat. Add the lemon juice and lemon zest, and toss well to combine. Garnish with the parsley and the fennel fronds.

Nutrition: Calories: 240
Fat: 9g Sodium: 335mg
Carbohydrates: 13g
Protein: 25g

Fish Amandine

Preparation time: 15 minutes Cooking time: 15 minutes Servings: 4
Ingredients:
- 4-ounce skinless tilapia, trout, or halibut fillets, 1/2- to 1-inch thick
- ¼ cup buttermilk
- ½ teaspoon dry mustard
- 1/8 teaspoon crushed red pepper 1 tablespoon butter, melted
- ¼ teaspoon salt
- ½ cup panko bread crumbs 2 tbsp chopped fresh parsley
- ¼ cup sliced almonds, coarsely chopped
- 2 tablespoons grated Parmesan cheese

Directions:
1. Defrost fish, if frozen. Preheat oven to 450oF. Grease a shallow baking pan; set aside. Rinse fish; pat dry with paper towels.

2. Pour buttermilk into a shallow dish. In an extra shallow dish, mix bread crumbs, dry mustard, parsley, and salt. Soak fish into buttermilk, then into crumb mixture, turning to coat. Put coated fish in the ready baking pan.

3. Flavor the fish with almonds plus Parmesan cheese; drizzle with melted butter. Sprinkle with crinkled red pepper. Bake for 5 minutes per 1/2- inch thickness of fish or until fish flakes easily when checked with a fork.

Nutrition: Calories 209
Fat 8.7 g
Sodium 302 mg
Carbohydrates 6.7 g
Protein 26.2 g

Baked Fish & Potatoes

Preparation time: 15 minutes Cooking time: 20 minutes Servings: 4
Ingredients:
- 1/2 lb. small red potato es (about 4)
- 4 RITZ Reduced Fat Crackers, finely crushed
- 2 tbsp. KRAFT Sun-Dried Tomato Vinaigrette Dressing 2 tbsp. KRAFT Grated Parmesan Cheese, divided
- 1/2 lb. cod fillet 2 lemon wedges
- tbsp. KRAFT Light Mayo Reduced Fat Mayonnaise 2 cups fresh broccoli florets, steamed

Directions:
1. Heat the oven to 400ºF. Slice each potato into 6 pieces and put it in a large bowl. Add dressing; toss to coat. Put, cut sides down, on a rimmed baking sheet sprayed with cooking spray and bake for 10 mins.

2. In the meantime, mix cracker crumbs and 1 tbsp cheese in a shallow dish. Slice the fish crosswise into 1-inch-wide sticks; spread tops and sides with mayo. Roll in crumb mixture until evenly covered.

3. Turn potatoes and move to ends of pan. Put the fish, coated sides up, in the middle of the pan, and bake for 8 to 10 minutes. Sprinkle remaining cheese over potatoes. Serve fish with lemon wedges, broccoli, and potatoes.

Nutrition: Calories 330 Fat 11g Sodium 560mg
Carbohydrates 33g
Protein 28g

Steamed Salmon Teriyaki

Preparation time: 15 minutes Cooking time: 15 minutes Servings: 4
Ingredients:
- green onions, minced 2 packet Stevia
- 1 tbsp freshly grated ginger
- 1 clove garlic, minced 2 tsp sesame seeds
- tbsp sesame oil
- ¼ cup mirin
- tbsp low sodium soy sauce 1/2-lb salmon filet

Directions:
1. Mix stevia, ginger, garlic, oil, mirin, and

soy sauce in a heat-proof dish that fits inside a saucepan. Add salmon and cover generously with sauce.

2. Put sesame seeds and green onions on top of the salmon. Cover dish with foil. Place on top of the trivet. Cover and steam for 15 minutes. Let it rest for 5 minutes in the pan. Serve and enjoy.

Nutrition: Calories: 242.7 Carbs: 1.2g Protein: 35.4g Fats: 10.7g Sodium: 285mg

Easy Steamed Alaskan Cod

Preparation time: 15 minutes Cooking time: 15 minutes Servings: 3
Ingredients:
- 2 tbsp butter Pepper to taste
- 1 cup cherry tomatoes, halved
- large Wild Alaskan cod filet, cut into 3 smaller pieces

Directions:

1. In a heat-proof dish that fits inside a saucepan, add all ingredients. Cover dish with foil. Place on trivet and steam for 15 minutes. Serve and enjoy.

Nutrition: Calories: 132.9 Carbs: 1.9g Protein: 12.2g Fats: 8.5g Sodium: 296mg

Dill and Lemon Cod Packets

Preparation time: 15 minutes Cooking time: 10 minutes Servings: 2
Ingredients:
- tsp olive oil, divided 4 slices lemon, divided
- 2 sprigs fresh dill, divided
- ½ tsp garlic powder, divided Pepper to taste
- 1/2-lb cod filets

Directions:

1. Cut two pieces of 15-inch lengths foil. Put one filet in the middle in one foil. Season with pepper to taste. Sprinkle ¼ tsp garlic. Add a tsp of oil on top of the filet. Top with 2 slices of lemon and a sprig of dill.

2. Fold over the foil and seal the filet inside. Repeat process for the rest of the fish. Place packet on the trivet. Cover and steam for 10 minutes. Serve.

Nutrition: Calories: 164.8 Carbs: 9.4g Protein: 18.3g Fats: 6g Sodium: 347mg

Steamed Fish Mediterranean Style

Preparation time: 15 minutes Cooking time: 15 minutes Servings: 4
Ingredients:
- Pepper to taste
- 1 clove garlic, smashed 2 tsp olive oil
- 1 bunch fresh thyme 2 tbsp pickled capers
- 1 cup black salt-cured olives
- 1-lb cherry tomatoes halved 1 ½-lbs. cod filets

Directions:

1. In a heat-proof dish that fits inside a saucepan, layer half of the halved cherry tomatoes. Season with pepper.

2. Add filets on top of tomatoes and season with pepper. Drizzle oil. Sprinkle 3/4s of thyme on top and the smashed garlic.

3. Cover top of fish with remaining cherry tomatoes, then place the dish on the trivet. Cover it with foil, then steam for 15 minutes. Serve and enjoy.

Nutrition: Calories: 263.2 Carbs: 21.8g Protein: 27.8g Fats: 7.2g Sodium: 264mg

Preparation time: 15 minutes Cooking time: 10 minutes Servings: 5
Ingredients:
- 1 tbsp olive oil
- onion, chopped
- cloves of garlic, minced 2 cups chicken broth
- 1 teaspoon crushed red pepper flakes 1-pound wild Haddock fillets
- ½ cup heavy cream 1 tablespoon basil
- 1 cup kale leaves, chopped
- Pepper to taste

Directions:

1. Place a pot on medium-high fire within 3 minutes. Put oil, then sauté the onion and garlic for 5 minutes. Put the rest of the fixing, except for basil, and mix well. Boil on lower fire within 5 minutes. Serve with a sprinkle of basil.

Nutrition: Calories: 130.5 Carbs: 5.5g Protein: 35.7g Fats: 14.5g Sodium: 278mg

Coconut Curry Sea Bass

Preparation time: 15 minutes Cooking time: 15 minutes Servings: 3
Ingredients:
- 1 can coconut milk
- Juice of 1 lime, freshly squeezed 1

tablespoon red curry paste
- teaspoon coconut aminos 1 teaspoon honey
- teaspoons sriracha
- 2 cloves of garlic, minced 1 teaspoon ground turmeric 1 tablespoon curry powder
- ¼ cup fresh cilantro Pepper

Directions:

1. Place a heavy-bottomed pot on medium-high fire. Mix in all ingredients, then simmer on lower fire to a simmer and simmer for 5 minutes. Serve and enjoy.

Nutrition: Calories: 241.8 Carbs: 12.8g Protein: 3.1g Fats: 19.8g Sodium: 19mg

Stewed Cod Filet with Tomatoes

Preparation time: 15 minutes Cooking time: 15 minutes Servings: 6
Ingredients:

- 1 tbsp olive oil 1 onion, sliced
- 1 ½ pound fresh cod fillets
- Pepper
- 1 lemon juice, freshly squeezed 1 can diced tomatoes

Directions:

1. Sauté the onion for 2 minutes in a pot on medium-high fire. Stir in diced tomatoes and cook for 5 minutes. Add cod filet and season with pepper. Simmer on lower fire within 5 minutes. Serve with freshly squeezed lemon juice.

Nutrition: Calories: 106.4 Carbs: 2.5g Protein: 17.8g Fats: 2.8g Sodium: 381mg

Lemony Parmesan Shrimps

Preparation time: 15 minutes Cooking time: 15 minutes Servings: 4
Ingredients:

- 1 tablespoon olive oil
- ½ cup onion, chopped
- 3 cloves of garlic, minced
- 1-pound shrimps, peeled and deveined
- ½ cup parmesan cheese, low fat 1 cup spinach, shredded
- ½ cup chicken broth, low sodium
- ¼ cup of water Pepper

Directions:

1. Sauté the onion and garlic within 5 minutes in a pot with oil on a medium-high fire. Stir in shrimps and cook for 2 minutes.

2. Add remaining ingredients, except for

parmesan. Cover, bring to a boil, lower fire to a simmer, and simmer for 5 minutes. Serve and enjoy with a sprinkle of parmesan.

Nutrition: Calories: 252.6 Carbs: 5.4g Protein: 33.9g Fats: 10.6g Sodium: 344mg

Tuna and Carrots Casserole

Preparation time: 15 minutes Cooking time: 12 minutes Servings: 4
Ingredients:

- 2 carrots, peeled and chopped
- ¼ cup diced onions 1 cup frozen peas
- ¾ cup milk
- 2 cans tuna in water, drained 1 can cream of celery soup
- 1 tbsp olive oil
- ½ cup of water 2 eggs beaten Pepper

Directions:

1. Place a heavy-bottomed pot on medium-high fire and heat pot for 3 minutes. Once hot, add oil and stir around to coat pot with oil. Sauté the onion and carrots for 3 minutes.

2. Add remaining ingredients and mix well. Bring to a boil while constantly stirring, cook until thickened around 5 minutes. Serve and enjoy.

Nutrition: Calories: 281.3 Carbs: 14.3g Protein: 24.3g Fats: 14.1g Sodium: 275mg

Sweet-Ginger Scallops

Preparation time: 15 minutes Cooking time: 15 minutes Servings: 3
Ingredients:

- 1-pound sea scallops, shells removed
- ½ cup coconut aminos
- 3 tablespoons maple syrup
- ½ teaspoon garlic powder
- ½ teaspoon ground ginger

Directions:

1. In a heat-proof dish that fits inside a saucepan, add all ingredients. Mix well. Cover dish of scallops with foil and place on a trivet. Cover pan and steam for 10 minutes. Let it stand in the pan for another 5 minutes. Serve and enjoy.

Nutrition: Calories: 233.4 Carbs: 23.7g Protein: 31.5g Fats: 1.4g Sodium: 153mg

Savory Lobster Roll

Preparation time: 15 minutes Cooking time: 20 minutes Servings: 6

Ingredients:

- ½ cups chicken broth, low sodium 2 teaspoon old bay seasoning
- pounds lobster tails, raw and in the shell
- 1 lemon, halved
- 3 scallions, chopped
- 1 teaspoon celery seeds

Directions:

1. Place a heavy-bottomed pot on medium-high fire and add all ingredients and ½ of the lemon. Cover, bring to a boil, lower fire to a simmer, and simmer for 15 minutes. Let it rest for another 5 minutes. Serve and enjoy with freshly squeezed lemon juice.

Nutrition: Calories: 209 Carbs: 1.9g Protein: 38.2g Fats: 5.4g Sodium: 288mg

Garlic and Tomatoes on Mussels

Preparation time: 15 minutes Cooking time: 15 minutes Servings: 6

Ingredients:

- ¼ cup white wine
- ½ cup of water
- 3 Roma tomatoes, chopped 2 cloves of garlic, minced 1 bay leaf
- 2 pounds mussels, scrubbed
- ½ cup fresh parsley, chopped 1 tbsp oil
- Pepper

Directions:

1. Warm a pot on medium-high fire within 3 minutes. Put oil and stir around to coat pot with oil. Sauté the garlic, bay leaf, and tomatoes for 5 minutes.

2. Add remaining ingredients except for parsley and mussels. Mix well. Add mussels. Cover, and boil for 5 minutes. Serve with a sprinkle of parsley and discard any unopened mussels.

Nutrition: Calories: 172.8 Carbs: 10.2g Protein: 19.5g Fats: 6g Sodium: 261mg

Lemon Salmon with Kaffir Lime

Preparation time: 15 minutes Cooking time: 30 minutes Servings: 8

Ingredients:

- A whole side of salmon fillet 1 thinly sliced lemon
- 2 kaffir torn lime leaves

- 1 quartered and bruised lemongrass stalk 1 ½ cups fresh coriander leaves

Directions:

1. Warm-up oven to 350 F. Covers a baking pan with foil sheets, overlapping the sides (enough to fold over the fish).

2. Put the salmon on the foil, top with the lemon, lime leaves, the lemongrass, and 1 cup of the coriander leaves. Option: season with salt and pepper.

3. Bring the long side of the foil to the center before folding the seal. Roll the ends to close up the salmon. Bake for 30 minutes. Transfer the cooked fish to a platter. Top with fresh coriander. Serve with white or brown rice.

Nutrition: Calories 103 Protein 18g Carbohydrates 43.5g Fat 11.8g Sodium 170mg

Baked Fish Served with Vegetables

Preparation time: 15 minutes Cooking time: 30 minutes Servings: 4

Ingredients:

- 4 haddock or cod fillets, skinless
- 2 Zucchinis, sliced into thick pieces 2 red onions, sliced into thick pieces 3 large tomatoes, cut in wedges
- ¼ cup black olives pitted
- ¼ cup flavorless oil (olive, canola, or sunflower) 1 Tablespoon lemon juice
- 1 Tablespoon Dijon mustard 2 garlic cloves, minced
- Salt and pepper to season
- ½ cup chopped parsley

Directions:

1. Warm oven to 400 F. In a large baking dish, drizzle some oil over the bottom. Place the fish in the middle. Surround the fish with the zucchini, tomato, onion, and olives. Drizzle more oil over the vegetables and fish. Season with salt and pepper.

2. Place the baking dish in the oven. Bake within 30 minutes, or until the fish is flaky and vegetables are tender. In another bowl, whisk the lemon juice, garlic, mustard, and remaining oil. Set aside.

3. Split the cooked vegetables onto plates, then top with the fish. Drizzle the dressing over the vegetables, fish. Garnish with

parsley.

Nutrition: Calories 91 Protein 18.7g
Carbohydrates 41g Fat 7.6g
Sodium 199mg

Fish in A Vegetable Patch

Preparation time: 15 minutes Cooking time: 20 minutes Servings: 3

Ingredients:

- 1-pound halibut fillet, skinless
- 1 Tablespoon flavorless oil (olive, canola, or sunflower) 1 cup tomato sauce
- 1 ½ Tablespoons Worcestershire sauce 2 large lemons, juiced
- 1 celery stick, diced
- ½ green pepper, chopped 1 large carrot, diced
- ½ an onion, diced
- lemon, sliced

Directions:

1. Warm oven to 400 F. In a small saucepan, combine the tomato sauce, Worcestershire sauce, and lemon juice. Heat for 5 minutes.

2. In a shallow baking dish, drizzle oil along the bottom. Place the vegetables along the bottom and lay the fish over the vegetables. Pour the sauce over the fish. Cover with foil.

3. Bake fillet for 15 minutes, or until the fish is cooked and flaky. Dish out the vegetables, place the fish over the top. Garnish the fish with the lemon slices. Serve with white or brown rice.

Nutrition: Calories 80 Protein 18.9g
Carbohydrates 62g Fat 9g
Sodium 276mgSpicy Cod

Preparation time: 15 minutes Cooking time: 30 minutes Servings: 4

Ingredients:

- pounds cod fillets
- Tablespoon flavorless oil (olive, canola, or sunflower) 2 cups low sodium salsa
- tablespoons fresh chopped parsley

Directions:

1. Warm oven to 350 F. In a large, deep baking dish, drizzle the oil along the bottom. Place the cod fillets in the dish. Pour the salsa over the fish.

2. Cover with foil for 20 minutes. Remove the foil last 10 minutes of cooking. Bake in the oven for 20 – 30 minutes, until the fish is flaky. Serve with white or brown rice. Garnish with parsley.

Nutrition: Calories 110 Protein 16.5g
Carbohydrates 83g Fat 11g
Sodium 186mg

Easy Shrimp

Preparation time: 15 minutes Cooking time: 10 minutes Servings: 4

Ingredients:

- pound cooked shrimp
- 1 pack mixed frozen vegetables 1 garlic clove, minced
- 1 teaspoon butter or margarine
- ¼ cup of water
- 1 package shrimp-flavored instant noodles 3 teaspoons low sodium soy sauce
- ½ teaspoon ground ginger

Directions:

1. In a large skillet, melt the butter. Add the minced garlic, sweat it for 1 minute. Add the shrimp and vegetables to the skillet. Season with salt and pepper. Cover and simmer for 5 - 10 minutes, until the shrimp turns pink and the vegetables are tender.

2. Boil water in a separate pot. Add the noodles. Turn off the heat, cover the pot. Let it stand for 3 minutes. (Keep the water.)

3. Using a scoop or tongs, transfer the noodles to the skillet with the shrimp and vegetables. Stir in the seasoning packet. Mix, then serve immediately.

Nutrition: Calories 80 Protein 18.9g
Carbohydrates 62g Fat 9g
Sodium 276mg

Steamed Blue Crabs

Preparation time: 15 minutes Cooking time: 10 minutes Servings: 6

Ingredients:

- 30 live blue crabs
- ½ cup seafood seasoning
- ¼ cup of salt 3 cups beer
- cups distilled white vinegar

Directions:

1. In a large stockpot, combine the seasoning, salt, beer, and white vinegar. Bring it to a boil. Put each crab upside down, then stick a knife into the shell just before cooking

them. Cover the lid, leaving a crack for the steam to vent.

2. Steam the crabs until they turn bright orange and float to the top. Allow them to cook for another 2 - 3 minutes. Serve immediately.

Nutrition: Calories 77 Protein 9.8g
Carbohydrates 31g
Fat 7g
Sodium 119mg

Steamed Veggie and Lemon Pepper Salmon

Preparation time: 15 minutes Cooking time: 15 minutes Servings: 4
Ingredients:
- 1 carrot, peeled and julienned 1 red bell pepper, julienned
- 1 zucchini, julienned
- ½ lemon, sliced thinly 1 tsp pepper
- ½ tsp salt
- 1/2-lb salmon filet with skin on A dash of tarragon

Directions:

1. In a heat-proof dish that fits inside a saucepan, add salmon with skin side down. Season with pepper. Add slices of lemon on top.

2. Place the julienned vegetables on top of salmon and season with tarragon. Cover top of fish with remaining cherry tomatoes and place dish on the trivet. Cover dish with foil. Cover pan and steam for 15 minutes. Serve and enjoy.

Nutrition: Calories: 216.2 Carbs: 4.1g Protein: 35.1g Fats: 6.6g Sodium: 332mg

Steamed Fish with Scallions and Ginger

Preparation time: 15 minutes Cooking time: 15 minutes Servings: 3
Ingredients:
- ¼ cup chopped cilantro
- ¼ cup julienned scallions 2 tbsp julienned ginger
- 1 tbsp peanut oil 1-lb Tilapia filets 1 tsp garlic
- 1 tsp minced ginger 2 tbsp rice wine
- 1 tbsp low sodium soy sauce

Directions:

1. Mix garlic, minced ginger, rice wine, and

soy sauce in a heat-proof dish that fits inside a saucepan. Add the Tilapia filet and marinate for half an hour while turning over at the half time.

2. Cover dish of fish with foil and place on a trivet. Cover pan and steam for 15 minutes. Serve and enjoy.

Nutrition: Calories: 219 Carbs: 4.5g Protein: 31.8g Fats: 8.2g Sodium: 252mg

Steamed Tilapia with Green Chutney

Preparation time: 15 minutes Cooking time: 10 minutes Servings: 3
Ingredients:
- 1-pound tilapia fillets, divided into 3
- ½ cup green commercial chutney

Directions:

1. Cut 3 pieces of 15-inch lengths foil. In one foil, place one filet in the middle and 1/3 of chutney. Fold over the foil and seal the filet inside. Repeat process for remaining fish. Put packet on the trivet. Steam for 10 minutes. Serve and enjoy.

Nutrition: Calories: 151.5 Carbs: 1.1g Protein: 30.7g Fats: 2.7g Sodium: 79mg

Creamy Haddock with Kale

Ginger Sesame Salmon

Preparation time: 15 minutes Cooking time: 5 minutes Servings: 2
Ingredients:
- ounces salmon
- ¼ cup low-sodium soy sauce
- 2 Tablespoons Balsamic vinegar
- ½ teaspoon sesame oil
- inch chunk ginger, peeled and grated 1 garlic clove, minced
- 1 teaspoon flavorless oil (olive, canola, or sunflower) 1 teaspoon sesame seeds
- 1 teaspoon green onion, minced

Directions:

1. In a glass dish, combine the soy sauce, balsamic vinegar, sesame oil, garlic, and ginger. Place the salmon in the dish. Cover, marinate for 15-60 minutes in the fridge.

2. In a nonstick skillet, heat 1 teaspoon of oil. Sauté the fish until it becomes firm and golden on each side. Sprinkle the sesame

seeds in the pan. Heat for 1 minute. Serve immediately. Garnish with green onion.

Nutrition: Calories 422 Protein 10.8g
Carbohydrates 5.7g Fat 18g
Sodium 300mg

Sicilian Spaghetti with Tuna

Preparation time: 15 minutes Cooking time: 10 minutes Servings: 2

Ingredients:

- ½ cup fresh Tuna, cut into ½ inch pieces 85 grams whole wheat pasta
- ½ medium yellow onion, diced
- 1 garlic clove, minced
- ½ teaspoon anchovy paste
- ½ chipotle chili, minced
- 1 cup fresh tomatoes, chopped
- 1 teaspoon capers, drained and rinsed 1 cup fresh spinach, chopped
- ½ tablespoon fresh or dried marjoram
- 1 teaspoon flavorless oil (olive, canola, or sunflower)

Directions:

1. In a large skillet, drizzle oil over the bottom. Sweat the onion for 1 minute. Add the garlic, anchovy paste, and chipotle chili. Cook for 2 minutes.

2. Add the chopped tomatoes and capers. Sauté 2 minutes. Add the fresh spinach and tuna. Cover and cook for 2 - 5 minutes until the tuna is cooked. Turn off the heat. Sprinkle the mixture with the marjoram. Serve over cooked spaghetti.

Nutrition: Calories 166 Protein 11g
Carbohydrates 112g Fat 17.8g
Sodium 304mg

CHAPTER 9:

Poultry

Rosemary Roasted Chicken

Preparation time: 15 minutes Cooking time: 20 minutes Servings: 8
Ingredients:
- 8 rosemary springs
- 1 minced garlic clove Black pepper
- 1 tbsp. chopped rosemary 1 chicken
- 1 tbsp. organic olive oil

Directions:

1. In a bowl, mix garlic with rosemary, rub the chicken with black pepper, the oil and rosemary mix, place it inside roasting pan, introduce inside the oven at 350 0F, and roast for sixty minutes and 20 min. Carve chicken, divide between plates and serve using a side dish. Enjoy!

Nutrition: Calories: 325 Fat:5 g Carbs:15 g
Protein:14 g
Sodium: 950 mg

Artichoke and Spinach Chicken

Preparation time: 15 minutes Cooking time: 5 minutes Servings: 4
Ingredients:
- 10 oz baby spinach
- ½ tsp. crushed red pepper flakes 14 oz. chopped artichoke hearts 28 oz. no-salt-added tomato sauce 2 tbsps. Essential olive oil
- 4 boneless and skinless chicken breasts

Directions:

1. Heat-up a pan with the oil over medium-high heat, add chicken and red pepper flakes and cook for 5 minutes on them. Add spinach, artichokes, and tomato sauce, toss, cook for ten minutes more, divide between plates and serve. Enjoy!

Nutrition: Calories: 212 Fat:3 g Carbs:16 g
Protein:20 g Sugars:5 g Sodium:418 mg

Pumpkin and Black Beans Chicken

Preparation time: 15 minutes Cooking time: 25 minutes Servings: 4

Ingredients:
- 1 tbsp. essential olive oil 1 tbsp. Chopped cilantro 1 c. coconut milk
- 15 oz canned black beans, drained
- 1 lb. skinless and boneless chicken breasts 2 c. water
- ½ cpumpkin flesh

Directions:

1. Heat a pan when using oil over medium-high heat, add the chicken and cook for 5 minutes. Add the river, milk, pumpkin, and black beans toss, cover the pan, reduce heat to medium and cook for 20 mins. Add cilantro, toss, divide between plates and serve. Enjoy!

Nutrition: Calories: 254 Fat:6 g Carbs:16 g
Protein:22 g Sodium:92 mg

Chicken Thighs and Apples Mix

Preparation time: 15 minutes Cooking time: 60 minutes Servings: 4
Ingredients:
- 3 cored and sliced apples
- 1 tbsp apple cider vinegar treatment
- ¾ c. natural apple juice
- ¼ tsp. pepper and salt 1 tbsp. grated ginger 8 chicken thighs
- 3 tbsps. Chopped onion

Directions:

1. In a bowl, mix chicken with salt, pepper, vinegar, onion, ginger, and apple juice, toss well, cover, keep within the fridge for ten minutes, transfer with a baking dish, and include apples. Introduce inside the oven at 400 0F for just 1 hour. Divide between plates and serve. Enjoy!

Nutrition: Calories: 214 Fat:3 g Carbs:14 g
Protein:15 g Sodium:405 mg

Thai Chicken Thighs

Preparation time: 15 minutes Cooking time: 1 hour & 5minutes Servings: 6
Ingredients:

- ½ c. Thai chili sauce
- 1 chopped green onions bunch 4 lbs. chicken thighs

Directions:

1. Heat a pan over medium-high heat. Add chicken thighs, brown them for 5 minutes on both sides Transfer to some baking dish, then add chili sauce and green onions and toss.

2. Introduce within the oven and bake at 4000F for 60 minutes. Divide everything between plates and serve. Enjoy!

Nutrition: Calories: 220 Fat:4 g Carbs:12 g
Protein:10 g
Sodium: 870 mg

Falling "Off" The Bone Chicken

Preparation time: 15 minutes Cooking time: 40 minutes Servings: 4
Ingredients:
- 6 peeled garlic cloves
- 1 tbsp. organic extra virgin coconut oil 2 tbsps. Lemon juice
- 1 ½ c. pacific organic bone chicken broth
- tsp freshly ground black pepper
- ½ tsp. sea flavored vinegar
- 1 whole organic chicken piece 1 tsp. paprika
- 1 tsp. dried thyme

Directions:

1. Take a small bowl and toss in the thyme, paprika, pepper, and flavored vinegar and mix them. Use the mixture to season the chicken properly. Pour down the oil in your instant pot and heat it to shimmering; toss in the chicken with breast downward and let it cook for about 6-7 minutes

2. After the 7 minutes, flip over the chicken pour down the broth, garlic cloves, and lemon juice. Cook within 25 minutes on a high setting. Remove the dish from the cooker and let it stand for about 5 minutes before serving.

Nutrition: Calories: 664 Fat:44 g Carbs:44 g
Protein:27 g
Sugars:0.1 g Sodium:800 mg

Feisty Chicken Porridge

Preparation time: 15 minutes Cooking time: 30 minutes Servings: 4

Ingredients:
- 1 ½ c. fresh ginger
- 1 lb. cooked chicken legs Green onions
- Toasted cashew nuts 5 c. chicken broth
- 1 cup jasmine rice
- c. water

Directions:

1. Place the rice in your fridge and allow it to chill 1 hour before cooking.

2. Take the rice out and add them to your Instant Pot. Pour broth and water. Lock up the lid and cook on Porridge mode.

3. Separate the meat from the chicken legs and add the meat to your soup. Stir well over sauté mode. Season with a bit of flavored vinegar and enjoy with a garnish of nuts and onion.

Nutrition: Calories: 206 Fat:8 g Carbs:8 g
Protein:23 g Sugars:0 g
Sodium:950 mg

The Ultimate Faux-Tisserie Chicken

Preparation time: 15 minutes Cooking time: 35 minutes Servings: 5
Ingredients:
- c. low sodium broth 2 tbsps. Olive oil
- ½ quartered medium onion
- tbsps. Favorite seasoning 2 ½ lbs. whole chicken Black pepper
- 5 large fresh garlic cloves

Directions:

1. Massage the chicken with 1 tablespoon of olive oil and sprinkle pepper on top. Place onion wedges and garlic cloves inside the chicken. Take a butcher's twin and secure the legs

2. Set your pot to Sauté mode. Put olive oil in your pan on medium heat, allow the oil to heat up. Add chicken and sear both sides for 4 minutes per side. Sprinkle your seasoning over the chicken, remove the chicken and place a trivet at the bottom of your pot

3. Sprinkle seasoning over the chicken, making sure to rub it. Transfer the chicken to the trivet with the breast side facing up, lock up the lid. Cook on HIGH pressure for 25 minutes. Allow it to rest and serve!

Nutrition: Calories: 1010 Fat:64 g Carbs:47 g
Protein:60 g Sodium:209 mg

Oregano Chicken Thighs

Preparation time: 15 minutes Cooking time: 20 minutes Servings: 6
Ingredients:
- 12 chicken thighs 1 tsp dried parsley
- ¼ tsp. pepper and salt.
- ½ c. extra virgin essential olive oil 4 minced garlic cloves
- 1 c. chopped oregano
- ¼ c. low-sodium veggie stock

Directions:

1. In your food processor, mix parsley with oregano, garlic, salt, pepper, and stock and pulse. Put chicken thighs within the bowl, add ooregano paste, toss, cover, and then leave aside within the fridge for 10 minutes

2. Heat the kitchen grill over medium heat, add chicken pieces, close the lid and cook for twenty or so minutes with them. Divide between plates and serve!

Nutrition: Calories: 254 Fat:3 g Carbs:7 g
Protein:17 g Sugars:0.9 g
Sodium:730 mg

Pesto Chicken Breasts with Summer Squash

Preparation time: 15 minutes Cooking time: 10 minutes Servings: 4
Ingredients:
- 4 medium boneless, skinless chicken breast halves 1 tbsp. olive oil
- 2 tbsps. Homemade pesto
- 2 c. finely chopped zucchini
- 2 tbsps. Finely shredded Asiago

Directions:

1. Cook your chicken in hot oil on medium heat within 4 minutes in a large nonstick skillet. Flip the chicken then put the zucchini.

2. Cook within 4 to 6 minutes more or until the chicken is tender and no longer pink (170 F), and squash is crisp-tender, stirring squash gently once or twice. Transfer chicken and squash to 4 dinner plates. Spread pesto over chicken; sprinkle with Asiago.

Nutrition: Calories: 230 Fat:9 g Carbs:8 g
Protein:30 g
Sodium:578 mg

Chicken, Tomato and Green Beans

Preparation time: 15 minutes Cooking time: 25 minutes Servings: 4
Ingredients:
- 6 oz. low-sodium canned tomato paste 2 tbsps. Olive oil
- ¼ tsp. black pepper
- 2 lbs. trimmed green beans 2 tbsps. Chopped parsley
- 1 ½ lbs. boneless, skinless, and cubed chicken breasts
- 25 oz. no-salt-added canned tomato sauce

Directions:

1. Heat a pan with 50 % with the oil over medium heat, add chicken, stir, cover, cook within 5 minutes on both sides and transfer to a bowl. Heat inside the same pan while using rest through the oil over medium heat, add green beans, stir and cook for 10minutes.

2. Return chicken for that pan, add black pepper, tomato sauce, tomato paste, and parsley, stir, cover, cook for 10 minutes more, divide between plates and serve. Enjoy!

Nutrition: Calories: 190 Fat:4 g Carbs:12 g
Protein:9 g Sodium:168 mg

Chicken Tortillas

Preparation time: 15 minutes Cooking time: 5 minutes Servings: 4
Ingredients:
- 6 oz. boneless, skinless, and cooked chicken breasts Black pepper
- 1/3 c. fat-free yogurt
- 4 heated up whole-wheat tortillas 2 chopped tomatoes

Directions:

1. Heat-up a pan over medium heat, add one tortilla during those times, heat up, and hang them on the working surface. Spread yogurt on each tortilla, add chicken and tomatoes, roll, divide between plates and serve. Enjoy!

Nutrition: Calories:190 Fat:2 g Carbs:12 g Protein:6 g Sodium:300 mg

Chicken with Potatoes Olives & Sprouts

Preparation time: 15 minutes Cooking time: 35 minutes Servings: 4

Ingredients:

- 1 lb. chicken breasts, skinless, boneless, and cut into pieces
- ¼ cup olives, quartered 1 tsp oregano
- 1 ½ tsp Dijon mustard 1 lemon juice
- 1/3 cup vinaigrette dressing
- 1 medium onion, diced
- cups potatoes cut into pieces
- cups Brussels sprouts, trimmed and quartered
- ¼ tsp pepper
- ¼ tsp salt

Directions:

1. Warm-up oven to 400 F. Place chicken in the center of the baking tray, then place potatoes, sprouts, and onions around the chicken.

2. In a small bowl, mix vinaigrette, oregano, mustard, lemon juice, and salt and pour over chicken and veggies. Sprinkle olives and season with pepper.

3. Bake in preheated oven for 20 minutes. Transfer chicken to a plate. Stir the vegetables and roast for 15 minutes more. Serve and enjoy.

Nutrition: Calories: 397 Fat: 13g Protein: 38.3g
Carbs: 31.4g
Sodium 175 mg

Garlic Mushroom Chicken

Preparation time: 15 minutes Cooking time: 15 minutes Servings: 4
Ingredients:

- 4 chicken breasts, boneless and skinless 3 garlic cloves, minced
- onion, chopped
- cups mushrooms, sliced 1 tbsp olive oil
- ½ cup chicken stock
- ¼ tsp pepper
  ½ tsp salt

Directions:

1. Season chicken with pepper and salt. Warm oil in a pan on medium heat, then put season chicken in the pan and cook for 5-6 minutes on each side. Remove and place on a plate.

2. Add onion and mushrooms to the pan and sauté until tender, about 2-3 minutes. Add garlic and sauté for a minute. Add stock and bring to boil. Stir well and cook for 1-2

minutes. Pour over chicken and serve.
Nutrition: Calories: 331 Fat: 14.5g Protein: 43.9g
Carbs: 4.6g Sodium 420 mg

Grilled Chicken

Preparation time: 15 minutes Cooking time: 15 minutes Servings: 4
Ingredients:

- 4 chicken breasts, skinless and boneless 1 ½ tsp dried oregano
- 1 tsp paprika
- 5 garlic cloves, minced
- ½ cup fresh parsley, minced
- ½ cup olive oil
- ½ cup fresh lemon juice Pepper
- Salt

Directions:

1. Add lemon juice, oregano, paprika, garlic, parsley, and olive oil to a large zip-lock bag. Season chicken with pepper and salt and add to bag. Seal bag and shake well to coat chicken with marinade. Let sit chicken in the marinade for 20 minutes.

2. Remove chicken from marinade and grill over medium-high heat for 5-6 minutes on each side. Serve and enjoy.

Nutrition: Calories: 512 Fat: 36.5g Protein: 43.1g
Carbs: 3g Sodium 110mg

Delicious Lemon Chicken Salad

Preparation time: 15 minutes Cooking time: 5 minutes Servings: 4
Ingredients:

- lb. chicken breast, cooked and diced 1 tbsp fresh dill, chopped
- tsp olive oil
- 1/4 cup low-fat yogurt 1 tsp lemon zest, grated 2 tbsp onion, minced
- ¼ tsp pepper
- ¼ tsp salt

Directions:

1. Put all your fixing into the large mixing bowl and toss well. Season with pepper and salt. Cover and place in the refrigerator. Serve chilled and enjoy.

Nutrition: Calories: 165 Fat: 5.4g Protein: 25.2g
Carbs: 2.2g Sodium 153mg

Healthy Chicken Orzo

Preparation time: 15 minutes Cooking time: 15 minutes Servings: 4

Ingredients:

- 1 cup whole wheat orzo
- 1 lb. chicken breasts, sliced
- ½ tsp red pepper flakes
- ½ cup feta cheese, crumbled
- ½ tsp oregano
- 1 tbsp fresh parsley, chopped 1 tbsp fresh basil, chopped
- ¼ cup pine nuts
- 1 cup spinach, chopped
- ¼ cup white wine
- ½ cup olives, sliced
- 1 cup grape tomatoes, cut in half
- ½ tbsp garlic, minced 2 tbsp olive oil
- ½ tsp pepper
- ½ tsp salt

Directions:

1. Add water in a small saucepan and bring to boil. Heat 1 tablespoon of olive oil in a pan over medium heat. Season chicken with pepper and salt and cook in the pan for 5-7 minutes on each side. Remove from pan and set aside.

2. Add orzo in boiling water and cook according to the packet directions. Heat remaining olive oil in a pan on medium heat, then put garlic in the pan and sauté for a minute. Stir in white wine and cherry tomatoes and cook on high for 3 minutes.

3. Add cooked orzo, spices, spinach, pine nuts, and olives and stir until well combined. Add chicken on top of orzo and sprinkle with feta cheese. Serve and enjoy.

Nutrition: Calories: 518 Fat: 27.7g Protein: 40.6g Carbs: 26.2g Sodium 121mg

Lemon Garlic Chicken

Preparation time: 15 minutes Cooking time: 12 minutes Servings: 3

Ingredients:

- chicken breasts, cut into thin slices 2 lemon zest, grated
- ¼ cup olive oil
- garlic cloves, minced Pepper
- Salt

Directions:

1. Warm-up olive oil in a pan over medium heat. Add garlic to the pan and sauté for 30 seconds. Put the chicken in the pan and sauté within 10 minutes. Add lemon zest and lemon juice and bring to boil. Remove from heat and season with pepper and salt. Serve and enjoy.

Nutrition: Calories: 439 Fat: 27.8g Protein: 42.9g Carbs: 4.9g Sodium 306 mg

Baked Chicken

Preparation time: 15 minutes Cooking time: 35 minutes Servings: 4

Ingredients:

- lbs. chicken tenders 1 large zucchini
- cup grape tomatoes
- tbsp olive oil 3 dill sprigs
- For topping:
- 2 tbsp feta cheese, crumbled 1 tbsp olive oil
- 1 tbs fresh lemon juice
- tbsp fesh dill, chopped

Directions: Warm oven to 200 C/ 400 F. Drizzle the olive oil on a baking tray, then place chicken, zucchini, dill, and tomatoes on the tray. Season with salt. Bake chicken within 30 minutes.

1. Meanwhile, in a small bowl, stir all topping ingredients. Place chicken on the serving tray, then top with veggies and discard dill sprigs. Sprinkle topping mixture on top of chicken and vegetables. Serve and enjoy.

Nutrition: Calories: 557 Fat: 28.6g Protein: 67.9g Carbs: 5.2g Sodium 760 mg

Garlic Pepper Chicken

Preparation time: 15 minutes Cooking time: 21 minutes Servings: 2

Ingredients:

- chicken breasts, cut into strips 2 bell peppers, cut into strips
- 5 garlic cloves, chopped
- 3 tbsp water
- 2 tbsp olive oil 1 tbsp paprika
- 2 tsp black pepper 1/2 tsp salt

Directions:

1. Warm-up olive oil in a large saucepan over medium heat. Add garlic and sauté for 2-3 minutes. Add peppers and cook for 3 minutes. Add chicken and spices and stir to coat. Add water and stir well. Bring to boil. Cover and simmer for 10-15 minutes. Serve and enjoy.

Nutrition: Calories: 462 Fat: 25.7g Protein: 44.7g Carbs: 14.8g Sodium 720 mg

Mustard Chicken Tenders

Preparation time: 15 minutes Cooking time: 20 minutes Servings: 4

Ingredients:

- lb. chicken tenders
- tbsp fresh tarragon, chopped 1/2 cup whole grain mustard 1/2 tsp paprika
- garlic clove, minced 1/2 oz fresh lemon juice 1/2 tsp pepper
- 1/4 tsp kosher salt

Directions:

1. Warm oven to 425 F. Add all ingredients except chicken to the large bowl and mix well. Put the chicken in the bowl, then stir until well coated. Place chicken on a baking dish and cover. Bake within 15-20 minutes. Serve and enjoy.

Nutrition: Calories: 242 Fat: 9.5g Protein: 33.2g Carbs: 3.1g Sodium 240 mg

Salsa Chicken Chili

Preparation time: 15 minutes Cooking time: 20 minutes Servings: 8

Ingredients:

- 1/2 lbs. chicken breasts, skinless and boneless 1/2 tsp cumin powder
- garlic cloves, minced
- 1 onion, diced
- 16 oz salsa
- 1 tsp oregano 1 tbsp olive oil

Directions:

1. Add oil into the instant pot and set the pot on sauté mode. Add onion to the pot and sauté until softened, about 3 minutes. Add garlic and sauté for a minute. Add oregano and cumin and sauté for a minute. Add half salsa and stir well. Place chicken and pour remaining salsa over chicken.

2. Seal pot with the lid and select manual, and set timer for 10 minutes. Remove chicken and shred. Move it back to the pot, then stir well to combine. Serve and enjoy.

Nutrition: Calories: 308 Fat: 12.4g Protein: 42.1g Carbs: 5.4g Sodium 656 mg

Honey Crusted Chicken

Preparation time: 10 minutes Cooking time: 25 minutes Servings: 2

Ingredients:

- 1 teaspoon paprika

- 8 saltine crackers, 2 inches square
- 2 chicken breasts, each 4 ounces
- 4 tsp honey

Directions:

1. Set the oven to heat at 375 degrees F. Grease a baking dish with cooking oil. Smash the crackers in a Ziplock bag and toss them with paprika in a bowl. Brush chicken with honey and add it to the crackers.

2. Mix well and transfer the chicken to the baking dish. Bake the chicken for 25 minutes until golden brown. Serve.

Nutrition: Calories 219
Fat 17 g
Sodium 456 mg
Carbs 12.1 g
Protein 31 g

Paella with Chicken, Leeks, and Tarragon

Preparation time: 10 minutes Cooking time: 20 minutes Servings: 2

Ingredients:

- teaspoon extra-virgin olive oil 1 small onion, sliced
- leeks (whites only), thinly sliced
- garlic cloves, minced
- 1-pound boneless, skinless chicken breast, cut into strips 1/2-inch-wide and 2 inches long
- 2 large tomatoes, chopped 1 red pepper, sliced
- 2/3 cup long-grain brown rice 1 teaspoon tarragon, or to taste
- 2 cups fat-free, unsalted chicken broth 1 cup frozen peas
- 1/4 cup chopped fresh parsley
- 1 lemon, cut into 4 wedges

Directions:

1. Preheat a nonstick pan with olive oil over medium heat. Toss in leeks, onions, chicken strips, and garlic. Sauté for 5 minutes. Stir in red pepper slices and tomatoes. Stir and cook for 5 minutes.

2. Add tarragon, broth, and rice. Let it boil, then reduce the heat to a simmer. Continue cooking for 10 minutes, then add peas and continue cooking until the liquid is thoroughly cooked. Garnish with parsley

and lemon. Serve.
Nutrition: Calories 388
Fat 15.2 g
Sodium 572 mg
Carbs 5.4 g
Protein 27 g

Southwestern Chicken and Pasta

Preparation time: 10 minutes Cooking time: 10 minutes Servings: 2
Ingredients:
- 1 cup uncooked whole-wheat rigatoni 2 chicken breasts, cut into cubes
- 1/4 cup of salsa
- 1 1/2 cups of canned unsalted tomato sauce 1/8 tsp garlic powder
- 1 tsp cumin
- 1/2 tsp chili powder
- 1/2 cup canned black beans, drained 1/2 cup fresh corn
- 1/4 cup Monterey Jack and Colby cheese, shredded

Directions:

1. Fill a pot with water up to ¾ full and boil it. Add pasta to cook until it is al dente, then drain the pasta while rinsing under cold water. Preheat a skillet with cooking oil, then cook the chicken for 10 minutes until golden from both sides.

2. Add tomato sauce, salsa, cumin, garlic powder, black beans, corn, and chili powder. Cook the mixture while stirring, then toss in the pasta. Serve with 2 tablespoons cheese on top. Enjoy.

Nutrition: Calories 245
Fat 16.3 g
Sodium 515 mg
Carbs 19.3 g
Protein 33.3 g

Parmesan and Chicken Spaghetti Squash

Preparation time: 15 minutes Cooking time: 20 minutes Servings: 6
Ingredients:
- 16 oz. mozzarella
- 1 spaghetti squash piece 1 lb. cooked cube chicken 1 c. Marinara sauce

Directions:

1. Split up the squash in halves and remove the seeds. Arrange or put one cup of water in your pot, then put a trivet on top.

2. Add the squash halves to the trivet. Cook within 20 minutes at HIGH pressure. Remove the squashes and shred them using a fork into spaghetti portions

3. Pour sauce over the squash and give it a nice mix. Top them up with the cubed-up chicken and top with mozzarella. Broil for 1-2 minutes and broil until the cheese has melted

Nutrition: Calories: 237 Fat:10 g Carbs:32 g
Protein:11 g Sodium: 500 mg

Apricot Chicken

Preparation time: 15 minutes Cooking time: 6 minutes Servings: 4
Ingredients:
- 1 bottle creamy French dressing
- ¼ c. flavorless oil White cooked rice
- 1 large jar Apricot preserve
- 4 lbs. boneless and skinless chicken 1 package onion soup mix

Directions:

1. Rinse and pat dry the chicken. Dice into bite-size pieces. In a large bowl, mix the apricot preserve, creamy dressing, and onion soup mix. Stir until thoroughly combined. Place the chicken in the bowl. Mix until coated.

2. In a large skillet, heat the oil. Place the chicken in the oil gently. Cook 4-6 minutes on each side, until golden brown. Serve over rice.

Nutrition: Calories: 202 Fat:12 g Carbs:75 g
Protein:20 g Sugars:10 g Sodium: 630 mg

Oven-Fried Chicken Breasts

Preparation time: 15 minutes Cooking time: 30 minutes Servings: 8
Ingredients:
- ½ pack Ritz crackers
- 1 c. plain non-fat yogurt
- 8 boneless, skinless, and halved chicken breasts

Directions:

1. Preheat the oven to 350 0F. Rinse and pat dry the chicken breasts. Pour the yogurt into a shallow bowl. Dip the chicken pieces

in the yogurt, then roll in the cracker crumbs. Place the chicken in a single layer in a baking dish. Bake within 15 minutes per side. Serve.
Nutrition: Calories: 200 Fat:13 g Carbs:98 g Protein:19 g Sodium:217 mg

Stuffed Chicken Breasts

Preparation time: 15 minutes Cooking time: 30 minutes Servings: 4
Ingredients:
- 3 tbsp seedless raisins 1/2 cup of chopped onion
- 1/2 cup of chopped celery
- 1/4 tsp garlic, minced 1 bay leaf
- cup apple with peel, chopped
- tbsp chopped water chestnuts
- 4 large chicken breast halves, 5 ounces each 1 tablespoon olive oil
- 1 cup fat-free milk
- teaspoon curry powder
- tablespoons all-purpose (plain) flour 1 lemon, cut into 4 wedges

Directions:

1. Set the oven to heat at 425 degrees F. Grease a baking dish with cooking oil. Soak raisins in warm water until they swell. Grease a heated skillet with cooking spray.

2. Add celery, garlic, onions, and bay leaf. Sauté for 5 minutes. Discard the bay leaf, then toss in apples. Stir cook for 2 minutes. Drain the soaked raisin and pat them dry to remove excess water.

3. Add raisins and water chestnuts to the apple mixture. Pull apart the chicken's skin and stuff the apple raisin mixture between the skin and the chicken. Preheat olive oil in another skillet and sear the breasts for 5 minutes per side.

4. Place the chicken breasts in the baking dish and cover the dish. Bake for 15 minutes until temperature reaches 165 degrees F. Prepare sauce by mixing milk, flour, and curry powder in a saucepan.

5. Stir cook until the mixture thickens, about 5 minutes. Pour this sauce over the baked chicken. Bake again in the covered dish for 10 minutes. Serve.

Nutrition: Calories 357
Fat 32.7 g
Sodium 277 mg
Carbs 17.7 g
Protein 31.2 g

Buffalo Chicken Salad Wrap

Preparation time: 10 minutes Cooking time: 10 minutes Servings: 4
Ingredients:
- 3-4 ounces chicken breasts 2 whole chipotle peppers 1/4 cup white wine vinegar
- 1/4 cup low-calorie mayonnaise 2 stalks celery, diced
- 2 carrots, cut into matchsticks
- small yellow onion, diced
- 1/2 cup thinly sliced rutabaga or another root vegetable 4 ounces spinach, cut into strips
- whole-grain tortillas (12-inch diameter)

Directions:

1. Set the oven or a grill to heat at 375 degrees F. Bake the chicken first for 10 minutes per side. Blend chipotle peppers with mayonnaise and wine vinegar in the blender. Dice the baked chicken into cubes or small chunks.

2. Mix the chipotle mixture with all the ingredients except tortillas and spinach. Spread 2 ounces of spinach over the tortilla and scoop the stuffing on top. Wrap the tortilla and cut it into half. Serve.

Nutrition: Calories 300
Fat 16.4 g
Sodium 471 mg
Carbs 8.7 g
Protein 38.5 g

Chicken Sliders

Preparation time: 10 minutes Cooking time: 10 minutes Servings: 4
Ingredients:
- 10 ounces ground chicken breast 1 tablespoon black pepper
- 1 tablespoon minced garlic
- 1 tablespoon balsamic vinegar 1/2 cup minced onion
- 1 fresh chili pepper, minced
- 1 tablespoon fennel seed, crushed 4 whole-wheat mini buns
- 4 lettuce leaves

- 4 tomato slices

Directions:

1. Combine all the ingredients except the wheat buns, tomato, and lettuce.

2. Mix well and refrigerate the mixture for 1 hour. Divide the mixture into 4 patties.

3. Broil these patties in a greased baking tray until golden brown. Place the chicken patties in the wheat buns along with lettuce and tomato. Serve.

Nutrition: Calories 224
Fat 4.5 g
Sodium 212 mg
Carbs 10.2 g
Protein 67.4 g

White Chicken Chili

Preparation time: 20 minutes Cooking time: 15 minutes Servings: 4
Ingredients:

- can white chunk chicken
- cans low-sodium white beans, drained 1 can low-sodium diced tomatoes
- 4 cups of low-sodium chicken broth 1 medium onion, chopped
- 1/2 medium green pepper, chopped
- medium red pepper, chopped 2 garlic cloves, minced
- teaspoons chili powder
- 1 teaspoon ground cumin 1 teaspoon dried oregano Cayenne pepper, to taste
- 8 tablespoons shredded reduced-fat Monterey Jack cheese 3 tablespoons chopped fresh cilantro

Directions:

1. In a soup pot, add beans, tomatoes, chicken, and chicken broth. Cover this soup pot and let it simmer over medium heat. Meanwhile, grease a nonstick pan with cooking spray. Add peppers, garlic, and onions. Sauté for 5 minutes until soft.

2. Transfer the mixture to the soup pot. Add cumin, chili powder, cayenne pepper, and oregano. Cook for 10 minutes, then garnish the chili with cilantro and 1 tablespoon cheese. Serve.

Nutrition: Calories 225
Fat 12.9 g
Sodium 480 mg
Carbs 24.7 g Protein 25.3g

Sweet Potato-Turkey Meatloaf

Preparation time: 15 minutes Cooking time: 25 minutes Servings: 4
Ingredients:

- 1 large sweet potato, peeled and cubed 1-pound ground turkey (breast)
- 1 large egg
- small sweet onion, finely chopped 2 cloves garlic, minced
- slices whole-wheat bread, crumbs
- ¼ cup honey barbecue sauce
- ¼ cup ketchup
- 2 Tablespoons Dijon Mustard
- 1 Tablespoon fresh ground pepper
- ½ Tablespoon salt

Directions:

1. Warm oven to 350 F. Grease a baking dish. In a large pot, boil a cup of lightly salted water, add the sweet potato. Cook until tender. Drain the water. Mash the potato.

2. Mix the honey barbecue sauce, ketchup, and Dijon mustard in a small bowl. Mix thoroughly. In a large bowl, mix the turkey and the egg. Add the sweet onion, garlic. Pour in the combined sauces. Add the bread crumbs. Season the mixture with salt and pepper.

3. Add the sweet potato. Combine thoroughly with your hands. If the mixture feels wet, add more bread crumbs. Shape the mixture into a loaf. Place in the loaf pan. Bake for 25 – 35 minutes until the meat is cooked through. Broil for 5 minutes. Slice and serve.

Nutrition: Calories - 133
Protein - 85g Carbohydrates - 50g Fat - 34g
Sodium - 202mg

Oaxacan Chicken

Preparation time: 15 minutes Cooking time: 28 minutes Servings: 2
Ingredients:

- 1 4-ounce chicken breast, skinned and halved
- ½ cup uncooked long-grain rice
- teaspoon of extra-virgin olive oil
- ½ cup low-sodium salsa

- ½ cup chicken stock, mixed with 2 Tablespoons water
- ¾ cup baby carrots
- tablespoons green olives, pitted and chopped 2 Tablespoons dark raisins
- ½ teaspoon ground Cinnamon
- 2 Tablespoons fresh cilantro or parsley, coarsely chopped

Directions:

1. Warm oven to 350 F. In a large saucepan that can go in the oven, heat the olive oil. Add the rice. Sauté the rice until it begins to pop, approximately 2 minutes.

2. Add the salsa, baby carrots, green olives, dark raisins, halved chicken breast, chicken stock, and ground cinnamon. Bring the mix to a simmer, stir once.

3. Cover the mixture tightly, bake in the oven until the chicken stock has been completely absorbed, approximately 25 minutes. Sprinkle fresh cilantro or parsley, mix. Serve immediately.

Nutrition: Calories - 143 Protein - 102g
Carbohydrates - 66g
Fat - 18g Sodium - 97mg

Spicy Chicken with Minty Couscous

Preparation time: 15 minutes Cooking time: 25 minutes Servings: 2
Ingredients:

- 2 small chicken breasts, sliced
- red chili pepper, finely chopped 1 garlic clove, crushed
- ginger root, 2 cm long peeled and grated 1 teaspoon ground cumin
- ½ teaspoon turmeric
- Tablespoons extra-virgin olive oil 1 pinch sea salt
- ¾ cup couscous
- Small bunch mint leaves, finely chopped 2 lemons, grate the rind and juice them

Directions:

1. In a large bowl, place the chicken breast slices and chopped chili pepper. Sprinkle with the crushed garlic, ginger, cumin, turmeric, and a pinch of salt. Add the grated rind of both lemons and the juice from 1 lemon. Pour 1 tablespoon of the olive oil over the chicken, coat evenly.

2. Cover the dish with plastic and refrigerate within 1 hour. After 1 hour, coat a skillet with olive oil and fry the chicken. As the chicken is cooking, pour the couscous into a bowl and pour hot water over it, let it absorb the water (approximately 5 minutes).

3. Fluff the couscous. Add some chopped mint, the other tablespoon of olive oil, and juice from the second lemon. Top the couscous with the chicken. Garnish with chopped mint. Serve immediately.

Nutrition: Calories - 166
Protein - 106g Carbohydrates - 52g Sugars - 0.1g
Fat - 17g Sodium - 108mg

Chicken, Pasta and Snow Peas

Preparation time: 15 minutes Cooking time: 20 minutes Servings: 2
Ingredients:

- 1-pound chicken breasts 2 ½ cups penne pasta
- 1 cup snow peas, trimmed and halved
- 1 teaspoon olive oil
- 1 standard jar Tomato and Basil pasta sauce Fresh ground pepper

Directions:

1. In a medium frying pan, heat the olive oil. Flavor the chicken breasts with salt and pepper. Cook the chicken breasts until cooked through (approximately 5 – 7 minutes each side).

2. Cook the pasta, as stated in the instruction of the package. Cook the snow peas with the pasta. Scoop 1 cup of the pasta water. Drain the pasta and peas, set aside.

3. Once the chicken is cooked, slice diagonally. Return back the chicken in the frying pan. Add the pasta sauce. If the mixture seems dry, add some of the pasta water to the desired consistency. Heat, then divide into bowls. Serve immediately.

Nutrition: Calories - 140 Protein - 34g
Carbohydrates - 52g Fat - 17g
Sodium - 118mg

Chicken with Noodles

Preparation time: 15 minutes Cooking time: 30 minutes Servings: 6
Ingredients:

- 4 chicken breasts, skinless, boneless
- 1-pound pasta (angel hair, or linguine, or

ramen)

- ½ teaspoon sesame oil 1 Tablespoon canola oil
- 2 Tablespoons chili paste 1 onion, diced
- garlic cloves, chopped coarsely
- ½ cup of soy sauce
- ½ medium cabbage, sliced 2 carrots, chopped coarsely

Directions:

1. Cook your pasta in a large pot. Mix the canola oil, sesame oil, and chili paste and heat for 25 seconds in a large pot. Add the onion, cook for 2 minutes. Put the garlic and fry within 20 seconds. Add the chicken, cook on each side 5 - 7 minutes, until cooked through.

2. Remove the mix from the pan, set aside. Add the cabbage, carrots, cook until the vegetables are tender. Pour everything back into the pan. Add the noodles. Pour in the soy sauce and combine thoroughly. Heat for 5 minutes. Serve immediately.

Nutrition: Calories - 110 Protein - 30g
Carbohydrates - 32g Sugars - 0.1g
Fat - 18g Sodium - 121mg

Teriyaki Chicken Wings

Preparation time: 15 minutes Cooking time: 30 minutes Servings: 6
Ingredients:

- pounds of chicken wings (15 – 20) 1/3 cup lemon juice
- ¼ cup of soy sauce
- ¼ cup of vegetable oil
- 3 tablespoons chili sauce
- 1 garlic clove, finely chopped
- ¼ teaspoon fresh ground pepper
- ¼ teaspoon celery seed Dash liquid mustard

Directions:

1. Prepare the marinade. Combine lemon juice, soy sauce, chili sauce, oil, celery seed, garlic, pepper, and mustard. Stir well, set aside. Rinse and dry the chicken wings.

2. Pour marinade over the chicken wings. Coat thoroughly. Refrigerate for 2 hours. After 2 hours. Preheat the broiler in the oven. Drain off the excess sauce.

3. Place the wings on a cookie sheet with parchment paper. Broil on each side for 10 minutes. Serve immediately.

Nutrition: Calories - 96 Protein - 15g
carbohydrates - 63g Fat - 15g
Sodium- 145mg

Hot Chicken Wings

Preparation time: 15 minutes Cooking time: 25 minutes Servings: 4
Ingredients:

- 10 - 20 chicken wings
- ½ stick margarine
- 1 bottle Durkee hot sauce 2 Tablespoons honey
- 10 shakes Tabasco sauce
- 2 Tablespoons cayenne pepper

Directions:

1. Warm canola oil in a deep pot. Deep-fry the wings until cooked, approximately 20 minutes. Mix the hot sauce, honey, Tabasco, and cayenne pepper in a medium bowl. Mix well.

2. Place the cooked wings on paper towels. Drain the excess oil. Mix the chicken wings in the sauce until coated evenly.

Nutrition: Calories - 102 Protein - 23g
Carbohydrates - 55g Sugars - 0.1g
Fat - 14g
Sodium- 140mg

Crispy Cashew Chicken

Preparation time: 15 minutes Cooking time: 30 minutes Servings: 5
Ingredients:

- 2 chicken breasts, skinless, boneless 2 egg whites
- cup cashew nuts
- ¼ cup bread crumbs
- cups of peanut oil or vegetable oil
- ¼ cup of corn starch
- 1 teaspoon brown sugar 2 teaspoons salt
- teaspoon dry sherry

Directions:

1. Warm oven to 400 F. Put the cashews in a blender. Pulse until they are finely chopped. Place in a shallow bowl and stir in the bread crumbs.

2. Wash the chicken breasts. Pat them dry. Cut into small cubes. In a separate shallow bowl, mix the salt, corn starch, brown sugar, and sherry. In a separate bowl, beat the egg white.

3. Put the oil into a large, deep pot. Heat to high temp. Place the chicken pieces on a plate. Arrange the bowls in a row; flour, eggs, cashews & bread crumbs. Prepare a baking tray with parchment paper.

4. Dunk the chicken pieces in the flour, then the egg, and then the cashew mixture. Shake off the excess mixture. Gently place the chicken in the oil. Fry on each side for 2 minutes. Place on the baking tray.

5. Once done, slide the baking tray into the oven. Cook for an additional 4 minutes, flip, cook for an additional 4 minutes, until golden brown. Serve immediately, or cold, with your favorite low-fat dip.

Nutrition:
Calories - 86 Protein - 21g Carbohydrates - 50g
Sugars - 0.1g
Fat - 16g Sodium- 139mg

Chicken Tortellini Soup

Preparation time: 15 minutes Cooking time: 30 minutes Servings: 5
Ingredients:
- chicken breasts, boneless, skinless; diced into cubes
- Tablespoon flavorless oil (olive oil, canola, sunflower) 1 teaspoon butter
- cups cheese tortellini 2 cups frozen broccoli
- 2 cans cream of chicken soup
- 4 cups of water
- large onion, diced
- garlic cloves, minced 2 large carrots, sliced 1 celery stick, sliced
- 1 teaspoon Oregano
- ½ teaspoon Basil

Directions:
1. Pull the broccoli out of the freezer. Set in a bowl. Rinse and pat dry the chicken breasts. Dice into cubes. In a large pot, heat the oil. Fry the cubes of chicken breast. Pull from the pot, place on paper to drain off the oil.

2. Add the teaspoon of butter to the hot pot. Sauté the onion, garlic, carrots, and celery, broccoli. Once the vegetable el dente, add the chicken soup and water. Stir the ingredients until they are combined. Bring it to a simmer.

3. Add the chicken and tortellini back to the

pot. Cook on low within 10 minutes, or until the tortellini is cooked. Serve immediately.

Nutrition: Calories - 79 Protein - 15g
Carbohydrates - 55g Sugars - 0g
Fat - 13g
Sodium- 179mg

Chicken Divan

Preparation time: 15 minutes Cooking time: 30 minutes Servings: 4
Ingredients:
- 1/2-pound cooked chicken, boneless, skinless, diced in bite-size pieces 1 cup broccoli, cooked, diced into bite-size pieces
- 1 cup extra sharp cheddar cheese, grated
- can mushroom soup
- cup of water 1 cup croutons

Directions:
1. Warm oven to 350 F. In a large pot, heat the soup and water. Add the chicken, broccoli, and cheese. Combine thoroughly. Pour into a greased baking dish. Place the croutons over the mixture. Bake within 30 minutes or until the casserole is bubbling, and the croutons are golden brown.

Nutrition: Calories - 380 Protein - 25g
Carbohydrates - 10g
Sugars - 1g Fat - 22g
Sodium- 397mg

Creamy Chicken Fried Rice

Preparation time: 15 minutes Cooking time: 45 minutes Servings: 4
Ingredients:
- pounds of chicken; white and dark meat (diced into cubes) 2 Tablespoons butter or margarine
- 1 ½ cups instant rice
- 1 cup mixed frozen vegetables
- 1 can condensed cream of chicken soup 1 cup of water
- 1 cube instant chicken bouillon Salt and pepper to taste

Directions:
1. Take the vegetables out of the freezer. Set aside. Warm large, deep skillet over medium heat, add the butter or margarine. Place the chicken in the skillet, season with salt and pepper. Fry until both sides are brown.

2. Remove the chicken, then adjust the heat and add the rice. Add the water and bouillon. Cook the rice, then add the chicken, the vegetables. Mix in the soup, then simmer until the vegetables are tender. Serve immediately.

Nutrition: Calories - 119 Protein - 22g
Carbohydrates - 63g
Fat - 18g Sodium - 180mg

Chicken Tikka

Preparation time: 15 minutes Cooking time: 20 minutes Servings: 6
Ingredients:

- 4 chicken breasts, skinless, boneless; cubed 2 large onion, cubed
- 10 Cherry tomatoes
- 1/3 cup plain non-fat yogurt 4 garlic cloves, crushed
- 1 ½ inch fresh ginger, peeled and chopped
- 1 small onion, grated
- 1 ½ teaspoon chili powder
- Tablespoon ground coriander 1 teaspoon salt
- tablespoons of coriander leaves

Directions:

1. In a large bowl, combine the non-fat yogurt, crushed garlic, ginger, chili powder, coriander, salt, and pepper. Add the cubed chicken, stir until the chicken is coated. Cover with plastic film, place in the fridge. Marinate 2 – 4 hours. Heat the broiler or barbecue.

2. After marinating the chicken, get some skewers ready. Alternate pieces of chicken cubes, cherry tomatoes, and cubed onions onto the skewers.

3. Grill within 6 – 8 minutes on each side. Once the chicken is cooked through, pull the meat and vegetables off the skewers onto plates. Garnish with coriander. Serve immediately.

Nutrition: Calories - 117 Protein - 19g
Carbohydrates - 59g Fat - 19g
Sodium - 203mg

Honey Spiced Cajun Chicken

Preparation time: 15 minutes Cooking time: 20 minutes Servings: 4
Ingredients:

- 2 chicken breasts, skinless, boneless 1

Tablespoon butter or margarine
- 1 pound of linguini
- 3 large mushrooms, sliced 1 large tomato, diced
- 2 Tablespoons regular mustard
- 4 Tablespoons honey
- ounces low-fat table cream Parsley, roughly chopped

Directions:

1. Wash and dry the chicken breasts. Warm 1 tablespoon of butter or margarine in a large pan. Add the chicken breasts. Season with salt and pepper. Cook on each side 6 – 10 minutes, until cooked thoroughly. Pull the chicken breasts from the pan. Set aside.

2. Cook the linguine as stated to instructions on the package in a large pot. Save 1 cup of the pasta water. Drain the linguine. Add the mushrooms, tomatoes to the pan from cooking the chicken. Heat until they are tender.

3. Add the honey, mustard, and cream. Combine thoroughly. Add the chicken and linguine to the pan. Stir until coated. Garnish with parsley. Serve immediately.

Nutrition: Calories - 112 Protein - 12g
Carbohydrates - 56g
Fat - 20g Sodium - 158mg

Italian Chicken

Preparation time: 15 minutes Cooking time: 35 minutes Servings: 4
Ingredients:

- chicken breasts, skinless boneless
- 1 large jar of pasta sauce, low sodium
- 1 Tablespoon flavorless oil (olive, canola, or sunflower) 1 large onion, diced
- 1 large green pepper, diced
- ½ teaspoon garlic salt Salt and pepper to taste
- cup low-fat mozzarella cheese, grated Spinach leaves, washed, dried, rough chop

Directions:

1. Wash the chicken breasts, pat dry. In a large pot, heat the oil. Add the onion, cook, until it sweats and becomes translucent. Add the chicken. Season with salt, pepper, and garlic salt. Cook the chicken. 6 – 10 minutes on each side.

2. Add the peppers. Cook for 2 minutes. Pour

the pasta sauce over the chicken. Mix well. Simmer on low for 20 minutes. Serve on plates, sprinkle the cheese over each piece. Garnish with spinach.

Nutrition: Calories - 142 Protein - 17g Carbohydrates - 51g Fat - 15g Sodium - 225mg

Simple Mediterranean Chicken

Preparation time: 15 minutes Cooking time: 15 minutes Servings: 12
Ingredients:

- 2 chicken breasts, skinless and boneless 1 ½ cup grape tomatoes, cut in half
- ½ cup olives
- 2 tbsp olive oil
- 1 tsp Italian seasoning
- ¼ tsp pepper
- ¼ tsp salt

Directions:

1. Season chicken with Italian seasoning, pepper, and salt. Warm-up olive oil in a pan over medium heat. Add season chicken to the pan and cook for 4-6 minutes on each side. Transfer chicken on a plate.

2. Put tomatoes plus olives in the pan and cook for 2-4 minutes. Pour olive and tomato mixture on top of the chicken and serve.

Nutrition: Calories: 468 Fat: 29.4g Protein: 43.8g Carbs: 7.8g Sodium 410 mg

Roasted Chicken Thighs

Preparation time: 15 minutes Cooking time: 55 minutes Servings: 4
Ingredients:

- 8 chicken thighs
- 3 tbsp fresh parsley, chopped 1 tsp dried oregano
- 6 garlic cloves, crushed
- ¼ cup capers, drained
- 10 oz roasted red peppers, sliced 2 cups grape tomatoes
- 1 ½ lbs. potatoes, cut into small chunks 4 tbsp olive oil
- Pepper Salt

Directions:

1. Warm oven to 200 400 F. Season chicken with pepper and salt. Heat-up 2 tablespoons of olive oil in a pan over medium heat. Add chicken to the pan and sear until lightly golden brown from all the sides.

2. Transfer chicken onto a baking tray. Add tomato, potatoes, capers, oregano, garlic, and red peppers around the chicken. Season with pepper and salt and drizzle with remaining olive oil. Bake in preheated oven for 45-55 minutes. Garnish with parsley and serve.

Nutrition: Calories: 848 Fat: 29.1g Protein: 91.3g Carbs: 45.2g Sodium 110 mg

Mediterranean Turkey Breast

Preparation time: 15 minutes
Cooking time: 4 minutes & 30 minutes Servings: 6
Ingredients:

- 4 lbs. turkey breast 3 tbsp flour
- ¾ cup chicken stock
- 4 garlic cloves, chopped 1 tsp dried oregano
- ½ fresh lemon juice
- ½ cup sun-dried tomatoes, chopped
- ½ cup olives, chopped 1 onion, chopped
- ¼ tsp pepper
- ½ tsp salt

Directions:

1. Add turkey breast, garlic, oregano, lemon juice, sun-dried tomatoes, olives, onion, pepper, and salt to the slow cooker. Add half stock. Cook on high within 4 hours.

2. Whisk remaining stock and flour in a small bowl and add to slow cooker. Cover and cook for 30 minutes more. Serve and enjoy.

Nutrition: Calories: 537 Fat: 9.7g Protein: 79.1g Carbs: 29.6g Sodium 330 mg

Olive Capers Chicken

Preparation time: 15 minutes Cooking time: 16 minutes Servings: 4
Ingredients:

- 2 lbs. chicken
- 1/3 cup chicken stock
- 3.5 oz Capers 6 oz olives
- 1/4 cup fresh basil 1 tbsp olive oil
- tsp oregano
- garlic cloves, minced 2 tbsp red wine vinegar 1/8 tsp pepper
- 1/4 tsp salt

Directions:

1. Put olive oil in your instant pot and set the pot on sauté mode. Add chicken to the pot and sauté for 3-4 minutes. Add remaining

ingredients and stir well. Seal pot with the lid and select manual, and set timer for 12 minutes. Serve and enjoy.

Nutrition: Calories: 433 Fat: 15.2g Protein: 66.9g Carbs: 4.8g Sodium 244 mg

Chicken with Mushrooms

Preparation time: 15 minutes Cooking time: 6 hours & 10 minutes Servings: 2
Ingredients:

- 2 chicken breasts, skinless and boneless 1 cup mushrooms, sliced
- 1 onion, sliced
- cup chicken stock 1/2 tsp thyme, dried Pepper
- Salt

Directions:

1. Add all ingredients to the slow cooker. Cook on low within 6 hours.

2. Serve and enjoy.

Nutrition: Calories: 313 Fat: 11.3g Protein: 44.3g Carbs: 6.9g Sodium 541 mg

Lemon-Parsley Chicken Breast

Preparation time: 15 minutes Cooking time: 15 minutes Servings: 2
Ingredients:

- chicken breasts, skinless, boneless 1/3 cup white wine
- 1/3 cup lemon juice
- garlic cloves, minced
- Tablespoons bread crumbs
- 2 Tablespoons flavorless oil (olive, canola, or sunflower)
- ¼ cup fresh parsley

Directions:

1. Mix the wine, lemon juice, plus garlic in a measuring cup. Pound each chicken breast until they are ¼ inch thick. Coat the chicken with bread crumbs, and heat the oil in a large skillet.

2. Fry the chicken within 6 minutes on each side, until they turn brown. Stir in the wine mixture over the chicken. Simmer for 5 minutes. Pour any extra juices over the chicken. Garnish with parsley.

Nutrition: Calories - 117 Protein - 14g Carbohydrates - 74 g Fat - 12g Sodium - 189mg

CHAPTER 10:

Vegetables

Moroccan-Inspired Tagine with Chickpeas & Vegetables

Preparation time: 15 minutes Cooking time: 45 minutes Servings: 3
Ingredients:

- 2 teaspoons olive oil 1 cup chopped carrots
- ½ cup finely chopped onion 1 sweet potato, diced
- 1 cup low-sodium vegetable broth
- ¼ teaspoon ground cinnamon 1/8 teaspoon salt
- 1½ cups chopped bell peppers, any color
- 3 ripe plum tomatoes, chopped 1 tablespoon tomato paste
- 1 garlic clove, pressed or minced
- (15-ounce) can chickpeas, drained and rinsed
- ½ cup chopped dried apricots 1 teaspoon curry powder
- ½ teaspoon paprika
- ½ teaspoon turmeric

Directions:

1. Warm-up oil over medium heat in a large Dutch oven or saucepan. Add the carrots and onion and cook until the onion is translucent about 4 minutes. Add the sweet potato, broth, cinnamon, and salt and cook for 5 to 6 minutes, until the broth is slightly reduced.

2. Add the peppers, tomatoes, tomato paste, and garlic. Stir and cook for another 5 minutes. Add the chickpeas, apricots, curry powder, paprika, and turmeric to the pot. Bring all to a boil, then reduce the heat to low, cover, simmer for about 30 minutes, and serve.

Nutrition: Calories: 469 Fat: 9g
Carbohydrates: 88g Protein: 16g Sodium: 256mg

Roasted Brussels Sprouts

Preparation time: 5 minutes Cooking time: 20 minutes Servings: 4
Ingredients:

- 1½ pounds Brussels sprouts, trimmed and halved 2 tablespoons olive oil
- ¼ teaspoon salt
- ½ teaspoon freshly ground black pepper

Directions:

1. Preheat the oven to 400°f. Combine the Brussels sprouts and olive oil in a large mixing bowl and toss until they are evenly coated

2. Turn the Brussels sprouts out onto a large baking sheet and flip them over, so they are cut-side down with the flat part touching the baking sheet. Sprinkle with salt and pepper.

3. Bake within 20 to 30 minutes or until the Brussels sprouts are lightly charred and crisp on the outside and toasted on the bottom. The outer leaves will be extra dark, too. Serve immediately.

Nutrition: Calories: 134 Fat: 8g Sodium: 189mg
Carbohydrate: 15g Protein: 6g

Broccoli with Garlic and Lemon

Preparation time: 2 minutes Cooking time: 4 minutes Servings: 4
Ingredients:

- 1 cup of water
- 4 cups broccoli florets 1 teaspoon olive oil
- 1 tablespoon minced garlic 1 teaspoon lemon zest
- Salt
- Freshly ground black pepper

Directions:

1. Put the broccoli in the boiling water in a small saucepan and cook within 2 to 3 minutes. The broccoli should retain its bright-green color. Drain the water from the broccoli.

2. Put the olive oil in a small sauté pan over medium-high heat. Add the garlic and sauté for 30 seconds. Put the broccoli, lemon zest, salt, plus pepper. Combine well and serve.

Nutrition: Calories: 38g Fat: 1g Sodium: 24mg

Carbohydrate: 5g Protein: 3g

Brown Rice Pilaf

Preparation time: 5 minutes Cooking time: 10 minutes Servings: 4
Ingredients:

- 1 cup low-sodium vegetable broth
- ½ tablespoon olive oil 1 clove garlic, minced 1 scallion, thinly sliced
- 1 tablespoon minced onion flakes 1 cup instant brown rice
- 1/8 teaspoon freshly ground black pepper

Directions:

1. Mix the vegetable broth, olive oil, garlic, scallion, and minced onion flakes in a saucepan and boil. Put rice, then boil it again, adjust the heat and simmer within 10 minutes. Remove and let stand within 5 minutes. Fluff with a fork and season with black pepper.

Nutrition: Calories: 100g Fat: 2g Sodium: 35mg
Carbohydrate: 19g Protein: 2g

Chunky Black-Bean Dip

Preparation time: 5 minutes Cooking time: 1 minute
Servings: 2
Ingredients:

- 1 (15-ounce) can black beans, drained, with liquid reserved
- ½-can of chipotle peppers in adobo sauce
- ¼ cup plain Greek yogurt Freshly ground black pepper

Directions:

1. Combine beans, peppers, and yogurt in a food processor or blender and process until smooth. Add some of the bean liquid, 1 tablespoon at a time, for a thinner consistency. Season to taste with black pepper. Serve.

Nutrition: Calories: 70g Fat: 1g Sodium: 159mg
Carbohydrate: 11g Protein: 5g

Sweet Potato Rice with Spicy Peanut Sauce

Preparation time: 15 minutes Cooking time: 25 minutes Servings: 2
Ingredients:

- ½ cup basmati rice
- teaspoons olive oil, divided
- (8-ounce) can chickpeas, drained and rinsed

- 2 medium sweet
- potatoes, small cubes
- ¼ teaspoon ground cumin 1 cup of water
- 1/8 teaspoon salt
- tablespoons chopped cilantro 3 tablespoons peanut butter
- tablespoon sriracha
- teaspoons reduced-sodium soy sauce
- ½ teaspoon garlic powder
- ¼ teaspoon ground ginger

Directions:

1. Heat-up 1 teaspoon of oil in a large nonstick skillet over medium-high heat. Add the chickpeas and heat for 3 minutes. Stir and cook until lightly browned. Transfer the chickpeas to a small bowl.

2. Put the rest of the1 teaspoon of oil to the skillet, then add the potatoes and cumin, distributing them evenly. Cook the potatoes until they become lightly browned before turning them.

3. While the potatoes are cooking, boil the water with the salt in a large saucepan over medium-high heat. Put the rice in the boiling water, adjust the heat to low, cover, and simmer for 20 minutes.

4. When the potatoes have fully cooked, about 10 minutes in total, remove the skillet from the heat. Transfer the potatoes and chickpeas to the rice, folding all gently. Add the chopped cilantro.

5. In a small bowl, whisk the peanut butter, sriracha, soy sauce, garlic powder, and ginger until well blended. Divide the rice mixture between two serving bowls. Drizzle with the sauce and serve.

Nutrition: Calories: 667 Fat: 22g
Carbohydrates: 100g
Fiber: 14g Protein: 20g Sodium: 563mg Potassium: 963mg

Vegetable Red Curry

Preparation time: 15 minutes Cooking time: 25 minutes Servings: 2
Ingredients:

- 2 teaspoons olive oil 1 cup sliced carrots
- ½ cup chopped onion
- garlic clove, pressed or minced
- bell peppers, seeded and thinly sliced 1 cup chopped cauliflower

- 2/3 cup light coconut milk
- ½ cup low-sodium vegetable broth 1 tablespoon tomato paste
- teaspoon curry powder
- ½ teaspoon ground cumin
- ½ teaspoon ground coriander
- ¼ teaspoon turmeric
- cups fresh baby spinach
- 1 cup quick-cooking brown rice

Directions:

1. Heat-up oil in a large nonstick skillet over medium heat. Add the carrots, onion, and garlic and cook for 2 to 3 minutes. Reduce the heat to medium-low, add the peppers and cauliflower to the skillet, cover, and cook within 5 minutes.

2. Add the coconut milk, broth, tomato paste, curry powder, cumin, coriander, and turmeric, stirring to combine. Simmer, covered (vent the lid slightly), for 10 to 15 minutes until the curry is slightly reduced and thickened.

3. Uncover, add the spinach, and stir for 2 minutes until it is wilted and mixed into the vegetables. Remove from the heat. Cook the rice as stated to the package instructions. Serve the curry over the rice.

Nutrition: Calories: 584 Fat: 16g
Carbohydrates: 101g Fiber: 10g
Protein: 13g Sodium: 102mg Potassium: 1430mg

Black Bean Burgers

Preparation time: 15 minutes Cooking time: 20 minutes Servings: 4
Ingredients:
- ½ cup quick-cooking brown rice 2 teaspoons canola oil, divided
- ½ cup finely chopped carrots
- ¼ cup finely chopped onion 1 can black beans, drained
- 1 tablespoon salt-free mesquite seasoning blend
- 4 small, hard rolls

Directions:

1. Cook the rice as stated in the package directions and set aside. Heat-up

2. 1 teaspoon of oil in a large nonstick skillet over medium heat. Add the carrots and onions and cook until the onions are translucent about 4 minutes. Adjust the heat

to low, and cook again for 5 to 6 minutes, until the carrots are tender.

3. Add the beans and seasoning to the skillet and continue cooking for 2 to 3 more minutes. Pulse bean mixture in a food processor within 3 to 4 times or until the mixture is coarsely blended. Put the batter in a medium bowl and fold in the brown rice until well combined.

4. Divide the mixture evenly and form it into 4 patties with your hands. Heat the remaining oil in the skillet. Cook the patties within 4 to 5 minutes per side, turning once. Serve the burgers on the rolls with your choice of toppings.

Nutrition: Calories: 368 Fat: 6g
Carbohydrates: 66g
Fiber: 8g Protein: 13g Sodium: 322mg
Potassium: 413mg

Summer Barley Pilaf with Yogurt Dill Sauce

Preparation time: 15 minutes Cooking time: 30 minutes Servings: 3
Ingredients:
- 2 2/3 cups low-sodium vegetable broth 2 teaspoons avocado oil
- 1 small zucchini, diced
- 1/3 cup slivered almonds 2 scallions, sliced
- 1 cup barley
- ½ cup plain nonfat Greek yogurt 2 teaspoons grated lemon zest
- ¼ teaspoon dried dill

Directions:

1. Boil the broth in a large saucepan. Heat-up the oil in a skillet. Add the zucchini and sauté 3 to 4 minutes. Add the almonds and the white parts of the scallions and sauté for 2 minutes. Remove, and transfer it to a small bowl.

2. Add the barley to the skillet and sauté for 2 to 3 minutes to toast. Transfer the barley to the boiling broth and reduce the heat to low, cover, and simmer for 25 minutes or until tender. Remove, and let stand within 10 minutes or until the liquid is absorbed.

3. Simultaneously, mix the yogurt, lemon zest, and dill in a small bowl and set aside. Fluff the barley with a fork. Add the zucchini, almond, and onion mixture and mix gently.

To serve, divide the pilaf between two bowls and drizzle the yogurt over each bowl.

Nutrition: Calories: 545 Fat: 15g
Carbohydrates: 87g Fiber: 19g
Protein: 21g
Sodium: 37mg Potassium: 694mg

Lentil Quinoa Gratin with Butternut Squash

Preparation time: 15 minutes Cooking time: 1 hour & 15 minutes Servings: 3
Ingredients:

- For the Lentils and Squash: Nonstick cooking spray 2 cups of
- p dried green or red lentils, rinsed Pinch salt
- teaspoon olive oil, divided
- ½ cup quinoa
- ¼ cup diced shallot
- cups frozen cubed butternut squash
- ¼ cup low-fat milk
- 1 teaspoon chopped fresh rosemary Freshly ground black pepper
- For the Gratin Topping:
- ¼ cup panko bread crumbs 1 teaspoon olive oil
- 1/3 cup shredded Gruyère cheese

Directions:

1. Preheat the oven to 400°F. Spray a 1½-quart casserole dish or an 8-by- 8-inch baking dish with cooking spray.

2. In a medium saucepan, stir the water, lentils, and salt and boil over medium-high heat. Lower the heat once the water is boiling, cover, and simmer for 20 to 25 minutes. Then drain and transfer the lentils to a large bowl and set aside.

3. In the same saucepan, heat-up ½ teaspoon of oil over medium heat. Add the quinoa and quickly stir for 1 minute to toast it lightly. Cook according to the package directions, about 20 minutes.

4. While the quinoa cooks, heat the remaining olive oil in a medium skillet over medium-low heat, add the shallots, and sauté them until they are translucent, about 3 minutes. Add the squash, milk, and rosemary and cook for 1 to 2 minutes.

5. Remove, then transfer to the lentil bowl.

Add in the quinoa and gently toss all. Season with pepper to taste. Transfer the mixture to the casserole dish.

6. For the gratin topping, mix the panko bread crumbs with the olive oil in a small bowl. Put the bread crumbs over the casserole and top them with the cheese. Bake the casserole for 25 minutes and serve.

Nutrition: Calories: 576 Fat: 15g
Carbohydrates: 87g Fiber: 12g
Protein: 28g Sodium: 329mg Potassium: 1176mg

Brown Rice Casserole with Cottage Cheese

Preparation time: 15 minutes Cooking time: 45 minutes Servings: 3
Ingredients:

- Nonstick cooking spray
- 1 cup quick-cooking brown rice 1 teaspoon olive oil
- ½ cup diced sweet onion
- 1 (10-ounce) bag of fresh spinach 1½ cups low-fat cottage cheese
- tablespoon grated Parmesan cheese
- ¼ cup sunflower seed kernels

Directions:

1. Preheat the oven to 375°F. Spray a small 1½-quart casserole dish with cooking spray. Cook the rice, as stated in the package directions. Set aside.

2. Warm-up oil in a large nonstick skillet over medium-low heat. Add the onion and sauté for 3 to 4 minutes. Add the spinach and cover the skillet, cooking for 1 to 2 minutes until the spinach wilts. Remove the skillet from the heat.

3. In a medium bowl, mix the rice, spinach mixture, and cottage cheese. Transfer the mixture to the prepared casserole dish. Top with the Parmesan cheese and sunflower seeds, bake for 25 minutes until lightly browned, and serve.

Nutrition: Calories: 334 Fat: 9g
Carbohydrates: 47g Fiber: 5g
Protein: 19g Sodium: 425mg Potassium: 553mg

Quinoa-Stuffed Peppers

Preparation time: 15 minutes Cooking time: 35 minutes Servings: 2
Ingredients:

- large green bell peppers, halved 1½ teaspoons olive oil, divided
- ½ cup quinoa
- ½ cup minced onion
- 1 garlic clove, pressed or minced
- 1 cup chopped portobello mushrooms
- 3 tablespoons grated Parmesan cheese, divided 4 ounces tomato sauce

Directions:

1. Preheat the oven to 400°F. Put the pepper halves on your prepared baking sheet. Brush the insides of peppers with ½ teaspoon olive oil and bake for 10 minutes.

2. Remove the baking sheet, then set aside. While the peppers bake, cook the quinoa in a large saucepan over medium heat according to the package directions and set aside.

3. Warm-up the rest of the oil in a medium-size skillet over medium heat. Add the onion and sauté until it's translucent about 3 minutes. Put the garlic and cook within 1 minute.

4. Put the mushrooms in the skillet, adjust the heat to medium-low, cover, and cook within 5 to 6 minutes. Uncover, and if there's still liquid in the pan, reduce the heat and cook until the liquid evaporates.

5. Add the mushroom mixture, 1 tablespoon of Parmesan, and the tomato sauce to the quinoa and gently stir to combine. Carefully spoon the quinoa mixture into each pepper half and sprinkle with the remaining Parmesan. Return the peppers to the oven, bake for 10 to 15 more minutes until tender, and serve.

Nutrition: Calories: 292 Fat: 9g
Carbohydrates: 45g Fiber: 8g
Protein: 12g
Sodium: 154mg Potassium: 929mg

Greek Flatbread with Spinach, Tomatoes & Feta

Preparation time: 15 minutes Cooking time: 9 minutes Servings: 2
Ingredients:

- 2 cups fresh baby spinach, coarsely chopped 2 teaspoons olive oil
- 2 slices naan, or another flatbread
- ¼ cup sliced black olives
- 2 plum tomatoes, thinly sliced
- teaspoon salt-free Italian seasoning blend
- ¼ cup crumbled feta

Directions:

1. Preheat the oven to 400°F. Heat 3 tablespoons of water in a small skillet over medium heat. Add the spinach, cover, and steam until wilted, about 2 minutes. Drain off any excess water, then put aside.

2. Drizzle the oil evenly onto both flatbreads. Top each evenly with the spinach, olives, tomatoes, seasoning, and feta. Bake the flatbreads within 5 to 7 minutes, or until lightly browned. Cut each into four pieces and serve hot.

Nutrition: Calories: 411 Fat: 15g
Carbohydrates: 53g Fiber: 7g
Protein: 15g Sodium: 621mg Potassium: 522mg

Mushroom Risotto with Peas

Preparation time: 15 minutes Cooking time: 20 minutes Servings: 2
Ingredients:

- cups low-sodium vegetable or chicken broth 1 teaspoon olive oil
- 8 ounces baby portobello mushrooms, thinly sliced
- ½ cup frozen peas 1 teaspoon butter 1 cup arborio rice
- 1 tablespoon grated Parmesan cheese

Directions:

1. Pour the broth into a microwave-proof glass measuring cup. Microwave on high for 1½ minutes or until hot. Warm-up oil over medium heat in a large saucepan. Add the mushrooms and stir for 1 minute. Cover and cook until soft, about 3 more minutes. Stir in the peas and reduce the heat to low.

2. Put the mushroom batter to the saucepan's sides and add the butter to the middle, heating until melted. Put the rice in the saucepan and stir for 1 to 2 minutes to lightly toast. Add the hot broth, ½ cup at a time, and stir gently.

3. As the broth is cooked into the rice, continue adding more broth, ½ cup at a time, stirring after each addition, until all broth is added. Once all of the liquid is absorbed (this should take 15 minutes), remove from the heat. Serve immediately,

topped with Parmesan cheese.
Nutrition: Calories: 430 Fat: 6g
Carbohydrates: 83g
Fiber: 5g Protein: 10g Sodium: 78mg
Potassium: 558mg

Loaded Tofu Burrito with Black Beans

Preparation time: 15 minutes Cooking time: 20
minutes Servings: 2
Ingredients:
- 4 ounces extra-firm tofu, pressed and cut into 2-inch cubes 2 teaspoons mesquite salt-free seasoning, divided
- 2 teaspoons canola oil
- cup thinly sliced bell peppers
- ½ cup diced onions
- 2/3 cup of black beans, drained 2 (10-inch) whole-wheat tortillas 1 tablespoon sriracha
- Nonfat Greek yogurt, for serving

Directions:
1. Put the tofu and 1 teaspoon of seasoning in a medium zip-top plastic freezer bag and toss until the tofu is well coated.
2. Heat-up the oil in a medium skillet over medium-high heat. Put the tofu in the skillet. Don't stir; allow the tofu to brown before turning. When lightly browned, about 6 minutes, transfer the tofu from the skillet to a small bowl and set aside.
3. Put the peppers plus onions in the skillet and sauté until tender, about 5 minutes. Lower the heat to medium-low, then put the beans and the remaining seasoning. Cook within 5 minutes.
4. For the burritos, lay each tortilla flat on a work surface. Place half of the tofu in the center of each tortilla, top with half of the pepper-bean mixture, and drizzle with the sriracha.
5. Fold the bottom portion of each tortilla up and over the tofu mixture. Then fold each side into the middle, tuck in, and tightly roll it up toward the open end. Serve with a dollop of yogurt.

Nutrition: Calories: 327 Fat: 12g
Carbohydrates: 41g Fiber: 11g
Protein: 16g
Sodium: 282mg

Southwest Tofu Scramble

Preparation time: 15 minutes Cooking time: 15
minutes Servings: 1
Ingredients:
- ½ tablespoon olive oil
- ½ red onion, chopped
- cups chopped spinach
- 8 ounces firm tofu, drained well 1 teaspoon ground cumin
- ½ teaspoon garlic powder
- Optional for serving: sliced avocado or sliced tomatoes

Directions:
1. Heat-up the olive oil in a medium skillet over medium heat. Put the onion and cook within 5 minutes. Add the spinach and cover to steam for 2 minutes.
2. Using a spatula, move the veggies to one side of the pan. Crumble the tofu into the open area in the pan, breaking it up with a fork. Add the cumin and garlic to the crumbled tofu and mix well. Sauté for 5 to 7 minutes until the tofu is slightly browned.
3. Serve immediately with whole-grain bread, fruit, or beans. Top with optional sliced avocado and tomato, if using.

Nutrition: Calories: 267 Fat: 17g Sodium: 75mg
Carbohydrate: 13g Protein: 23g

Black-Bean and Vegetable Burrito

Preparation time: 15 minutes Cooking time: 15
minutes Servings: 4
Ingredients:
- ½ tablespoon olive oil
- 2 red or green bell peppers, chopped 1 zucchini or summer squash, diced
- ½ teaspoon chili powder 1 teaspoon cumin
- Freshly ground black pepper
- 2cans black beans drained and rinsed 1 cup cherry tomatoes, halved
- 4 (8-inch) whole-wheat tortillas
- Optional for serving: spinach, sliced avocado, chopped scallions, or hot sauce

Directions:
1. Heat-up the oil in a large sauté pan over medium heat. Add the bell peppers and sauté until crisp-tender, about 4 minutes. Add the zucchini, chili powder, cumin, and black pepper to taste, and continue to sauté until the vegetables are tender, about 5 minutes.

2. Add the black beans and cherry tomatoes and cook within 5 minutes. Divide between 4 burritos and serve topped with optional ingredients as desired. Enjoy immediately.

Nutrition: Calories: 311 Fat: 6g Sodium: 499mg
Carbohydrate: 52g
Protein: 19g

Baked Eggs in Avocado

Preparation time: 15 minutes Cooking time: 15 minutes Servings: 2
Ingredients:

- 2 avocados Juice of 2 limes
- Freshly ground black pepper
- 4 eggs
- 2 (8-inch) whole-wheat or corn tortillas, warmed
- Optional for serving: halved cherry tomatoes and chopped cilantro

Directions:

1. Adjust the oven rack to the middle position and preheat the oven to 450°F. Scrape out the center of halved avocado using a spoon about 1½ tablespoons.

2. Press lime juice over the avocados and season with black pepper to taste, and then place it on a baking sheet. Crack an egg into the avocado.

3. Bake within 10 to 15 minutes. Remove from oven and garnish with optional cilantro and cherry tomatoes and serve with warm tortillas.

Nutrition: Calories: 534 Fat: 39g Sodium: 462mg
Potassium: 1,095mg Carbohydrate: 30g Fiber: 20g
Sugars: 3g Protein: 23g

Red Beans and Rice

Preparation time: 15 minutes Cooking time: 45 minutes Servings: 2
Ingredients:

- ½ cup dry brown rice
- 1 cup water, plus ¼ cup 1 can red beans, drained
- 1 tablespoon ground cumin Juice of 1 lime
- 4 handfuls of fresh spinach
- Optional toppings: avocado, chopped tomatoes, Greek yogurt, onions

Directions:

1. Mix rice plus water in a pot and bring to a boil. Cover and reduce heat to a low

simmer. Cook within 30 to 40 minutes or according to package directions.

2. Meanwhile, add the beans, ¼ cup of water, cumin, and lime juice to a medium skillet. Simmer within 5 to 7 minutes.

3. Once the liquid is mostly gone, remove from the heat and add the spinach. Cover and let spinach wilt slightly, 2 to 3 minutes. Mix in with the beans. Serve beans with rice. Add toppings, if using.

Nutrition: Calories: 232 Fat: 2g Sodium: 210mg
Carbohydrate: 41g Protein: 13g

Hearty Lentil Soup

Preparation time: 15 minutes Cooking time: 30 minutes Servings: 4
Ingredients:

- tablespoon olive oil
- carrots, peeled and chopped 2 celery stalks, diced
- 1 onion, chopped
- 1 teaspoon dried thyme
- ½ teaspoon garlic powder Freshly ground black pepper
- 1 (28-ounce) can no-salt diced tomatoes, drained 1 cup dry lentils
- 5 cups of water Salt

Directions:

1. Heat-up the oil in a large Dutch oven or pot over medium heat. Once the oil is simmering, add the carrot, celery, and onion. Cook, often stirring within 5 minutes.

2. Add the thyme, garlic powder, and black pepper. Cook within 30 seconds. Pour in the drained diced tomatoes and cook for a few more minutes, often stirring to enhance their flavor.

3. Put the lentils, water, plus a pinch of salt. Raise the heat and bring to a boil, then partially cover the pot and reduce heat to maintain a gentle simmer.

4. Cook within 30 minutes, or until lentils are tender but still hold their shape. Ladle into serving bowls and serve with a fresh green salad and whole-grain bread.

Nutrition:
Calories: 168 Fat: 4g Sodium: 130mg
Carbohydrate: 35g Protein: 10g

Black-Bean Soup

Preparation time: 15 minutes Cooking time: 20 minutes Servings: 4
Ingredients:

- 1 yellow onion
- tablespoon olive oil
- cans black beans, drained 1 cup diced fresh tomatoes
- 5 cups low-sodium vegetable broth
- ¼ teaspoon freshly ground black pepper
- ¼ cup chopped fresh cilantro

Directions:

1. Cook or sauté the onion in the olive oil within 4 to 5 minutes in a large saucepan over medium heat. Put the black beans, tomatoes, vegetable broth, and black pepper. Boil, then adjust heat to simmer within 15 minutes.

2. Remove, then working in batches, ladle the soup into a blender and process until somewhat smooth. Put it back to the pot, add the cilantro, and heat until warmed through. Serve immediately.

Nutrition: Calories: 234 Fat: 5g Sodium: 363mg Carbohydrate: 37g Protein: 11g

Loaded Baked Sweet Potatoes

Preparation time: 15 minutes Cooking time: 20 minutes Servings: 4
Ingredients:

- 4 sweet potatoes
- ½ cup nonfat or low-fat plain Greek yogurt Freshly ground black pepper
- 1 teaspoon olive oil
- 1 red bell pepper, cored and diced
- ½ red onion, diced
- 1 teaspoon ground cumin
- 1 (15-ounce) can chickpeas, drained and rinsed

Directions:

1. Prick the potatoes using a fork and cook on your microwave's potato setting until potatoes are soft and cooked through, about 8 to 10 minutes for 4 potatoes. If you don't have a microwave, bake at 400°F for about 45 minutes.

2. Combine the yogurt and black pepper in a small bowl and mix well. Heat the oil in a medium pot over medium heat. Add bell pepper, onion, cumin, and additional black

pepper to taste.

3. Add the chickpeas, stir to combine, and heat through about 5 minutes. Slice the potatoes lengthwise down the middle and top each half with a portion of the bean mixture followed by 1 to 2 tablespoons of the yogurt. Serve immediately.

Nutrition: Calories: 264 Fat: 2g Sodium: 124mg Carbohydrate: 51g
Protein: 11g

White Beans with Spinach and Pan-Roasted Tomatoes

Preparation time: 15 minutes Cooking time: 10 minutes Servings: 2
Ingredients:

- 1 tablespoon olive oil
- 4 small plum tomatoes, halved lengthwise
- 10 ounces frozen spinach, defrosted and squeezed of excess water 2 garlic cloves, thinly sliced
- 2 tablespoons water
- ¼ teaspoon freshly ground black pepper 1 can white beans, drained
- Juice of 1 lemon

Directions:

1. Heat-up the oil in a large skillet over medium-high heat. Put the tomatoes, cut-side down, and cook within 3 to 5 minutes; turn and cook within 1 minute more. Transfer to a plate.

2. Reduce heat to medium and add the spinach, garlic, water, and pepper to the skillet. Cook, tossing until the spinach is heated through, 2 to 3 minutes.

3. Return the tomatoes to the skillet, put the white beans and lemon juice, and toss until heated through 1 to 2 minutes.

Nutrition: Calories: 293 Fat: 9g Sodium: 267mg Carbohydrate: 43g Protein: 15g

Spaghetti Squash with Maple Glaze & Tofu Crumbles

Preparation time: 15 minutes Cooking time: 22 minutes Servings: 3
Ingredients:

- ounces firm tofu, well-drained
- 1 small spaghetti squash, halved lengthwise 2½ teaspoons olive oil, divided
- 1/8 teaspoon salt

- ½ cup chopped onion
- teaspoon dried rosemary
- ¼ cup dry white wine
- tablespoons maple syrup
- ½ teaspoon garlic powder
- ¼ cup shredded Gruyère cheese

Directions:

1. Put the tofu in a large mesh colander and place over a large bowl to drain. Score the squash using a paring knife so the steam can vent while it cooks. Place the squash in a medium microwave-safe dish and microwave on high for 5 minutes. Remove the squash from the microwave and allow it to cool.

2. Cut the cooled squash in half on a cutting board. Remove the seeds, then put the squash halves into a 9-by-11-inch baking dish.

3. Drizzle the squash with half a teaspoon of olive oil and season it with the salt, then wrap it using wax paper and put it back in the microwave for 5 more minutes on high. Once it's cooked, scrape the squash strands with a fork into a small bowl and cover it to keep it warm.

4. While the squash is cooking, heat 1 teaspoon of oil in a large skillet over medium-high heat. Put the onion and sauté for within minutes. Add the rosemary and stir for 1 minute, until fragrant.

5. Put the rest of the oil in the same skillet. Crumble the tofu into the skillet, stir fry until lightly browned, about 4 minutes, and transfer it to a small bowl.

6. Add the wine, maple syrup, and garlic powder to the skillet and stir to combine. Cook for 2 minutes until slightly reduced and thickened. Remove from the heat. Evenly divide the squash between two plates, then top it with the tofu mixture. Drizzle the maple glaze over the top, then add the grated cheese.

Nutrition: Calories: 330 Fat: 15g
Carbohydrates: 36g
Fiber: 5g Protein: 12g Sodium: 326mg
Potassium: 474mg

Stuffed Tex-Mex Baked Potatoes

Preparation time: 15 minutes Cooking time: 45 minutes Servings: 2
Ingredients:

- 2 large Idaho potatoes
- ½ cup black beans, rinsed and drained
- ¼ cup store-bought salsa 1 avocado, diced
- teaspoon freshly squeezed lime juice
- ½ cup nonfat plain Greek yogurt
- ¼ teaspoon reduced-sodium taco seasoning
- ¼ cup shredded sharp cheddar cheese

Directions:

1. Preheat the oven to 400°F. Scrub the potatoes, then slice an "X" into the top of each using a paring knife. Put the potatoes on the oven rack, then bake for 45 minutes until they are tender.

2. In a small bowl, stir the beans and salsa and set aside. In another small bowl, mix the avocado and lime juice and set aside. In a third small bowl, stir the yogurt and the taco seasoning until well blended.

3. When the potatoes are baked, carefully open them up. Top each potato with the bean and salsa mixture, avocado, seasoned yogurt, and cheddar cheese, evenly dividing each component, and serve.

Nutrition: Calories: 624 Fat: 21g
Carbohydrates: 91g Fiber: 21g
Protein: 24g
Sodium: 366mg Potassium: 2134mg

Lentil-Stuffed Zucchini Boats

Preparation time: 15 minutes Cooking time: 45 minutes Servings: 2
Ingredients:

- medium zucchinis, halved lengthwise and seeded 2¼ cups water, divided
- cup green or red lentils, dried & rinsed
- teaspoons olive oil 1/3 cup diced onion
- 2 tablespoons tomato paste
- ½ teaspoon oregano
- ¼ teaspoon garlic powder Pinch salt
- ¼ cup grated part-skim mozzarella cheese

Directions:

1. Preheat the oven to 375°F. Line a baking sheet with parchment paper.

2. Place the zucchini, hollow sides up, on the baking sheet, and set aside.

3. Boil 2 cups of water to a boil over high heat in a medium saucepan and add the lentils.

Lower the heat, then simmer within 20 to 25 minutes. Drain and set aside.

4. Heat-up the olive oil in a medium skillet over medium-low heat. Sauté the onions until they are translucent, about 4 minutes. Lower the heat and add the cooked lentils, tomato paste, oregano, garlic powder, and salt.

5. Add the last quarter cup of water and simmer for 3 minutes, until the liquid reduces and forms a sauce. Remove from heat.

6. Stuff each zucchini half with the lentil mixture, dividing it evenly, top with cheese, bake for 25 minutes and serve. The zucchini should be fork-tender, and the cheese should be melted.

Nutrition: Calories: 479 Fat: 9g
Carbohydrates: 74g Fiber: 14g
Protein: 31g
Sodium: 206mg Potassium: 1389mg

Baked Eggplant Parmesan

Preparation time: 15 minutes Cooking time: 35 minutes Servings: 4
Ingredients:
- 1 small to medium eggplant, cut into ¼-inch slices
- ½ teaspoon salt-free Italian seasoning blend 1 tablespoon olive oil
- ¼ cup diced onion
- ½ cup diced yellow or red bell pepper 2 garlic cloves, pressed or minced
- 1 (8-ounce) can tomato sauce
- 3 ounces fresh mozzarella, cut into 6 pieces
- tablespoon grated Parmesan cheese, divided 5 to 6 fresh basil leaves, chopped

Directions:

1. Preheat an oven-style air fryer to 400°F.

2. Working in two batches, place the eggplant slices onto the air-fryer tray and sprinkle them with Italian seasoning. Bake for 7 minutes. Repeat with the remaining slices, then set them aside on a plate.

3. In a medium skillet, heat the oil over medium heat and sauté the onion and peppers until softened about 5 minutes. Add the garlic and sauté for

4. 1 to 2 more minutes. Add the tomato sauce

and stir to combine. Remove the sauce from the heat.

5. Spray a 9-by-6-inch casserole dish with cooking spray. Spread one- third of the sauce into the bottom of the dish. Layer eggplant slices onto the sauce. Sprinkle with half of the Parmesan cheese.

6. Continue layering the sauce and eggplant, ending with the sauce. Place the mozzarella pieces on the top. Sprinkle the remaining Parmesan evenly over the entire dish. Bake in the oven for 20 minutes. Garnish with fresh basil, cut into four servings, and serve.

Nutrition: Calories: 213 Fat: 12g
Carbohydrates: 20g Fiber: 7g
Protein: 10g Sodium: 222mg Potassium: 763mg

Black-Eyed Peas and Greens Power Salad

Preparation time: 15 minutes Cooking time: 6 minutes Servings: 2
Ingredients:
- 1 tablespoon olive oil
- 3 cups purple cabbage, chopped 5 cups baby spinach
- 1 cup shredded carrots
- 1 can black-eyed peas, drained Juice of ½ lemon
- Salt
- Freshly ground black pepper

Directions:

1. In a medium pan, add the oil and cabbage and sauté for 1 to 2 minutes on medium heat. Add in your spinach, cover for 3 to 4 minutes on medium heat, until greens are wilted. Remove from the heat and add to a large bowl.

2. Add in the carrots, black-eyed peas, and a splash of lemon juice. Season with salt and pepper, if desired. Toss and serve.

Nutrition: Calories: 320 Fat: 9g Sodium: 351mg Potassium: 544mg Carbohydrate: 49g Protein: 16g

Butternut-Squash Macaroni and Cheese

Preparation time: 15 minutes Cooking time: 20 minutes Servings: 2
Ingredients:
- cup whole-wheat ziti macaroni
- cups peeled and cubed butternut squash 1

cup nonfat or low-fat milk, divided Freshly ground black pepper

- 1 teaspoon Dijon mustard 1 tablespoon olive oil
- ¼ cup shredded low-fat cheddar cheese

Directions:

1. Cook the pasta al dente. Put the butternut squash plus ½ cup milk in a medium saucepan and place over medium-high heat. Season with black pepper. Bring it to a simmer. Lower the heat, then cook until fork-tender, 8 to 10 minutes.

2. To a blender, add squash and Dijon mustard. Purée until smooth. Meanwhile, place a large sauté pan over medium heat and add olive oil. Add the squash purée and the remaining ½ cup of milk. Simmer within 5 minutes. Add the cheese and stir to combine.

3. Add the pasta to the sauté pan and stir to combine. Serve immediately. Nutrition:

Calories: 373 Fat: 10g Sodium: 193mg
Carbohydrate: 59g Protein: 14g

Pasta with Tomatoes and Peas

Preparation time: 15 minutes Cooking time: 15 minutes Servings: 2
Ingredients:

- ½ cup whole-grain pasta of choice 8 cups water, plus ¼ for finishing 1 cup frozen peas
- 1 tablespoon olive oil
- 1 cup cherry tomatoes, halved
- ¼ teaspoon freshly ground black pepper 1 teaspoon dried basil
- ¼ cup grated Parmesan cheese (low-sodium)

Directions:

1. Cook the pasta al dente. Add the water to the same pot you used to cook the pasta, and when it's boiling, add the peas. Cook within 5 minutes. Drain and set aside.

2. Heat-up the oil in a large skillet over medium heat. Add the cherry tomatoes, put a lid on the skillet and let the tomatoes soften for about 5 minutes, stirring a few times.

3. Season with black pepper and basil. Toss in the pasta, peas, and ¼ cup of water, stir and remove from the heat. Serve topped with

Parmesan.
Nutrition: Calories: 266 Fat: 12g Sodium: 320mg
Carbohydrate: 30g Protein: 13g

Healthy Vegetable Fried Rice

Preparation time: 15 minutes Cooking time: 10 minutes Servings: 4
Ingredients:
For the sauce:

- 1/3 cup garlic vinegar
- 1½ tablespoons dark molasses 1 teaspoon onion powder
- For the fried rice:
- teaspoon olive oil
- lightly beaten whole eggs + 4 egg whites 1 cup of frozen mixed vegetables
- cup frozen edamame
- cups cooked brown rice

Directions:

1. Prepare the sauce by combining the garlic vinegar, molasses, and onion powder in a glass jar. Shake well.

2. Heat-up oil in a large wok or skillet over medium-high heat. Add eggs and egg whites, let cook until the eggs set, for about 1 minute.

3. Break up eggs with a spatula or spoon into small pieces. Add frozen mixed vegetables and frozen edamame. Cook for 4 minutes, stirring frequently.

4. Add the brown rice and sauce to the vegetable-and-egg mixture. Cook for 5 minutes or until heated through. Serve immediately.

Nutrition: Calories: 210 Fat: 6g Sodium: 113mg
Carbohydrate: 28g Protein: 13g

Portobello-Mushroom Cheeseburgers

Preparation time: 15 minutes Cooking time: 10 minutes Servings: 4
Ingredients:

- 4 portobello mushrooms, caps removed and brushed clean 1 tablespoon olive oil
- ½ teaspoon freshly ground black pepper
- 1 tablespoon red wine vinegar
- 4 slices reduced-fat Swiss cheese, sliced thin 4 whole-wheat 100-calorie sandwich thins
- ½ avocado, sliced thin

Directions:

1. Heat-up a skillet or grill pan over medium-high heat. Clean the mushrooms and remove the stems. Brush each cap with olive oil and sprinkle with black pepper. Place in skillet cap-side up and cook for about 4 minutes. Flip and cook for another 4 minutes.

2. Sprinkle with the red wine vinegar and flip. Add the cheese and cook for 2 more minutes. For optimal melting, place a lid loosely over the pan. Meanwhile, toast the sandwich thins. Create your burgers by topping each with sliced avocado. Enjoy immediately.

Nutrition: Calories: 245 Fat: 12g Sodium: 266mg Carbohydrate: 28g Protein: 14g

Baked Chickpe -And-Rosemary Omelet

Preparation time: 15 minutes Cooking time: 15 minutes Servings: 2
Ingredients:
- ½ tablespoon olive oil 4 eggs
- ¼ cup grated Parmesan cheese
- 1 (15-ounce) can chickpeas, drained and rinsed 2 cups packed baby spinach
- cup button mushrooms, chopped
- sprigs rosemary, leaves picked (or 2 teaspoons dried rosemary) Salt
- Freshly ground black pepper

Directions:

1. Warm oven to 400 F and puts a baking tray on the middle shelf. Line an 8-inch springform pan with baking paper and grease generously with olive oil. If you don't have a springform pan, grease an oven-safe skillet (or cast-iron skillet) with olive oil.

2. Lightly whisk the eggs and Parmesan. Place chickpeas in the prepared pan. Layer the spinach and mushrooms on top of the beans. Pour the egg mixture on top and scatter the rosemary. Season to taste with salt and pepper.

3. Place the pan on the preheated tray and bake until golden and puffy and the center feels firm and springy about 15 minutes. Remove from the oven, slice, and serve immediately.

Nutrition: Calories: 418 Fat: 19g Sodium: 595mg Carbohydrate: 33g Protein: 30g

Chilled Cucumber-And-Avocado Soup with Dill

Preparation time: 15 minutes Cooking time: 30 minutes Servings: 4
Ingredients:
- 2 English cucumbers, peeled and diced, plus ¼ cup reserved for garnish 1 avocado, peeled, pitted, and chopped, plus ¼ cup reserved for garnish 1½ cups nonfat or low-fat plain Greek yogurt
- ½ cup of cold water
- 1/3 cup loosely packed dill, plus sprigs for garnish 1 tablespoon freshly squeezed lemon juice
- ¼ teaspoon freshly ground black pepper
- ¼ teaspoon salt 1 clove garlic

Directions:

1. Purée ingredients in a blender until smooth. If you prefer a thinner soup, add more water until you reach the desired consistency. Divide soup among 4 bowls. Cover with plastic wrap and refrigerate within 30 minutes. Garnish with cucumber, avocado, and dill sprigs, if desired.

Nutrition: Calories: 142 Fat: 7g Sodium: 193mg Carbohydrate: 12g Protein: 11g

Southwestern Bean-And-Pepper Salad

Preparation time: 6 minutes Cooking time: 0 minutes Servings: 4
Ingredients:
- can pinto beans, drained
- bell peppers, cored and chopped 1 cup corn kernels
- Salt
- Freshly ground black pepper Juice of 2 limes
- 1 tablespoon olive oil 1 avocado, chopped

Directions:

1. Mix beans, peppers, corn, salt, plus pepper in a large bowl. Press fresh lime juice, then mix in olive oil. Let the salad stand in the fridge within 30 minutes. Add avocado just before serving.

Nutrition: Calories: 245 Fat: 11g Sodium: 97mg Carbohydrate: 32g Protein: 8g

Cauliflower Mashed Potatoes

Preparation time: 10 minutes Cooking time: 10 minutes Servings: 4

Ingredients:

- 16 cups water (enough to cover cauliflower)
- 1 head cauliflower (about 3 pounds), trimmed and cut into florets 4 garlic cloves
- 1 tablespoon olive oil
- ¼ teaspoon salt
- 1/8 teaspoon freshly ground black pepper 2 teaspoons dried parsley

Directions:

1. Boil a large pot of water, then the cauliflower and garlic. Cook within 10 minutes, then strain. Move it back to the hot pan, and let it stand within 2 to 3 minutes with the lid on.

2. Put the cauliflower plus garlic in a food processor or blender. Add the olive oil, salt, pepper, and purée until smooth. Taste and adjust the salt and pepper.

3. Remove, then put the parsley, and mix until combined. Garnish with additional olive oil, if desired. Serve immediately.

Nutrition: Calories: 87g Fat: 4g Sodium: 210mg Carbohydrate: 12g Protein: 4g

Classic Hummus

Preparation time: 5 minutes Cooking time: 0 minutes Servings: 6–8
Ingredients:

- (15-ounce) can chickpeas, drained and rinsed 3 tablespoons sesame tahini
- tablespoons olive oil
- garlic cloves, chopped Juice of 1 lemon
- Salt
- Freshly ground black pepper

Directions:

1. Mix all the ingredients until smooth but thick in a food processor or blender. Add water if necessary to produce a smoother hummus. Store covered for up to 5 days.

Nutrition: Calories: 147g Fat: 10g Sodium: 64mg Carbohydrate: 11g Protein: 6g.

Crispy Potato Skins

Preparation time: 2 minutes Cooking time: 19 minutes Servings: 2
Ingredients:

- 2 russet potatoes Cooking spray
- 1 teaspoon dried rosemary
- 1/8 teaspoon freshly ground black pepper

Directions:

1. Preheat the oven to 375°f. Prick or pierce the potatoes all over using a fork. Put on a plate. Cook on full power in the microwave within 5 minutes. Flip over, and cook again within 3 to 4 minutes more, or until soft.

2. Carefully—the potatoes will be very hot—scoop out the pulp of the potatoes, leaving a 1/8 inch of potato pulp attached to the skin. Set aside.

3. Spray the inside of each potato with cooking spray. Press in the rosemary and pepper. Place the skins on a baking sheet and bake in a preheated oven for 5 to 10 minutes until slightly browned and crispy. Serve immediately.

Nutrition: Calories 114 Fat: 0g Sodium: 0mg Carbohydrate: 27g Protein: 3g

Roasted Chickpeas

Preparation time: 5 minutes Cooking time: 30 minutes Servings: 2
Ingredients:

- (15-ounce can) chickpeas, drained and rinsed
- ½ teaspoon olive oil
- teaspoons of your favorite herbs or spice blend
- ¼ teaspoon salt

Directions:

1. Preheat the oven to 400°f.

2. Wrap a rimmed baking sheet with paper towels, place the chickpeas on it in an even layer, and blot with more paper towels until most of the liquid is absorbed.

3. In a medium bowl, gently toss the chickpeas and olive oil until combined. Sprinkle the mixture with the herbs and salt and toss again.

4. Place the chickpeas back on the baking sheet and spread in an even layer. Bake for 30 to 40 minutes, until crunchy and golden brown. Stir halfway through. Serve.

Nutrition: Calories: 175g Fat: 3g Sodium: 474mg Carbohydrate: 29g Protein: 11g

Carrot-Cake Smoothie

Preparation time 5 minutes Cooking time: 0 minutes Servings: 2

Ingredients:
- 1 frozen banana, peeled and diced
- 1 cup carrots, diced (peeled if preferred) 1 cup nonfat or low-fat milk
- ½ cup nonfat or low-fat vanilla Greek yogurt
- ½ cup ice
- ¼ cup diced pineapple, frozen
- ½ teaspoon ground cinnamon Pinch nutmeg
- Optional toppings: chopped walnuts, grated carrots

Directions:
1. Process all of the fixings to a blender. Serve immediately with optional toppings as desired.

Nutrition: Calories: 180g Fat: 1g Sodium: 114mg Carbohydrate: 36g Protein 10g

Vegetable Cheese Calzone

Preparation time: 15 minutes Cooking time: 20 minutes Servings: 4
Ingredients:
- 3 asparagus stalks, cut into pieces 1/2 cup spinach, chopped
- 1/2 cup broccoli, chopped
- 1/2 cup sliced
- 2 tablespoons garlic, minced 2 teaspoons olive oil, divided
- 1/2 lb. frozen whole-wheat bread dough, thawed 1 medium tomato, sliced
- 1/2 cup mozzarella, shredded
- 2/3 cup pizza sauce

Directions:
1. Prepare the oven to 400 degrees F to preheat. Grease a baking sheet with cooking oil and set it aside. Toss asparagus with mushrooms, garlic, broccoli, and spinach in a bowl. Stir in 1 teaspoon olive oil and mix well. Heat a greased skillet on medium heat.

2. Stir in vegetable mixture and sauté for 5 minutes. Set these vegetables aside. Cut the bread dough into quarters.

3. Spread each bread quarter on a floured surface into an oval. Add sautéed vegetables, 2 tbsp cheese, and tomato slice to half of each oval.

4. Wet the edges of each oval and fold the dough over the vegetable filling. Pinch and press the two edges.

5. Place these calzones on the baking sheet. Brush each calzone with foil and bake for 10 minutes. Heat pizza sauce in a saucepan for a minute. Serve the calzone with pizza sauce.

Nutritional:
Calories 198
Fat 8 g
Sodium 124 mg
Carbs 36 g
Protein 12 g

Mixed Vegetarian Chili

Preparation time: 10 minutes Cooking time: 36 minutes Servings: 4
Ingredients:
- 1 tablespoon olive oil
- 14 oz. canned black beans, rinsed and drained
- ½ cup yellow Onion, chopped
- 12 oz. extra-firm tofu, cut into pieces
- 14 oz. canned kidney beans, rinsed and drained 2 cans (14 oz.) diced tomatoes
- 3 tablespoons chili powder 1 tablespoon oregano
- 1 tablespoon chopped cilantro (fresh coriander)

Directions:
1. Take a soup pot and heat olive oil in it over medium heat. Add onions and sauté for 6 minutes until soft. Add tomatoes, beans, chili powder, oregano, and beans. Boil it first, then reduce the heat to a simmer. Cook for 30 minutes, then add cilantro. Serve warm.

Nutrition: Calories 314
Fat 6 g
Sodium 119 mg Carbs 46g Protein 19 g

Zucchini Pepper Kebabs

Preparation time: 15 minutes Cooking time: 40 minutes Servings: 2
Ingredients:
- 1 small zucchini, sliced into 8 pieces 1 red onion, cut into 4 wedges
- 1 green bell pepper, cut into 4 chunks
- 8 cherry tomatoes
- 8 button mushrooms
- 1 red bell pepper, cut into 4 chunks 1/2 cup Italian dressing, fat-free 1/2 cup brown rice
- 1 cup of water

- 4 wooden skewers, soaked and drained

Directions:

1. Toss tomatoes with zucchini, onion, peppers, and mushrooms in a bowl.

2. Stir in Italian dressing and mix well to coat the vegetables. Marinate them for 10 minutes. Boil water with rice in a saucepan, then reduce the heat to a simmer.

3. Cover the rice and cook for 30 minutes until rice is done. Meanwhile, prepare the grill and preheat it on medium heat. Grease the grilling rack with cooking spray and place it 4 inches above the heat.

4. Thread 2 mushrooms, 2 tomatoes, and 2 zucchini slices along with 1 onions wedge, 1 green and red pepper slice on each skewer. Grill these kebabs for 5 minutes per side. Serve warm with boiled rice.

Nutrition: Calories 335
Fat 8.2 g
Sodium 516 mg
Carbs 67 g
Protein 8.8 g

Asparagus Cheese Vermicelli

Preparation time: 10 minutes Cooking time: 15 minutes Servings: 4
Ingredients:

- 2 teaspoons olive oil, divided
- 6 asparagus spears, cut into pieces 4 oz. dried whole-grain vermicelli 1 medium tomato, chopped
- tablespoon garlic, minced
- tablespoons fresh basil, chopped
- 4 tablespoons Parmesan, freshly grated, divided 1/8 teaspoon black pepper, ground

Directions:

1. Add 1 tsp oil to a skillet and heat it. Stir in asparagus and sauté until golden brown.

2. Cut the sautéed asparagus into 1-inch pieces. Fill a sauce pot with water up to ¾ full. After boiling the water, add pasta and cook for 10 minutes until it is all done.

3. Drain and rinse the pasta under tap water. Add pasta to a large bowl, then toss in olive oil, tomato, garlic, asparagus, basil, garlic, and parmesan. Serve with black pepper on top.

Nutrition: Calories 325

Fat 8 g
Sodium 350 mg
Carbs 48 g
Protein 7.3 g

Corn Stuffed Peppers

Preparation time: 10 minutes Cooking time: 35 minutes Servings: 4
Ingredients:

- 4 red or green bell peppers 1 tablespoon olive oil
- ¼ cup onion, chopped
- green bell pepper, chopped 2 1/2 cups fresh corn kernels 1/8 teaspoon chili powder
- tablespoons chopped fresh parsley 3 egg whites
- 1/2 cup skim milk
- 1/2 cup water

Directions:

1. Prepare the oven to 350 F to preheat. Layer a baking dish with cooking spray. Cut the bell peppers from the top and remove their seeds from inside. Put the peppers in your prepared baking dish with their cut side up.

2. Add oil to a skillet, then heat it on medium flame. Stir in onion, corn, and green pepper. Sauté for 5 minutes. Add cilantro and chili powder. Switch the heat to low. Mix milk plus egg whites in a bowl. Pour this mixture into the skillet and cook for 5 minutes while stirring.

3. Divide this mixture into each pepper. Add some water to the baking dish. Cover the stuffed peppers with an aluminum sheet. Bake for 15 minutes, then serves warm.

Nutrition: Calories 197
Fat 5 g
Sodium 749 mg
Carbs 29 g
Protein 9 g

Stuffed Eggplant Shells

Preparation time: 10 minutes Cooking time: 25 minutes Servings: 2
Ingredients:

- 1 medium eggplant 1 cup of water
- 1 tablespoon olive oil
- 4 oz. cooked white beans 1/4 cup onion, chopped
- 1/2 cup red, green, or yellow bell peppers, chopped

- 1 cup canned unsalted tomatoes 1/4 cup tomatoes liquid
- 1/4 cup celery, chopped
- 1 cup fresh mushrooms, sliced
- 3/4 cup whole-wheat breadcrumbs Freshly ground black pepper, to taste

Directions:

1. Prepare the oven to 350 degrees F to preheat. Grease a baking dish with cooking spray and set it aside. Trim and cut the eggplant into half, lengthwise. Scoop out the pulp using a spoon and leave the shell about ¼ inch thick.

2. Place the shells in the baking dish with their cut side up. Add water to the bottom of the dish. Dice the eggplant pulp into cubes and set them aside. Add oil to an iron skillet and heat it over medium heat. Stir in onions, peppers, chopped eggplant, tomatoes, celery, mushrooms, and tomato juice.

3. Cook for 10 minutes on simmering heat, then stirs in beans, black pepper, and breadcrumbs. Divide this mixture into the eggplant shells. Cover the shells with a foil sheet and bake for 15 minutes. Serve warm.

Nutrition: Calories 334
Fat 10 g
Sodium 142 mg
Carbs 35 g
Protein 26 g

Southwestern Vegetables Tacos

Preparation time: 10 minutes Cooking time: 20 minutes Servings: 4

Ingredients:
- 1 tablespoon olive oil
- 1 cup red onion, chopped
- 1 cup yellow summer squash, diced 1 cup green zucchini, diced
- large garlic cloves, minced
- medium tomatoes, seeded and chopped 1 jalapeno chili, seeded and chopped
- 1 cup fresh corn kernels
- 1 cup canned pinto, rinsed and drained 1/2 cup fresh cilantro, chopped
- 8 corn tortillas
- 1/2 cup smoke-flavored salsa

Directions:

1. Add olive oil to a saucepan, then heat it over medium heat. Stir in onion and sauté until soft. Add zucchini and summer squash. Cook for 5 minutes.

2. Stir in corn kernels, jalapeno, garlic, beans, and tomatoes. Cook for another 5 minutes. Stir in cilantro, then remove the pan from the heat.

3. Warm each tortilla in a dry nonstick skillet for 20 secs per side. Place the tortilla on the serving plate. Spoon the vegetable mixture in each tortilla. Top the mixture with salsa. Serve.

Nutrition: Calories 310
Fat 6 g
Sodium 97 mg
Carbs 54 g Protein 10g

CHAPTER 11:

Soups

Soup for The Day

Preparation time: 15 minutes Cooking time: 10 hours & 10 minutes Servings: 8
Ingredients:

- 1 Beef Steak (cubed)
- 1 chopped onion (med.) 1 tbsp. Olive Oil
- 5 thinly sliced med. Carrots 4 cups Cabbage
- 4 diced Red Potatoes
- 2 diced Celery Stalks
- 2 cans Tomatoes, diced 2 cans Beef Broth
- 1 tsp. Sugar
- 1 can Tomato Soup
- 1 tsp. Parsley Flakes (dried) 2 tsp. Italian Seasoning

Directions:

1. In a skillet, sauté onion, and steak in oil. Transfer the sautéed mixture to the slow cooker. Put the rest of the fixing in the slow cooker. Cook on "low" for 10 hrs. Serve hot.

Nutrition: Calories 259.6
Fat 6.7 g
Cholesterol 29.8 mg
Sodium 699.2 mg
Carbohydrates 31.6 mg
Fiber 4.6 g
Protein 18.9 g

Chipotle Squash Soup

Preparation time: 15 minutes Cooking time: 4 hours & 20 minutes Servings: 6
Ingredients:

- 6 cups Butternut Squash (cubed)
- ½ cup chopped Onion 2 tsp. Adobo Chipotle 2 cups Chicken Broth 1 tbsp. Brown Sugar
- ¼ cup Tart Apple (chopped) 1 cup Yogurt (Greek style) 2 tbsp. Chives (chopped)

Directions:

1. Except for yogurt, chives, and apple, place all the ingredients in the slow cooker. Cook on "low" for 4 hrs. Now, in a blender or food processer, puree the cooked ingredients. Transfer puree to slow cooker.

2. Put the yogurt and cook on "Low" within 20 more mins. Garnish with chives and apples. Serve hot in heated bowls.

Nutrition: Calories 102
Fat 11 g
Cholesterol 2 mg
Sodium 142 mg
Carbohydrates 22 mg
Fiber 3 g
Protein 4 g

Kale Verde

Preparation time: 15 minutes Cooking time: 6 hours
Servings: 6
Ingredients:

- ¼ cup Olive Oil (extra virgin) 1 Yellow Onion (large)
- 2 cloves Garlic
- 2 ounces Tomatoes, dried
- 2 cups Yellow Potatoes (diced) 14-ounce Tomatoes (diced)
- 6 cups Chicken broth White pepper (ground) 1-pound o chopped Kale

Directions:

1. Sauté onion for 5 mins in oil. Add the garlic and sauté again for 1 minute. Transfer the sautéed mixture to the slow cooker. Put the rest of the fixing except pepper into the slow cooker. Cook on "low" for 6 hrs. Season with white pepper to taste. Serve hot in heated bowls

Nutrition: Calories 257
Fat 22 g
Cholesterol 3 mg
Sodium 239 mg
Carbohydrates 27 mg
Fiber 6 g
Protein 14 g

Escarole with Bean Soup

Preparation time: 15 minutes Cooking time: 6 hours
Servings: 6
Ingredients:

- 1 tbsp. Olive Oil
- 8 crushed cloves Garlic 1 cup chopped

Onions 1 diced Carrot

- 3 tsp. Basil (dried)
- 3 tsp. Oregano (dried) 4 cups Chicken Broth
- 3 cups chopped Escarole
- 1 cup of Northern Beans (dried) Parmesan Cheese (grated)
- 14 ounces o Tomatoes (diced)

Directions:

1. Sauté garlic for 2 mins in oil using a large soup pot. Except for the cheese, broth, and beans, add the rest of the ingredients and cook for 5 mins. Transfer the cooked ingredients to the slow cooker.

2. Mix in the broth and beans. Cook on "low" for 6 hrs. Garnish with cheese. Serve hot in heated bowls.

Nutrition: Calories 98
Fat 33 g
Cholesterol 1 mg
Sodium 115 mg
Carbohydrates 14 mg
Fiber 3 g
Protein 8 g

Chicken Squash Soup

Preparation time: 15 minutes Cooking time: 5 hours & 30 minutes Servings: 3
Ingredients:

- ½ Butternut Squash (large) 1 clove Garlic
- 1 ¼ quarts broth (vegetable or chicken)
- 1/8 tsp. Pepper (white)
- ½ tbsp. chopped Parsley 2 minced Sage leaves
- 1 tbsp. Olive Oil
- ¼ chopped onion (white)
- 1/16 tsp. Black Pepper (cracked) 1/2 tbsp. of Pepper Flakes (chili)
- ½ tsp. chopped rosemary

Directions:

1. Preheat oven to 400 degrees. Grease a baking sheet. Roast the squash in a preheated oven for 30 mins. Transfer it to a plate and let it cool. Sauté onion and garlic in the oil.

2. Now, scoop out the flesh from the roasted squash and add to the sautéed onion & garlic. Mash all of it well. Pour ½ quart of the broth into the slow cooker. Add the squash mixture. Cook on "low" for 4 hrs.

Using a blender, make a smooth puree.

3. Transfer the puree to the slow cooker. Add in the rest of the broth and other ingredients. Cook again for 1 hr. on "high". Serve in heated soup bowls.

Nutrition: Calories 158
Fats 6 g
Sodium 699 mg
Carbohydrates 24 mg
Fiber 6 g
Protein 3 g

Veggie and Beef Soup

Preparation time: 15 minutes Cooking time: 4 hours
Servings: 4
Ingredients:

- 1 chopped Carrot
- 1 chopped Celery Rib
- ¾ l. Sirloin (ground) 1 cup Water
- ½ Butternut Squash (large) 1 clove Garlic
- ½ quart Beef broth
- 7 ounces diced Tomatoes (unsalted)
- ½ tsp. Kosher Salt
- 1 tbsp. chopped parsley
- ¼ tsp. Thyme (dried)
- ¼ tsp. Black Pepper (ground)
- ½ Bay Leaf

Directions:

1. Sauté all the vegetables in oil. Put the vegetables to the side, then place sirloin in the center. Sauté, using a spoon to crumble the meat. When cooked, combine with the vegetables on the sides of the pan.

2. Now, pour the rest of the ingredients into the slow cooker. Add cooked meat and vegetables. Stir well. Cook on "low" for 3 hrs. Serve in soup bowls.

Nutrition: Calories 217
Fats 7 g
Cholesterol 53 mg
Sodium 728 mg
Carbohydrates 17 mg
Fiber 5 g
Protein 22 g

Collard, Sweet Potato and Pea Soup

Preparation time: 15 minutes Cooking time: 4 hours
Servings: 4
Ingredients:

- 3 1/2 oz. Ham Steak, chopped
- ½ chopped Yellow Onion

- ½ lb. sliced Sweet Potatoes
- ¼ tsp. Red Pepper (hot and crushed)
- ½ cup frozen Peas (black-eyed)
- ½ tbsp. Canola Oil
- minced clove of Garlic 1 ½ cup Water
- ¼ tsp. Salt
- cups Collard Greens (julienned and without stems)

Directions:

1. Sauté ham with garlic and onion in oil. In a slow cooker, place other ingredients except for collard greens and peas.

2. Add in the ham mixture. Cook on "low" for 3 hrs. Now, add collard green and peas and cook again for an hour on "low." Serve in soup bowls.

Nutrition: Calories 172
Fats 4 g
Sodium 547 mg
Carbohydrates 24 mg
Fiber 4 g
Protein 11 g

Bean Soup

Preparation time: 15 minutes Cooking time: 5 hours
Servings: 4
Ingredients:
- ½ cup Pinto Beans (dried)
- ½ Bay Leaf
- clove Garlic
- ½ onion (white) 2 cups Water
- tbsp. Cilantro (chopped)
- cubed Avocado
- 1/8 cup White Onion (chopped)
- ¼ cup Roma Tomatoes (chopped) 2 tbsp. Pepper Sauce (chipotle)
- ¼ tsp. Kosher Salt
- tbsp. chopped Cilantro
- 2 tbsp. Low Fat Monterrey Jack Cheese, shredded

Directions:

1. Place water, salt, onion, pepper, garlic, bay leaf, and beans in the slow cooker. Cook on high for 5-6 hours. Discard the Bay leaf. Serve in heated bowls.

Nutrition: Calories 258
Fats 19 g
Cholesterol 2 mg
Sodium 620 mg
Carbohydrates 25 mg

Fiber 11 g
Protein 8 g

Brown Rice and Chicken Soup

Preparation time: 15 minutes Cooking time: 4 hours
Servings: 4
Ingredients:
- 1/3 cups Brown Rice 1 chopped Leek
- 1 sliced Celery Rib
- 1 ½ cups water
- ½ tsp. Kosher Salt
- ½ Bay Leaf
- 1/8 tsp. Thyme (dried)
- ¼ tsp. Black Pepper (ground) 1 tbsp. chopped parsley
- ½ quart Chicken Broth (low sodium) 1 sliced Carrot
- ¾ lb. of Chicken Thighs (skin and boneless)

Directions:

1. Boil 1 cup of water with ½ tsp. of salt in a saucepan. Add the rice. Cook for 30 mins on medium flame. Brown chicken pieces in the oil. Transfer the chicken to a plate when done.

2. In the same pan, sauté the vegetables for 3 mins. Now, place the chicken pieces in the slow cooker. Add water and broth. Cook on "low" for 3 hrs. Put the rest of the fixing, the rice last. Cook again for 10 mins on "high." After discarding Bay leaf, serve in soup bowls

Nutrition: Calories 208
Fats 6 g
Cholesterol 71 mg
Sodium 540 mg
Carbohydrates 18 mg
Fiber 2 g
Protein 20 g

Broccoli Soup

Preparation time: 15 minutes Cooking time: 3 hours
Servings: 2
Ingredients:
- 4 cups chopped broccoli
- ½ cup chopped onion (white)
- 1 ½ cup Chicken Broth (low sodium) 1/8 tsp. Black Pepper (cracked)
- 1 tbsp. Olive Oil 1 Garlic Clove
- 1/16 tsp. Pepper Flakes (chili)
- ¼ cup Milk (low fat)

Directions:

1. In the slow cooker, cover the broccoli with water and cook for an hour on "high." Set aside after draining. Sauté onion and garlic in oil and transfer them to slow cooker when done. Add the broth.

2. Cook on "low" for 2 hrs. Transfer the mixture to a blender and make a smooth puree. Add black pepper, milk, and pepper flakes to the puree. Boil briefly. Serve the soup in heated bowls.

Nutrition: Calories 291
Fats 14 g
Cholesterol 24 mg
Sodium 227 mg
Carbohydrates 28 mg
Fiber 6 g
Protein 17 g

Hearty Ginger Soup

Preparation Time: 5 minutes Cooking Time: 5 minutes Servings: 4
Ingredients:

- 3 cups coconut almond milk 2 cups of water
- ½ pound boneless chicken breast halves, cut into chunks
- 3 tablespoons fresh ginger root, minced 2 tablespoons fish sauce
- ¼ cup fresh lime juice
- 2 tablespoons green onions, sliced
- 1 tablespoon fresh cilantro, chopped

Directions:

1. Take a saucepan and add coconut almond milk and water. Bring the mixture to a boil and add the chicken strips. Adjust the heat to medium, then simmer for 3 minutes. Stir in the ginger, lime juice, and fish sauce. Sprinkle a few green onions and cilantro.

Nutrition: Calories: 415 Fat: 39g
Carbohydrates: 8g Protein: 14g Sodium: 150 mg

Tasty Tofu and Mushroom Soup

Preparation time: 15 minutes Cooking time: 10 minutes Servings: 8
Ingredients:

- 3 cups prepared dashi stock
- ¼ cup shiitake mushrooms, sliced 1 tablespoon miso paste
- 1 tablespoon coconut aminos 1/8 cup cubed soft tofu

- 1 green onion, diced

Directions:

1. Take a saucepan and add the stock; bring to a boil. Add mushrooms, cook for 4 minutes. Take a bowl and add coconut aminos, miso pastes, and mix well. Pour the mixture into stock and let it cook for 6 minutes on simmer. Add diced green onions and enjoy!

Nutrition: Calories: 100 Fat: 4g
Carbohydrates: 5g
Protein: 11
Sodium: 87 mg

Ingenious Eggplant Soup

Preparation time: 15 minutes Cooking time: 15 minutes Servings: 8
Ingredients:

- 1 large eggplant, washed and cubed 1 tomato, seeded and chopped
- small onion, diced
- tablespoons parsley, chopped
- 2 tablespoons extra virgin olive oil 2 tablespoons distilled white vinegar
- ½ cup parmesan cheese, crumbled Sunflower seeds as needed

Directions:

1. Preheat your outdoor grill to medium-high. Pierce the eggplant a few times using a knife/fork. Cook the eggplants on your grill for about 15 minutes until they are charred. Put aside and allow them to cool.

2. Remove the eggplant's skin and dice the pulp. Put it in a mixing bowl and add parsley, onion, tomato, olive oil, feta cheese, and vinegar. Mix well and chill for 1 hour. Season with sunflower seeds and enjoy!

Nutrition: Calories: 99 Fat: 7g
Carbohydrates: 7g
Protein:3.4g Sodium: 90 mg

Loving Cauliflower Soup

Preparation time: 15 minutes Cooking time: 10 minutes Servings: 6
Ingredients:

- 4 cups vegetable stock
- 1-pound cauliflower, trimmed and chopped 7 ounces Kite ricotta/cashew cheese
- 4 ounces almond butter
- Sunflower seeds and pepper to taste

Directions:

1. Put almond butter and melt in a skillet over medium heat. Add cauliflower and sauté for 2 minutes. Add stock and bring the mix to a boil.

2. Cook until cauliflower is al dente. Stir in cream cheese, sunflower seeds, and pepper. Puree the mix using an immersion blender. Serve and enjoy!

Nutrition: Calories: 143 Fat: 16g
Carbohydrates: 6g
Protein: 3.4g Sodium: 510 mg

Garlic and Lemon Soup

Preparation time: 15 minutes Cooking time: 0 minutes Servings: 3
Ingredients:
- avocado, pitted and chopped 1 cucumber, chopped
- bunches spinach
- 1 ½ cups watermelon, chopped
- bunch cilantro, roughly chopped Juice from 2 lemons
- ½ cup coconut aminos
- ½ cup lime juice

Directions:

1. Add cucumber, avocado to your blender, and pulse well. Add cilantro, spinach, and watermelon and blend. Add lemon, lime juice, and coconut amino. Pulse a few more times. Transfer to a soup bowl and enjoy!

Nutrition: Calories: 100 Fat: 7g
Carbohydrates: 6g Protein: 3g Sodium: 0 mg

Italian Wedding Soup

Preparation time: 15 minutes Cooking time: 7 hours
Servings: 6
Ingredients:
- 1-pound ground turkey breast 1½ cups cooked Brown Rice 1 onion, grated
- ¼ cup chopped fresh parsley 1 egg, beaten
- 1 teaspoon garlic powder
- 1 teaspoon sea salt, divided
- 6 cups Poultry Broth or store-bought
- 1/8 teaspoon freshly ground black pepper Pinch red pepper flakes
- 1-pound kale, tough stems removed, leaves chopped

Directions:

1. In a small bowl, combine the turkey breast, rice, onion, parsley, egg, garlic powder, and ½ teaspoon of sea salt. Roll the mixture into

½-inch meatballs and put them in the slow cooker.

2. Add the broth, black pepper, red pepper flakes, and the remaining ½ teaspoon of sea salt. Cover and cook on low for 7 to 8 hours. Before serving, stir in the kale. Cover and cook until the kale wilts.

Nutrition: Calories: 302 Fat: 7g
Carbohydrates: 29g Fiber: 3g
Protein: 29g
Sodium: 320 mg

Taco Soup

Preparation time: 15 minutes Cooking time: 8 hours
Servings: 6
Ingredients:
- 1-pound ground turkey breast 1 onion, chopped
- 1 can tomatoes and green chilis, with their juice
- 6 cups Poultry Broth or store-bought 1 teaspoon chili powder
- 1 teaspoon ground cumin
- ½ teaspoon of sea salt
- ¼ cup chopped fresh cilantro Juice of 1 lime
- ½ cup grated low-fat Cheddar cheese

Directions:

1. Crumble the turkey into the slow cooker. Add the onion, tomatoes, green chilis (with their juice), broth, chili powder, cumin, and salt. Cover and cook on low within 8 hours. Stir in the cilantro and lime juice. Serve garnished with the cheese.

Nutrition: Calories: 281 Fat: 10g
Carbohydrates: 20g Fiber: 5g
Protein: 30g Sodium: 470 mg

Italian Sausage & Fennel Soup

Preparation time: 15 minutes Cooking time: 8 hours
Servings: 6
Ingredients:
- 1-pound Italian chicken or turkey sausage, cut into ½-inch slices 2 onions, chopped
- 1 fennel bulb, chopped
- 6 cups Poultry Broth or store-bought
- ¼ cup dry sherry
- 1½ teaspoons garlic powder 1 teaspoon dried thyme
- ½ teaspoon of sea salt
- ¼ teaspoon freshly ground black pepper

Pinch red pepper flakes

Directions:

1. In your slow cooker, combine all the ingredients. Cover and cook on low within 8 hours.

Nutrition: Calories: 311 Fat: 22g
Carbohydrates: 8g Fiber: 2g
Protein: 18g Sodium: 660 mg

Beef & Barley Soup

Preparation time: 15 minutes Cooking time: 8 hours
Servings: 6
Ingredients:

- 1-pound extra-lean ground beef 2 onions, chopped
- 3 carrots, peeled and sliced
- 1-pound fresh mushrooms, quartered 1½ cups dried barley
- 6 cups Beef Broth or store-bought
- 1 teaspoon ground mustard 1 teaspoon dried thyme
- 1 teaspoon garlic powder
- ¼ teaspoon of sea salt
- 1/8 teaspoon freshly ground black pepper

Directions:

1. In your slow cooker, crumble the ground beef into small pieces. Add the remaining ingredients. Cover and cook on low within 8 hours.

Nutrition: Calories: 319 Fat: 5g
Carbohydrates: 44g Fiber: 11g
Protein: 28g
Sodium: 380 mg

Cucumber Soup

Preparation time: 15 minutes Cooking time: 0
minutes Servings: 4
Ingredients:

- tablespoons garlic, minced
- 4 cups English cucumbers, peeled and diced
- ½ cup onions, diced
- 1 tablespoon lemon juice 1 ½ cups vegetable broth
- ½ teaspoon sunflower seeds
- ¼ teaspoon red pepper flakes
- ¼ cup parsley, diced
- ½ cup Greek yogurt, plain

Directions:

1. Put the listed fixing in a blender and blend

to emulsify (keep aside ½ cup of chopped cucumbers). Blend until smooth. Divide the soup amongst 4 servings and top with extra cucumbers. Enjoy chilled!

Nutrition: Calories: 371 Fat: 36g
Carbohydrates: 8g
Protein: 4g Sodium: 40 mg

Roasted Garlic Soup

Preparation time: 15 minutes Cooking time: 60
minutes Servings: 10
Ingredients:

- 1 tablespoon olive oil 2 bulbs garlic, peeled 3 shallots, chopped
- 1 large head cauliflower, chopped 6 cups vegetable broth
- Sunflower seeds and pepper to taste

Directions:

1. Warm your oven to 400 degrees F. Slice ¼ inch top of the garlic bulb and place it in aluminum foil. Oiled it using olive oil and roast in the oven for 35 minutes. Squeeze flesh out of the roasted garlic.

2. Heat-up oil in a saucepan and add shallots, sauté for 6 minutes. Add garlic and remaining ingredients. Adjust heat to low. Let it cook for 15- 20 minutes.

3. Puree the mixture using an immersion blender. Season soup with sunflower seeds and pepper. Serve and enjoy!

Nutrition: Calories: 142 Fat: 8g
Carbohydrates: 3.4g Protein: 4g
Sodium: 548 mg

Roasted Carrot Soup

Preparation time: 15 minutes Cooking time: 50
minutes Servings: 4
Ingredients:

- 8 large carrots, washed and peeled 6 tablespoons olive oil
- 1-quart broth
- Cayenne pepper to taste
- Sunflower seeds and pepper to taste

Directions:

1. Warm your oven to 425 degrees F. Take a baking sheet, add carrots, drizzle olive oil, and roast for 30-45 minutes. Put roasted carrots into a blender and add broth, puree. Pour into saucepan and heat soup. Season with sunflower seeds, pepper and cayenne.

Drizzle olive oil. Serve and enjoy!
Nutrition: Calories: 222 Fat: 18g
Net Carbohydrates: 7g Protein: 5g
Sodium: 266 mg

Pumpkin Soup

Preparation time: 15 minutes Cooking time: 6 hours
Servings: 4
Ingredients:

- 1 small pumpkin, halved, peeled, seeds removed, cubed 2 cups chicken broth
- cup of coconut milk
- Pepper and thyme to taste

Directions:

1. Add all the ingredients to a crockpot. Cook for 6-8 hours on low. Make a smooth puree by using a blender. Garnish with roasted seeds. Serve and enjoy!

Nutrition: Calories: 60 Fat: 2g
Carbohydrates: 10g Protein: 3g Sodium: 10 mg

Coconut Avocado Soup

Preparation time: 15 minutes Cooking time: 10 minutes Servings: 4
Ingredients:

- cups vegetable stock
- 2 teaspoons Thai green curry paste Pepper as needed
- 1 avocado, chopped
- 1 tablespoon cilantro, chopped Lime wedges
- cup of coconut milk

Directions:

1. Add milk, avocado, curry paste, pepper to a blender, and blend. Take a pan and place it over medium heat. Add mixture and heat, simmer for 5 minutes. Stir in seasoning, cilantro, and simmer for 1 minute. Serve and enjoy!

Nutrition: Calories: 250 Fat: 30g
Carbohydrates: 2g Protein: 4g Sodium: 378 mg

Coconut Arugula Soup

Preparation time: 15 minutes Cooking time: 10 minutes Servings: 4
Ingredients:

- Black pepper as needed 1 tablespoon olive oil
- tablespoons chives, chopped
- 2 garlic cloves, minced 10 ounces baby arugula

- 2 tablespoons tarragon, chopped
- 4 tablespoons coconut milk yogurt 6 cups chicken stock
- 2 tablespoons mint, chopped
- 1 onion, chopped
- ½ cup of coconut milk

Directions:

1. Take a saucepan and place it over medium-high heat, add oil and let it heat up. Put onion and garlic and fry within 5 minutes. Stir in stock and reduce the heat, let it simmer.

2. Stir in tarragon, arugula, mint, parsley, and cook for 6 minutes. Mix in seasoning, chives, coconut yogurt, and serve.

Nutrition: Calories: 180 Fat: 14g
Carbohydrates: 20g Protein: 2g Sodium: 362 mg

Cabbage Soup

Preparation time: 15 minutes Cooking time: 25 minutes Servings: 3
Ingredients:

- 3 cups non-fat beef stock 2 garlic cloves, minced
- tablespoon tomato paste
- cups cabbage, chopped
- ½ yellow onion
- ½ cup carrot, chopped
- ½ cup green beans
- ½ cup zucchini, chopped
- ½ teaspoon basil
- ½ teaspoon oregano
- Sunflower seeds and pepper as needed

Directions:

1. Grease a pot with non-stick cooking spray. Place it over medium heat and allow the oil to heat up. Add onions, carrots, and garlic, and sauté for 5 minutes. Add broth, tomato paste, green beans, cabbage, basil, oregano, sunflower seeds, and pepper.

2. Boil the whole mix and reduce the heat, simmer for 5-10 minutes until all veggies are tender. Add zucchini and simmer for 5 minutes more. Sever hot and enjoy!

Nutrition: Calories: 22 Fat: 0g
Carbohydrates: 5g Protein: 1g
Sodium: 200 mg

Ginger Zucchini Avocado Soup

Preparation time: 15 minutes Cooking time: 25

minutes Servings: 3
Ingredients:
- 1 red bell pepper, chopped 1 big avocado
- teaspoon ginger, grated
- Pepper as needed
- tablespoons avocado oil 4 scallions, chopped
- tablespoon lemon juice 29 ounces vegetable stock 1 garlic clove, minced
- zucchinis, chopped 1 cup of water

Directions:

1. Take a pan and place over medium heat, add onion and fry for 3 minutes. Stir in ginger, garlic and cook for 1 minute. Mix in seasoning, zucchini stock, water, and boil for 10 minutes.

2. Remove soup from fire and let it sit; blend in avocado and blend using an immersion blender. Heat over low heat for a while. Adjust your seasoning and add lemon juice, bell pepper. Serve and enjoy!

Nutrition: Calories: 155 Fat: 11g
Carbohydrates: 10g Protein: 7g Sodium: 345 mg

Greek Lemon and Chicken Soup

Preparation time: 15 minutes Cooking time: 30 minutes Servings: 4
Ingredients:
- 2 cups cooked chicken, chopped 2 medium carrots, chopped
- ½ cup onion, chopped
- ¼ cup lemon juice
- 1 clove garlic, minced
- can cream of chicken soup, fat-free and low sodium 2 cans of chicken broth, fat-free
- ¼ teaspoon ground black pepper 2/3 cup long-grain rice
- tablespoons parsley, snipped

Directions:

1. Put all of the listed fixings in a pot (except rice and parsley). Season

2. with sunflower seeds and pepper. Bring the mix to a boil over medium- high heat. Stir in rice and set heat to medium.

3. Simmer within 20 minutes until rice is tender. Garnish parsley, and enjoy!

Nutrition: Calories: 582 Fat: 33g
Carbohydrates: 35g Protein: 32g Sodium: 210 mg

Garlic and Pumpkin Soup

Preparation time: 15 minutes Cooking time: 5 hours
Servings: 4
Ingredients:
- 1-pound pumpkin chunks 1 onion, diced
- 2 cups vegetable stock
- 1 2/3 cups coconut cream
- ½ stick almond butter
- 1 teaspoon garlic, crushed 1 teaspoon ginger, crushed Pepper to taste

Directions:

1. Add all the fixing into your Slow Cooker. Cook for 4-6 hours on high. Puree the soup by using your immersion blender. Serve and enjoy!

Nutrition: Calories: 235 Fat: 21g
Carbohydrates: 11g Protein: 2g Sodium: 395 mg

Golden Mushroom Soup

Preparation time: 15 minutes Cooking time: 8 hours
Servings: 6
Ingredients:
- 1 onion, finely chopped
- 1 carrot, peeled and finely chopped 1 fennel bulb, finely chopped
- 1-pound fresh mushrooms, quartered
- 8 cups Vegetable Broth, Poultry Broth, or store-bought
- ¼ cup dry sherry
- teaspoon dried thyme 1 teaspoon garlic powder
- ½ teaspoon of sea salt
- 1/8 teaspoon freshly ground black pepper

Directions:

1. In your slow cooker, combine all the ingredients, mixing to combine.

2. Cover and set on low. Cook for 8 hours.

Nutrition: Calories: 71 Fat: 0g
Carbohydrates: 15g Fiber: 3g
Protein: 3g Sodium: 650 mg

Minestrone

Preparation time: 15 minutes Cooking time: 9 hours
Servings: 6
Ingredients:
- carrots, peeled and sliced 2 celery stalks, sliced
- onion, chopped
- cups green beans, chopped
- 1 (16-ounce) can crushed tomatoes 2 cups cooked kidney beans, rinsed

- 6 cups Poultry Broth, Vegetable Broth, or store-bought 1 teaspoon garlic powder
- 1 teaspoon dried Italian seasoning
- ¼ teaspoon of sea salt
- ¼ teaspoon freshly ground black pepper
- 1½ cups cooked whole-wheat elbow macaroni (or pasta shape of your choice)
- 1 zucchini, chopped

Directions:

1. In your slow cooker, combine the carrots, celery, onion, green beans, tomatoes, kidney beans, broth, garlic powder, Italian seasoning, salt, and pepper in the slow cooker. Cook on low within 8 hours. Stir in the macaroni and zucchini. Cook on low within 1 hour more.

Nutrition: Calories: 193 Fat: 0g
Carbohydrates: 39g
Fiber: 10g
Protein: 10g Sodium: 100 mg

Butternut Squash Soup

Preparation time: 15 minutes Cooking time: 8 hours
Servings: 6
Ingredients:

- 1 butternut squash, peeled, seeded, and diced 1 onion, chopped
- 1 sweet-tart apple (such as Braeburn), peeled, cored, and chopped
- 3 cups Vegetable Broth or store-bought 1 teaspoon garlic powder
- ½ teaspoon ground sage
- ¼ teaspoon of sea salt
- ¼ teaspoon freshly ground black pepper Pinch cayenne pepper
- Pinch nutmeg
- ½ cup fat-free half-and-half

Directions:

1. In your slow cooker, combine the squash, onion, apple, broth, garlic powder, sage, salt, black pepper, cayenne, and nutmeg. Cook on low within 8 hours.

2. Using an immersion blender, counter-top blender, or food processor, purée the soup, adding the half-and-half as you do. Stir to combine, and serve.

Nutrition: Calories: 106 Fat: 0g
Carbohydrates: 26g Fiber: 4g
Protein: 3g
Sodium: 550 mg

Black Bean Soup

Preparation time: 15 minutes Cooking time: 8 hours
Servings: 6
Ingredients:

- 1-pound dried black beans, soaked overnight and rinsed 1 onion, chopped
- carrot, peeled and chopped
- jalapeño peppers, seeded and diced
- 6 cups Vegetable Broth or store-bought 1 teaspoon ground cumin
- 1 teaspoon ground coriander 1 teaspoon chili powder
- ½ teaspoon ground chipotle pepper
- ½ teaspoon of sea salt
- ¼ teaspoon freshly ground black pepper Pinch cayenne pepper
- ¼ cup fat-free sour cream, for garnish (optional)
- ¼ cup grated low-fat Cheddar cheese, for garnish (optional)

Directions:

1. In your slow cooker, combine all the fixing listed, then cook on low for 8 hours. If you'd like, mash the beans with a potato masher, or purée using an immersion blender, blender, or food processor. Serve topped with the optional garnishes, if desired.

Nutrition: Calories: 320 Fat: 3g
Carbohydrates: 57g
Fiber: 13g Protein: 18g Sodium: 430 mg

Chickpea & Kale Soup

Preparation time: 15 minutes Cooking time: 9 hours
Servings: 6
Ingredients:

- summer squash, quartered lengthwise and sliced crosswise 1 zucchini, quartered lengthwise and sliced crosswise
- cups cooked chickpeas, rinsed
- cup uncooked quinoa
- cans diced tomatoes, with their juice
- 5 cups Vegetable Broth, Poultry Broth, or store-bought 1 teaspoon garlic powder
- teaspoon onion powder 1 teaspoon dried thyme
- ½ teaspoon of sea salt
- cups chopped kale leaves

Directions:

1. In your slow cooker, combine the summer

squash, zucchini, chickpeas, quinoa, tomatoes (with their juice), broth, garlic powder, onion powder, thyme, and salt. Cover and cook on low within 8 hours. Stir in the kale. Cover and cook on low for 1 more hour.

Nutrition: Calories: 221 Fat: 3g
Carbohydrates: 40g Fiber: 7g
Protein: 10g
Sodium: 124 mg

Clam Chowder

Preparation time: 15 minutes Cooking time: 8 hours
Servings: 6
Ingredients:

- 1 red onion, chopped
- 3 carrots, peeled and chopped
- 1 fennel bulb and fronds, chopped
- 1 (10-ounce) can chopped clams, with their juice 1-pound baby red potatoes, quartered
- 4 cups Poultry Broth or store-bought
- ½ teaspoon of sea salt
- 1/8 teaspoon freshly ground black pepper 2 cups skim milk
- ¼ pound turkey bacon, browned and crumbled, for garnish

Directions:

1. In your slow cooker, combine the onion, carrots, fennel bulb and fronds, clams (with their juice), potatoes, broth, salt, and pepper. Cover and cook on low within 8 hours. Stir in the milk and serve garnished with the crumbled bacon.

Nutrition: Calories: 172 Fat: 1g
Carbohydrates: 29g Fiber: 4g
Protein: 10g Sodium: 517 mg

Chicken & Rice Soup

Preparation time: 15 minutes Cooking time: 8 hours
Servings: 6
Ingredients:

- 1-pound boneless, skinless chicken thighs, cut into 1-inch pieces 1 onion, chopped
- 3 carrots, peeled and sliced
- 2 celery stalks, sliced
- 6 cup Poultry Broth or store-bought 1 teaspoon garlic powder
- teaspoon dried rosemary
- ¼ teaspoon of sea salt
- ¼ teaspoon freshly ground black pepper 3 cups cooked Brown Rice

Directions:

1. In your slow cooker, combine the chicken, onion, carrots, celery, broth, garlic powder, rosemary, salt, and pepper. Cover and cook on low within 8 hours. Stir in the rice about 10 minutes before serving, and allow the broth to warm it.

Nutrition: Calories: 354 Fat: 7g
Carbohydrates: 43g Fiber: 3g
Protein: 28g Sodium: 610 mg

Tom Kha Gai

Preparation time 15 minutes Cooking time: 8 hours
Servings: 6
Ingredients:

- 1-pound boneless, skinless chicken thighs, cut into 1-inch pieces 1-pound fresh shiitake mushrooms halved
- tablespoons grated fresh ginger
- cups canned light coconut milk
- 3 cups Poultry Broth or store-bought 1 tablespoon Asian fish sauce
- teaspoon garlic powder
- ¼ teaspoon freshly ground black pepper Juice of 1 lime
- tablespoons chopped fresh cilantro

Directions:

1. In your slow cooker, combine the chicken thighs, mushrooms, ginger, coconut milk, broth, fish sauce, garlic powder, and pepper. Cover and cook on low within 8 hours. Stir in the lime juice and cilantro just before serving.

Nutrition: Calories: 481 Fat: 35g
Carbohydrates: 19g Fiber: 5g
Protein: 28g Sodium: 160 mg

Chicken Corn Chowder

Preparation time: 15 minutes Cooking time: 8 hours
Servings: 6
Ingredients:

- 1-pound boneless, skinless chicken thighs, cut into 1-inch pieces 2 onions, chopped
- jalapeño peppers, seeded and minced
- 2 red bell peppers, seeded and chopped 1½ cups fresh or frozen corn
- 6 cups Poultry Broth or store-bought
- 1 teaspoon garlic powder
- ½ teaspoon of sea salt
- ¼ teaspoon freshly ground black pepper 1 cup skim milk

Directions:

1. In your slow cooker, combine the chicken, onions, jalapeños, red bell peppers, corn, broth, garlic powder, salt, and pepper. Cover and cook on low within 8 hours. Stir in the skim milk just before serving.

Nutrition: Calories: 236 Fat: 6g
Carbohydrates: 17g Fiber: 3g
Protein: 27g Sodium: 790 mg

Turkey Ginger Soup

Preparation time: 15 minutes Cooking time: 8 hours
Servings: 6
Ingredients:

- 1-pound boneless, skinless turkey thighs, cut into 1-inch pieces 1-pound fresh shiitake mushrooms halved
- 3 carrots, peeled and sliced
- 2 cups frozen peas
- 1 tablespoon grated fresh ginger
- 6 cups Poultry Broth or store-bought 1 tablespoon low-sodium soy sauce 1 teaspoon toasted sesame oil
- 2 teaspoons garlic powder
- 1½ cups cooked Brown Rice

Directions:

1. In your slow cooker, combine the turkey, mushrooms, carrots, peas, ginger, broth, soy sauce, sesame oil, and garlic powder. Cover and cook on low within 8 hours. About 30 minutes before serving, stir in the rice to warm it through.

Nutrition: Calories: 318 Fat: 7g
Carbohydrates: 42g Fiber: 6g
Protein: 24g Sodium: 690 mg

Chicken and Tortilla Soup

Preparation time: 15 minutes Cooking time: 6 hours
Servings: 12
Ingredients:

- 3 Chicken Breasts (boneless and skinless) 15 ounces diced Tomatoes
- 10 ounces Enchilada Sauce
- 1 chopped onion (med.)
- 4 ounces chopped Chili Pepper (green) 3 minced cloves Garlic
- 2 cups Water
- 14.5-ounces Chicken Broth (fat-free) 1 tbsp. Cumin
- 1 tbs. Chile Powder 1 tsp. Salt
- ¼ tsp. Black Pepper

- Bay Leaf
- 1 tbsp. Cilantro (chopped) 10 ounces Frozen Corn
- 3 tortillas, cut into thin slices

Directions:

1. Put all the listed fixing in the slow cooker. Stir well to mix. Cook on low heat within 8 hrs. or high heat for 6 hrs. Shred the chicken breasts to a plate. Add chicken to other ingredients. Serve hot, garnished with tortilla slices.

Nutrition: Calories 93.4
Fat 1.9 g
Cholesterol 18.6
Sodium 841.3 mg
Carbohydrates 11.9 g
Fiber 2.1 g
Protein 8.3 g

Stuffed Pepper Soup

Preparation time: 15 minutes Cooking time: 8 hours & 10 minutes Servings: 6
Ingredients:

- lb. ground Beef (drained) 1 chopped onion (large)
- cups Tomatoes (diced)
- 2 chopped Green Peppers 2 cups Tomato Sauce
- 1 tbs. Beef Bouillon
- 3 cups of water Pepper
- 1 tsp. of Salt
- 1 cup of cooked rice (white)
- Directions:

1. Place all ingredients in a cooker. Cook for 8 hours on "low." Serve hot.
Nutrition: Calories 216.1
Fat 5.1 g
Cholesterol 43.4 mg
Sodium 480.7 mg
Carbohydrates 21.8 mg
Fiber 2.5 g
Protein 18.8 g

Ham and Pea Soup

Preparation time: 15 minutes Cooking time: 8 hours
Servings: 8
Ingredients:

- 1 lb. Split Peas (dried) 1 cup sliced Celery
- 1 cup sliced Carrots
- cup sliced Onion

- cups chopped ham (cooked) 8 cups of water

Directions:

1. Place all the listed fixing in the slow cooker. Cook on "high" within 4 hrs. Serve hot.

Nutrition:

Calories 118.6

Fat 1.9 g

Cholesterol 15.9 mg

Sodium 828.2 mg

Carbohydrates 14.5 mg

Fiber 5.1 g

Protein 11.1 g

Pea Soup

Preparation time: 15 minutes Cooking time: 8 hours

Servings: 8

Ingredients:

- 16 oz. Split Peas (dried)
- 1 cup chopped Baby Carrots 1chopped onion (white)
- 3 Bay Leaves
- 10 oz. cubed Turkey Ham 4 cubes Chicken Bouillon 7 cups of water

Directions:

1. Rinse and drain peas. Place all the fixing in the slow cooker. Cook on "low" for 8 hrs. Serve hot.

Nutrition: Calories 122.7

Fat 2 g

Cholesterol 24 mg

Sodium 780.6 mg

Carbohydrates 15 mg

Fiber 5.2 g

Protein 11.8 g

CHAPTER 12:

Salads

Bean Salad with Orange Vinaigrette

Preparation time: 15 minutes Cooking time: 0 minutes Servings: 6
Ingredients:
- 1 (15-ounce) can no-salt-added kidney beans
- (15-ounce) can no-salt-added garbanzo beans 1 (15-ounce) can no-salt-added pinto beans
- shallots, chopped
- medium carrot, shredded 1 small bell pepper, diced 1 small stalk celery, diced 1/4 cup pure maple syrup 1/3 cup apple cider vinegar
- tablespoons freshly squeezed orange juice 1 tablespoon olive oil
- 1 teaspoon grated orange zest
- 1/2 teaspoon freshly ground black pepper

Directions:

1. Drain and rinse all the canned beans, then place them in a mixing bowl.

2. Add the chopped shallot, shredded carrot, bell pepper, and celery and stir to combine.

3. Place the remaining fixing into a small mixing bowl and whisk well. Mix the dressing on the salad, then serve immediately.

Nutrition: Calories: 393
Fat: 5 g
Protein: 19 g
Sodium: 70 mg
Fiber: 16 g
Carbohydrates: 69 g
Sugar: 13 g

Fresh Corn, Pepper, and Avocado Salad

Preparation time: 15 minutes Cooking time: 0 minutes Servings: 6
Ingredients:
- 3 ears freshly cooked corn 1 medium red bell pepper 1 ripe avocado
- 1 jalapeño pepper, minced 1 scallion, thinly sliced

- clove garlic, minced
- Juice of 1 fresh lime
- tablespoons olive oil
- Freshly ground black pepper, to taste

Directions:

1. Slice the kernels using a very sharp knife. Place in a mixing bowl. Core and dice the red pepper and peel and dice the avocado. Add to the bowl, along with the jalapeño, sliced scallion (white and green parts), and minced garlic.

2. Mix the lime juice and oil in a small bowl. Drizzle over the salad and toss to coat. Flavor with freshly ground black pepper. Serve immediately.

Nutrition: Calories: 135
Fat: 9 g
Protein: 2 g
Sodium: 5 mg
Fiber: 3 g
Carbohydrates: 13 g
Sugar: 2 g

Garlic Potato Salad

Preparation time: 15 minutes Cooking time: 25 minutes Servings: 6
Ingredients:
- 6 medium potatoes
- 6 garlic scapes or 3 cloves garlic 1 cup sliced scallions
- 1/4 cup olive oil
- 2 tablespoons unflavored rice vinegar 2 teaspoons chopped fresh rosemary Freshly ground black pepper, to taste

Directions:

1. Boil the potatoes into a pot with water to cover by 1 inch over high heat. Boil until fork-tender but still solid, depending upon size, roughly 20–25 minutes.

2. Once cooked, remove from heat and place under cold running water. Drain and set potatoes aside to cool, then slice into cubes. Place cubed potato, garlic, and scallions into a mixing bowl and toss to combine.

3. Measure the olive oil, vinegar, and rosemary into a small mixing bowl. Put ground black pepper, and whisk well to combine. Pour the dressing over the salad and stir gently to coat. Cover and refrigerate within a few hours before serving.

Nutrition: Calories: 204
Fat: 9 g
Protein: 2 g
Sodium: 6 mg
Fiber: 2 g
Carbohydrates: 28 g
Sugar: 1 g

Creamy Low-Sodium Coleslaw

Preparation time: 15 minutes Cooking time: 0 minutes Servings: 6
Ingredients:

- 1/2 medium head green cabbage, shredded 1 medium carrot, shredded
- 1 small onion, grated
- 1/3 cup Salt-Free Mayonnaise 3 tablespoons sugar
- 3 tablespoons apple cider vinegar
- 1/2 teaspoon dry ground mustard
- 1/2 teaspoon freshly ground black pepper

Directions:

1. Mix all the fixing in a large mixing bowl and stir well. Cover and refrigerate until ready to serve.

Nutrition: Calories: 133
Fat: 8 g
Protein: 2 g
Sodium: 32 mg
Fiber: 3 g
Carbohydrates: 13 g
Sugar: 10 g

Southwestern Beet Slaw

Preparation time: 15 minutes Cooking time: 0 minutes Servings: 6
Ingredients:

- 3 small-medium beets
- 3 scallions, sliced
- 2 medium carrots, shredded 1/4 cup chopped fresh cilantro 2 cloves garlic
- Juice of 2 fresh limes
- teaspoon olive oil
- 1/2 teaspoon salt-free chili seasoning
- 1/4 teaspoon freshly ground black pepper

Directions:

1. Trim and peel the beets, then shred. Place into a mixing bowl. Add the scallions, carrots, cilantro, and garlic and stir well to combine.

2. Mix the lime juice, olive oil, chili seasoning, and black pepper in a small bowl. Pour dressing over the salad, then serve immediately.

Nutrition: Calories: 38
Fat: 1 g
Protein: 1 g
Sodium: 46 mg
Fiber: 2 g
Carbohydrates: 7 g
Sugar: 4 g

Warm Kale Salad

Preparation time: 15 minutes Cooking time: 12 minutes Servings: 4
Ingredients:

- teaspoons olive oil
- 1 small red onion, diced 2 garlic cloves, minced
- 1 small red bell pepper, diced 8 cups chopped kale
- Juice of 1 fresh orange
- 1 medium carrot, shredded 1/4 teaspoon ground cumin
- 1/8 teaspoon dried red pepper flakes
- 1 teaspoon grated orange zest Freshly ground black pepper, to taste

Directions:

1. Heat-up oil in a large skillet or sauté pan over medium. Add the onion and cook, stirring, for 2 minutes. Add the garlic, bell pepper, kale, and orange juice and stir well to combine. Adjust heat to medium-low, cover, and cook within 5 minutes.

2. Remove lid, add remaining ingredients, and stir well to combine. Cover and cook for another 5 minutes. Remove from heat and serve immediately.

Nutrition: Calories: 137
Fat: 3 g
Protein: 5 g
Sodium: 76 mg
Fiber: 4 g
Carbohydrates: 25 g
Sugar: 7 g

Tabouleh Salad

Preparation time: 15 minutes Cooking time: 0 minutes Servings: 4

Ingredients:

- 2/3 cup dry couscous 1 cup boiling water
- 1 small ripe tomato, diced
- 1 small green bell pepper, diced 1 shallot, finely diced
- 1/3 cup chopped fresh parsley
- clove garlic, minced Juice of 1 fresh lemon 1 tablespoon olive oil
- 1/2 teaspoon freshly ground black pepper

Directions:

1. Mix the dry couscous into a small bowl. Mix in the boiling water, cover, and set aside within 5 minutes. Place the tomato, green pepper, shallot, and parsley into a salad bowl.

2. Mix the garlic, lemon juice, oil, and pepper in a small mixing bowl. Put the cooked couscous in the salad bowl. Put the dressing over the top and stir well to combine. Serve immediately.

Nutrition: Calories: 120

Fat: 3 g

Protein: 3 g

Sodium: 6 mg

Fiber: 1 g

Carbohydrates: 20 g

Sugar: 1 g

Tart Apple Salad with Fennel and Honey Yogurt Dressing

Preparation time: 15 minutes Cooking time: 0 minutes Servings: 6

Ingredients:

- tart green apples, diced
- small bulb fennel, chopped
- 11/2 cups seedless red grapes, halved
- tablespoons freshly squeezed lemon juice 1/4 cup low-fat vanilla yogurt
- teaspoon honey

Directions:

1. Mix all the fixing into a mixing bowl, then serve immediately.

Nutrition:

Calories: 70

Fat: 1 g

Protein: 1 g

Sodium: 26 mg

Fiber: 3 g

Carbohydrates: 16 g

Sugar: 11 g

Orchid Salad

Preparation time: 15 minutes Cooking time: 0 minutes Servings: 4

Ingredients:

- cups shredded red cabbage
- tablespoons freshly squeezed orange juice 1 teaspoon balsamic vinegar
- 1/8 teaspoon freshly ground black pepper 2 tart green apples, sliced thinly
- 1/2 teaspoon freshly squeezed lemon juice
- 1 medium ripe cantaloupe 1/4 cup chopped walnuts

Directions:

2. Place the cabbage into a mixing bowl. Add the orange juice, vinegar, and pepper and toss well to coat. Set aside. Place the apple slices in another bowl, add the lemon juice, and toss gently to coat. Set aside.

3. Slice the cantaloupe in half and discard the seeds. Slice each half into 8 wedges and remove the rind. Slice each wedge in half across the middle, so you're left with 16 triangular parts.

4. Place 2 cantaloupe parts in the middle of a plate, cut-sides, so they look rejoined. Pull them slightly apart and then do the same with another two parts so that you have a sort of X with a space in the middle.

5. Arrange a trio of fanned apple slices in each of the 4 empty spots between the cantaloupe points. Then place 1/4 of the cabbage mixture in the space in the middle of the X. Top with 1/4 of the chopped walnuts. Serve immediately.

Nutrition: Calories: 166

Fat: 5 g

Protein: 3 g

Sodium: 36 mg

Fiber: 4 g

Carbohydrates: 30 g

Sugar: 24 g

Thai Pasta Salad

Preparation time: 15 minutes Cooking time: 14 minutes Servings: 8

Ingredients:

- 1 (16-ounce) package dry spaghetti 2

tablespoons peanut oil
- 1 medium yellow squash, julienned
- 1 medium zucchini, julienned
- 1 medium green bell pepper, julienned 1 red bell pepper, julienned
- 1 orange bell pepper, julienned 6 scallions, sliced
- 3 cloves garlic, minced
- 1 jalpeño pepper, minced 3/4 cup chopped walnuts 1/3 cup peanut oil
- tablespoon sesame oil
- 1/4 cup unflavored rice vinegar
- tablespoons salt-free peanut butter
- 1 tablespoon no-salt-added tomato paste 1/4 cup chopped fresh cilantro
- 1 tablespoon minced fresh ginger 1 teaspoon sugar
- 1/4 teaspoon salt-free chili seasoning

Directions:

1. Cook the spaghetti in the pot with boiling water. Cook within 10 minutes, stirring once or twice. Remove from heat, drain, and set aside.

2. Warm 2 tablespoons peanut oil in a large sauté pan over medium heat. Add the julienned vegetables, scallions, garlic, jalapeño, and walnuts and cook, stirring, for 3–4 minutes.

3. Remove from heat and transfer to a huge bowl. Add cooked spaghetti. Whisk the remaining ingredients in a mixing bowl. Mix over the pasta salad. Serve immediately.

Nutrition: Calories: 464
Fat: 24 g
Protein: 11 g
Sodium: 9 mg
Fiber: 5 g
Carbohydrates: 50 g
Sugar: 4 g

Whole-Wheat Couscous Salad with Citrus and Cilantro

Preparation time: 15 minutes Cooking time: 2 minutes Servings: 6
Ingredients:
- 11/2 cups water
- 1 cup whole-wheat couscous
- medium cucumber, slice in halve
- 1-pint grape or cherry tomatoes halved 1

jalapeño pepper, minced
- shallots, minced
- 2 scallions, sliced
- 2 cloves garlic, minced
- 2 tablespoons freshly squeezed lemon juice 2 tablespoons freshly squeezed lime juice 1 teaspoon olive oil
- 1/4 cup chopped fresh cilantro
- Freshly ground black pepper, to taste

Directions:

1. Mix water into a saucepan and boil over high heat. Once boiling, stir in the couscous, reduce heat to medium-low, cover, and simmer for 2 minutes.

2. Remove pot from heat, remove the lid, and fluff couscous with a fork. Set aside to cool for 5 minutes.

3. Scrape out the cucumber's seeds using a spoon, then dice and place into a mixing bowl. Put the rest of the fixing in the bowl along with the cooked couscous and toss well to coat. Flavor with freshly ground black pepper, then serve immediately.

Nutrition:
Calories: 126
Fat: 2 g
Protein: 4 g
Sodium: 5 mg
Fiber: 2 g
Carbohydrates: 24 g
Sugar: 3 g

Salad Niçoise

Preparation time: 15 minutes Cooking time: 35 minutes Servings: 2
Ingredients:
- small head butter lettuce 1 small cucumber
- medium red potatoes
- 1 tablespoon white distilled vinegar 2 eggs
- bunch fresh green beans, trimmed
- tablespoons olive oil
- 2 tablespoons red wine vinegar
- 1 teaspoon salt-free prepared mustard 1 clove garlic, minced
- 1/2 teaspoon freshly ground black pepper 2 small tomatoes, quartered
- 1 (5-ounce) can no-salt-added tuna in water, drained

Directions:

1. Rip-up the lettuce leaves into small pieces

and set aside. Peel the cucumber, halve lengthwise, and remove seeds using a spoon. Slice and set aside.

2. Boil the potatoes into a pan with water over high heat, reduce heat slightly, and simmer until tender, about 20 minutes. Once cooked, dice, toss with white vinegar and set aside.

3. Boil the eggs into a saucepan, with enough water to cover over high heat within 12 minutes. Once cooked, carefully crack, peel, and slice into quarters. Set aside.

4. Boil a small pot of water, then once it's boiling, add the green beans and cook for 2 minutes. Remove beans from the pot and immediately place them in a bowl of ice water. Set aside.

5. In a small bowl, add the oil, vinegar, mustard, garlic, and pepper and whisk well to combine.

6. Assemble the salad on a platter, placing lettuce on the bottom and then grouping the cucumber, potatoes, eggs, green beans, tomatoes, and tuna on top. Drizzle the dressing evenly over the salad. Serve immediately.

Nutrition: Calories: 471
Fat: 20 g
Protein: 30 g
Sodium: 111 mg
Fiber: 7 g
Carbohydrates: 41 g
Sugar: 5 g

Simple Green Salad

Preparation time: 5 minutes Cooking time: 5 minutes Servings: 4
Ingredients:
- ¼ cup extra-virgin olive oil
- 1 tablespoon fresh lemon juice
- ¼ teaspoon salt
- ¼ teaspoon freshly ground black pepper 6 cups loosely packed mixed greens
- ½ small red onion, thinly sliced
- 1 small cucumber, peeled and thinly sliced
- ¼ cup shredded Parmesan cheese

Directions:
1. Mix the oil, lemon juice, salt, plus pepper in a small bowl. Store the dressing in 4 condiment cups. Mix the mixed greens,

onion, and cucumber in a large bowl. Divide salad into 4 medium storage containers. Top each with 1 tablespoon of Parmesan cheese. To serve, toss the dressing and salad.

Directions: Nutrition: Calories: 162g Fat: 15g
Carbohydrates: 6g Fiber: 2g
Protein: 3g Sodium: 290mg

Kale-Poppy Seed Salad

Preparation time: 10 minutes Cooking time: 5 minutes Servings: 6
Ingredients:
- ½ cup nonfat plain Greek yogurt 2 tablespoons apple cider vinegar
- ½ tablespoon extra-virgin olive oil
- 1 teaspoon poppy seeds 1 teaspoon sugar
- 4 cups firmly packed finely chopped kale
- 2 cups broccoli slaw
- 2 cups thinly sliced Brussels sprouts 6 tablespoons dried cranberries
- 6 tablespoons hulled pumpkin seeds

Directions:

1. Mix the yogurt, vinegar, oil, poppy seeds, sugar in a small bowl. Store the dressing in 6 condiment cups.

2. In a large bowl, mix the kale, broccoli slaw, and Brussels sprout. Divide the greens into 6 large storage containers and top each salad with cranberries and pumpkin seeds. To serve, toss the greens with the poppy seed dressing to coat.

Directions: Nutrition: Calories: 129g Fat: 6g
Carbohydrates: 13g Fiber: 3g
Protein: 8g
Sodium: 26mg

Edamame Salad with Corn and Cranberries

Preparation time: 15 minutes Cooking time: 0 minutes Servings: 4
Ingredients:
- 11/4 cups shelled edamame 3/4 cup corn kernels
- red or orange bell pepper, chopped
- 1/4 cup dried cranberries 1 shallot, finely diced
- tablespoons red wine vinegar
- 1 tablespoon olive oil
- 1 teaspoon agave nectar
- 1 teaspoon no-salt-added prepared mustard

Freshly ground black pepper, to taste

Directions:

1. Place the edamame, corn, bell pepper, cranberries, and shallot in a mixing bowl and stir to combine. Mix the vinegar, oil, agave nectar, and mustard into a small mixing bowl.

2. Pour the dressing over the salad. Flavor with freshly ground black pepper, to taste. Serve.

Nutrition: Calories: 149
Fat: 5 g
Protein: 5 g
Sodium: 5 mg
Fiber: 3 g
Carbohydrates: 22 g
Sugar: 10 g

Warm Asian Slaw

Preparation time: 15 minutes Cooking time: 3 minutes Servings: 4

Ingredients:

- tablespoon sesame oil 1 tablespoon peanut oil 2 sliced scallions
- cloves garlic, minced
- tablespoon minced fresh ginger 1 medium bok choy, chopped
- medium carrots, shredded
- 1 tablespoon unflavored rice vinegar 1/2 teaspoon sugar
- 1/2 teaspoon ground white pepper
- 1/2 tablespoon toasted sesame seeds (optional)

Directions:

1. Heat both oils in a skillet over medium. Add scallions, garlic, and ginger and cook, stirring, for 1 minute. Add bok choy and carrots and sauté for 2 minutes. Remove from heat.

2. Place contents in a bowl. Stir in vinegar, sugar, and pepper. Garnish with sesame seeds, if desired. Serve immediately.

Nutrition: Calories: 112
Fat: 7 g
Protein: 3 g
Sodium: 72 mg
Fiber: 3 g
Carbohydrates: 9 g
Sugar: 4 g

Tangy Three-Bean Salad with Barley

Preparation time: 15 minutes Cooking time: 30 minutes Servings: 8

Ingredients:

- cup uncooked pearled barley 21/4 cups water
- cups of green beans, slice into 2-inch pieces
- 1 (15-ounce) can no-salt-added kidney beans
- 1 (15-ounce) can no-salt-added garbanzo beans 1 medium red bell pepper, diced
- small onion, finely chopped
- tablespoons chopped fresh cilantro or parsley 1/3 cup canola oil
- 1/3 cup apple cider vinegar 1/3 cup pure maple syrup
- Freshly ground black pepper, to taste

Directions:

1. Measure the barley and water into a saucepan and boil over high heat. Once boiling, adjust heat to low, cover, and simmer until water is absorbed, 25–30 minutes. Remove pan from heat, then drain and rinse well.

2. Put the green beans in a bowl, then put the drained canned beans, bell pepper, onion, barley, and chopped cilantro or parsley. Stir well.

3. Mix the oil, vinegar, plus maple syrup in a small mixing bowl. Put on the salad and toss to coat. Flavor with ground black pepper, then serve.

Nutrition: Calories: 367
Fat: 11 g
Protein: 11 g
Sodium: 10 mg
Fiber: 11 g
Carbohydrates: 57 g

Wedge Salad with Creamy Blue Cheese Dressing

Preparation time: 15 minutes Cooking time: 0 minutes Servings: 4

Ingredients:

- cup nonfat plain Greek yogurt Juice of ½ large lemon
- ¼ teaspoon freshly ground black pepper
- ¼ teaspoon salt
- 1/3 cup crumbled blue cheese
- heads romaine lettuce, stem end trimmed,

halved lengthwise 1 cup grape tomatoes, halved
- ½ cup slivered almonds

Directions:

1. Mix the yogurt, lemon juice, pepper, salt, and cheese in a small bowl. Store the dressing in 4 condiment cups. Divide the lettuce halves and tomatoes among 4 large storage containers. Store the almonds separately.

2. To serve, arrange a half-head of romaine on a plate and top with the tomatoes. Sprinkle with 2 tablespoons of almonds and drizzle with the dressing.

Nutrition: Calories: 216g Fat: 11g
Carbohydrates: 20g
Fiber: 9g Protein: 16g Sodium: 329mg

Southwestern Bean Salad with Creamy Avocado Dressing

Preparation time: 15 minutes Cooking time: 0 minutes Servings: 4
Ingredients:
- 1 head romaine lettuce, chopped
- can no-salt-added black beans, drained 2 cups fresh corn kernels
- cups grape tomatoes, halved
- small avocados, halved and pitted 1 cup chopped fresh cilantro 1 cup nonfat plain Greek yogurt 8 scallions, chopped
- garlic cloves, quartered zest, and juice of 1 large lime
- ½ teaspoon sugar

Directions:

1. Mix the lettuce, beans, corn, and tomatoes in a large bowl. Toss you well combined. Divide the salad into 4 large storage containers. Put the avocado flesh into your blender or food processor.

2. Add the yogurt, scallions, garlic, lime zest and juice, and sugar. Blend until well

combined. Divide the dressing into 4 condiment cups. To serve, toss the salad and the dressing.

Directions: Nutrition: Calories: 349g Fat: 11g
Carbohydrates: 53g Fiber: 16g
Protein: 19g Sodium: 77mg

Cobb Pasta Salad

Preparation time: 15 minutes Cooking time: 10 minutes Servings: 6
Ingredients:
- 1-pound whole wheat rotini pasta
- 2 cups cooked chicken breast, chopped
- 8 low-sodium turkey bacon slices, cooked and chopped 4 scallions, sliced
- 1½ cups cherry tomatoes halved
- ¼ teaspoon freshly ground black pepper
- 4 hard-boiled eggs, peeled and coarsely chopped 1/3 cup crumbled blue cheese
- 1 cup frozen avocado cubes
- ¾ cup Greek Yogurt Dill Dressing

Directions:

1. Cook the pasta until al dente as stated to package directions. Rinse under cold water, then drain. Mix the pasta, chicken, bacon, scallions, tomatoes, pepper in a large bowl. Toss until well combined.

2. Add the eggs and blue cheese and fold until mixed well. Divide the salad into 6 storage containers. Divide the avocado into 6 small storage containers. Make the dressing as directed and store in 6 condiment cups.

3. The night before you're planning on having a salad, add the portion off the avocado to the salad so they will be soft by mealtime the next day. Serve drizzled with the dressing.

Nutrition: Calories: 550g Fat: 18g
Carbohydrates: 62g
Fiber: 9.5g Protein: 40g Sodium: 619mg

CHAPTER 13:

Snacks

Mediterranean Pop Corn Bites

Preparation Time: 5 minutes + 20 minutes chill time Cooking Time: 2-3 minutes
- Servings: 4 Ingredients:
- 3 cups Medjool dates, chopped 12 ounces brewed coffee
- 1 cup pecan, chopped
- ½ cup coconut, shredded
- ½ cup of cocoa powder

Directions:

1. Soak dates in warm coffee for 5 minutes. Remove dates from coffee and mash them, making a fine smooth mixture. Stir in remaining ingredients (except cocoa powder) and form small balls out of the mixture. Coat with cocoa powder, serve and enjoy!

Nutrition: Calories: 265 Fat: 12g
Carbohydrates: 43g Protein 3g
Sodium: 75 mg

Hearty Buttery Walnuts

Preparation Time: 10 minutes Cooking Time: 0 minutes Servings: 4
Ingredients:
- 4 walnut halves
- ½ tablespoon almond butter

Directions:

1. Spread butter over two walnut halves. Top with other halves. Serve and enjoy!

Nutrition: Calories: 90 Fat: 10g
Carbohydrates: 0g Protein: 1g Sodium: 1 mg

Refreshing Watermelon Sorbet

Preparation Time: 20 minutes + 20 hours chill time
Cooking Time: 0 minutes
Servings: 4 Ingredients:
- cups watermelon, seedless and chunked
- ¼ cup of coconut sugar 2 tablespoons lime juice

Directions:

1. Add the listed fixing to a blender and puree. Freeze the mix for about 4- 6 hours until you have gelatin-like consistency.

2. Puree the mix once again in batches and return to the container. Chill overnight. Allow the sorbet to stand for 5 minutes before serving and enjoy!

Nutrition: Calories: 91 Fat: 0g
Carbohydrates: 25g Protein: 1g Sodium: 0mg

Garlic Cottage Cheese Crispy

Preparation Time: 5 minutes Cooking Time: 2 minutes Servings: 4
Ingredients:
- 1 cup cottage cheese
- ½ teaspoon Garlic powder Pinch of pepper
- Pinch of onion powder

Directions:

1. Take a bowl and mix in cheese and spices. Scoop half a teaspoon of the cheese mix and place it in the pan. Cook in a skillet over medium heat within 1 minute per side. Repeat until done.

Nutrition: Calories: 70 Fat: 6g
Carbohydrates: 1g Protein: 6g Sodium: 195 mg

Lemon Fat Bombs

Preparation Time: 10 minutes Cooking Time: 0 minutes Servings: 3
Ingredients:
- 1 whole lemon
- 4 ounces cream cheese 2 ounces butter
- 2 teaspoons natural sweetener

Directions:

2. Take a fine grater and zest your lemon. Squeeze lemon juice into a bowl alongside the zest. Add butter, cream cheese to a bowl, and add zest, salt, sweetener, and juice.

3. Stir well using a hand mixer until smooth. Spoon mix into molds and freeze for 2

hours. Serve and enjoy!
Nutrition: Calories: 404 Carbs: 4g Fiber: 1g
Protein: 4g Fat: 43g Sodium: 19 mg

Chocolate Coconut Bombs

Preparation Time: 20 minutes Cooking Time: 0
minutes Servings: 12
Ingredients:

- ½ cup dark cocoa powder
- ½tablespoon vanilla extract 5 drops stevia
- 1 cup coconut oil, solid 1tablespoon peppermint extract

Directions:

1. Take a high-speed food processor and add all the ingredients. Blend until combined. Take a teaspoon and drop a spoonful onto parchment paper. Refrigerate until solidified and keep refrigerated.

Nutrition: Calories: 126 Carbs: 0g Fiber: 0g
Protein: 0g Fat: 14g Sodium: 30 mg

Espresso Fat Bombs

Preparation Time: 20 minutes Cooking Time: 0
minutes Servings: 24
Ingredients:

- 5 tablespoons butter, tender 3 ounces cream cheese, soft 2 ounces espresso
- 4 tablespoons coconut oil
- 2 tablespoons coconut whipping cream 2 tablespoons stevia

Directions:

2. Prepare your double boiler and melt all ingredients (except stevia) for 3-4 minutes and mix. Add sweetener and mix using a hand mixer.

3. Spoon mixture into silicone muffin molds and freeze for 4 hours. Remove fat bombs and serve!

Nutrition: Carbs: 1.3g Fiber: 0.2g Protein: 0.3g Fat: 7g Sodium: 50 mg

Crispy Coconut Bombs

Preparation Time: 10 minutes Cooking Time: 0
minutes Servings: 6
Ingredients:

- 14 ½ ounces coconut milk
- ¾ cup of coconut oil
- cup unsweetened coconut flakes 20 drops stevia

Directions:

1. Microwave your coconut oil for 20 seconds in the microwave. Mix in coconut milk and stevia in the hot oil. Stir in coconut flakes and pour the mixture into molds. Let it chill for 60 minutes in the fridge. Serve and enjoy!

Nutrition: Carbs: 2g Fiber: 0.5g Protein: 1g Fat: 13g
Calories: 123 Carbs: 1g Sodium: 0mg

Pumpkin Pie Fat Bombs

Preparation Time: 35 minutes Cooking Time: 5
minutes Servings: 12
Ingredients:

- tablespoons coconut oil 1/3 cup pumpkin puree 1/3 cup almond oil
- ¼ cup almond oil
- ounces sugar-free dark chocolate
- 1 ½ teaspoon of pumpkin pie spice mix Stevia to taste

Directions:

2. Melt almond oil and dark chocolate over a double boiler. Take this mixture and layer the bottom of 12 muffin cups. Freeze until the crust has set. Meanwhile, take a saucepan and combine the rest of the ingredients.

3. Put the saucepan on low heat. Heat until softened and mix well. Pour this over the initial chocolate mixture. Let it chill within 1 hour, then serve.

Nutrition: Calories: 124 Carbs: 3g Fiber: 1g
Protein: 3g Fat: 13g Sodium: 0mg

Sweet Almond and Coconut Fat Bomb

Preparation Time: 10 minutes Cooking Time: 0
minutes Servings: 6
Ingredients:

- ¼ cup melted coconut oil
- 9 ½ tablespoons almond butter 90 drops liquid stevia
- 3 tablespoons cocoa
- 9 tablespoons melted butter, salted

Directions:
Take a bowl and add all of the listed ingredients. Mix them well. Pour scant 2 tablespoons of the mixture into as many muffin molds as you like. Chill for 20 minutes and pop them out. Serve and enjoy!
Nutrition: Calories: 72 Carbs: 2g Fiber: 0g Protein: 2.53g Fat: 14g Sodium: 0mg

Almond and Tomato Balls

Preparation Time: 10 minutes Cooking Time: 0 minutes Servings: 6
Ingredients:

- 1/3 cup pistachios, de-shelled 10 ounces cream cheese
- 1/3 cup sun-dried tomatoes, diced

Directions:

1. Chop pistachios into small pieces. Add cream cheese, tomatoes in a bowl and mix well. Chill for 15-20 minutes and turn into balls. Roll into pistachios. Serve and enjoy!

Nutrition: Calories: 183 Fat: 18g Carb: 5g Protein: 5g
Sodium: 10 mg

Avocado Tuna Bites

Preparation Time: 10 minutes Cooking Time: 0 minutes Servings: 4
Ingredients:

- 1/3 cup coconut oil
- 1 avocado, cut into cubes
- 10 ounces of canned tuna, drained
- ¼ cup parmesan cheese, grated
- ¼ teaspoon garlic powder 1/4 teaspoon onion powder 1/3 cup almond flour
- ¼ teaspoon pepper
- ¼ cup low-fat mayonnaise Pepper as needed

Directions:

2. Take a bowl and add tuna, mayo, flour, parmesan, spices, and mix well. Fold in avocado and make 12 balls out of the mixture. Dissolve coconut oil in a pan and cook over medium heat until all sides are golden. Serve and enjoy!

Nutrition: Calories: 185 Fat: 18g
Carbohydrates: 1g Protein: 5g Sodium: 0mg

Faux Mac and Cheese

Preparation Time: 15 minutes Cooking Time: 45 minutes Servings: 4
Ingredients:

- cups cauliflower florets Salt and pepper to taste
- cup of coconut milk
- ½ cup vegetable broth
- tablespoons coconut flour, sifted 1 organic egg, beaten
- 2 cups cheddar cheese

Directions:

1. Warm your oven to 350 degrees F. Season florets with salt and steam until firm. Place florets in a greased ovenproof dish. Heat-up coconut milk over medium heat in a skillet; make sure to season the oil with salt and pepper.

2. Stir in broth and add coconut flour to the mix, stir. Cook until the sauce begins to bubble. Remove heat and add beaten egg. Pour the thick sauce over cauliflower and mix in cheese. Bake for 30-45 minutes. Serve and enjoy!

Nutrition: Calories: 229 Fat: 14g
Carbohydrates: 9g Protein: 15g Sodium: 125 mg

Banana Custard

Preparation Time: 10 minutes Cooking Time: 25 minutes Servings: 3
Ingredients:

- 2 ripe bananas, peeled and mashed finely
- ½ teaspoon of vanilla extract
- 14-onnce unsweetened almond milk 3 eggs

Directions:

1. Warm your oven to 350 degrees F. Grease 8 custard glasses lightly. Arrange the glasses in a large baking dish. Take a large bowl and mix all of the ingredients and mix them well until combined nicely.

2. Divide the mixture evenly between the glasses. Pour water into the baking dish. Bake for 25 minutes. Take out and serve.

Nutrition: Calories: 59 Fat: 2.4g
Carbohydrates: 7g Protein: 3g Sodium: 92 mg

Healthy Tahini Buns

Preparation Time: 10 minutes Cooking Time: 15-20 minutes Servings: 3
Ingredients:

- 1 whole egg
- 5 tablespoons Tahini paste
- ½ teaspoon baking soda 1 teaspoon lemon juice 1 pinch salt

Directions:

1. Warm your oven to 350 degrees F. Line a baking sheet with parchment paper and keep it on the side. Put the listed fixing in a blender and blend until you have a smooth batter.

2. Scoop batter onto prepared sheet forming

buns. Bake for 15-20 minutes. Remove, then let them cool. Serve and enjoy!

Nutrition: Calories: 172 Carbs: 7g Fiber: 2g Protein: 6g Fat: 14g Sodium: 112 mg

CHAPTER 14:

Desserts

Chocolate Truffles

Preparation time: 15 minutes Cooking time: 0 minutes Servings: 24

Ingredients:

For the truffles:

- ½ cup cacao powder
- ¼ cup chia seeds
- ¼ cup flaxseed meal
- ¼ cup maple syrup 1 cup flour
- tablespoons almond milk For the Coatings:
- Cacao powder
- Chia seeds Flour
- Shredded coconut, unsweetened

Directions:

1. Place all the fixing for the truffle in a blender; pulse until it is thoroughly blended; transfer contents to a bowl. Form into chocolate balls, then cover with the coating ingredients. Serve immediately.

Nutrition: Calories 70

Sodium 2 mg

Fats 1 g

Carbohydrates 4 g

Fibers 2 g

Sugar 11 g

Proteins 1 g

Grilled Pineapple Strips

Preparation time: 15 minutes Cooking time: 5 minutes Servings: 6

Ingredients:

- Vegetable oil
- Dash of iodized salt 1 pineapple
- 1 tablespoon lime juice extract 1 tablespoon olive oil
- 1 tablespoon raw honey
- 3 tablespoons brown sugar

Directions:

1. Peel the pineapple, remove the eyes of the fruit, and discard the core.

2. Slice lengthwise, forming six wedges. Mix the rest of the fixing in a bowl until blended.

3. Brush the coating mixture on the pineapple (reserve some for basting). Grease an oven or outdoor grill rack with vegetable oil.

4. Place the pineapple wedges on the grill rack and heat for a few minutes per side until golden brownish, basting it frequently with a reserved glaze. Serve on a platter.

Nutrition: Calories 97

Fats 2 g

Carbohydrates 20 g

Sodium 2 mg

Sugar 17 g

Fibers 1 g

Proteins 1 g

Raspberry Peach Pancake

Preparation time: 15 minutes Cooking time: 30 minutes Servings: 4

Ingredients:

- ½ teaspoon sugar
- ½ cup raspberries
- ½ cup fat-free milk
- ½ cup all-purpose flour
- ¼ cup vanilla yogurt
- 1/8 teaspoon iodized salt 1 tablespoon butter
- 2 medium peeled, thinly sliced peaches 3 lightly beaten organic eggs

Directions:

1. Preheat oven to 400 °F. Toss peaches and raspberries with sugar in a bowl. Melt butter in a 9-inch round baking plate. Mix eggs, milk, plus salt in a small bowl until blended; whisk in the flour.

2. Remove the round baking plate from the oven, tilt to coat the bottom and sides with the melted butter; pour in the flour mixture.

3. Put it in the oven until it becomes brownish and puffed. Remove the pancake from the oven. Serve immediately with more raspberries and vanilla yogurt.

Nutrition: Calories 199

Sodium 173 mg

Fats 7 g

Cholesterol 149 g
Carbohydrates 25 g
Sugar 11 g
Fibers 3 g
Proteins 9 g

Mango Rice Pudding

Preparation time: 15 minutes Cooking time: 35 minutes Servings: 4
Ingredients:

- ½ teaspoon ground cinnamon
- ¼ teaspoon iodized salt
- 1 teaspoon vanilla extract
- cup long-grain uncooked brown rice 2 mediums ripe, peeled, cored mango 1 cup vanilla soymilk
- tablespoons sugar 2 cups of water

Directions:

1. Bring saltwater to a boil in a saucepan to cook rice; after a few minutes, simmer covered within 30-35 minutes until the rice absorbs the water. Mash the mango with a mortar and pestle or stainless-steel fork.

2. Pour milk, sugar, cinnamon, and the mashed mango into the rice; cook uncovered on low heat, stirring frequently. Remove the mango rice pudding from the heat, then stir in the vanilla soymilk. Serve immediately.

Nutrition: Calories 275
Sodium 176 mg
Fats 3 g
Carbohydrates 58 mg
Sugar 20 g
Fibers 3 g

Choco Banana Cake

Preparation time: 15 minutes Cooking time: 30 minutes Servings: 18
Ingredients:

- ½ cup semisweet dark chocolate
- ½ cup brown sugar
- ½ teaspoon baking soda
- ¼ cup unsweetened cocoa powder
- ¼ cup canola oil
- ¾ cup soymilk 1 large egg
- 1 egg white
- 1 large, ripe, mashed banana
- tablespoon lemon juice extract 1 teaspoon vanilla extract
- cups all-purpose flour

Directions:

1. Preheat the oven to 350 °F. Coat a baking pan with a non-stick spray. Whisk brown sugar, flour, baking soda, and cocoa powder in a bowl.

2. In another bowl, whisk bananas, lemon juice extract, vanilla extract, oil, soymilk, egg, and egg whites. Create a hole in the flour mixture's core or center, then pour in the banana mixture and mix in the dark chocolate.

3. Stir all the fixing with a spoon until thoroughly blended; spoon the batter onto the baking pan. Place in the oven and bake within 25-30 minutes until the center springs back when pressed lightly using your fingertips.

Nutrition:
Calories 150
Sodium 52 mg
Cholesterol 12 mg
Fats 3 g
Carbohydrates 27 g
Proteins 3 g

Zesty Zucchini Muffins

Preparation time: 15 minutes Cooking time: 30 minutes Servings: 12
Ingredients:

- Vegetable oil cooking spray
- ½ cup of sugar
- ¼ teaspoon iodized salt
- ¼ teaspoon ground nutmeg
- ¾ cup skim milk
- 1 cup shredded zucchini
- tablespoon baking powder 1 large egg
- teaspoons grated lemon rind
- 2 cups of all-purpose flour 3 tablespoons vegetable oil

Directions:

1. Mix the flour, baking powder, sugar, salt, plus lemon rinds in a bowl. Create a well in the center of the flour batter. In another bowl, mix zucchini, milk, vegetable oil, and egg. Coat muffin cups with vegetable oil cooking spray.

2. Divide the batter equally into 12 muffin cups. Transfer the muffin cups to the baking pan, put it in a microwave oven, and bake at 400 °F within 30 minutes until light

golden brown. Remove, then allow to cool on a wire rack before serving.

Nutrition: Calories 169
Sodium 211.5 mg
Fats 4.8 g
Potassium 80.2 g
Carbohydrates 29.1 g
Fibers 2.5 g
Sugar 12.8 g
Proteins 0 g

Blueberry Oat Muffins

Preparation time: 15 minutes Cooking time: 30 minutes Servings: 12
Ingredients:

- ½ cup raw oatmeal
- ½ teaspoon baking powder
- ½ teaspoon iodized salt
- ½ cup dry milk
- ¼ cup of vegetable oil
- ¼ teaspoon baking soda 1/3 cup sugar
- 1 ½ cup flour 1 cup milk
- cup blueberries

Directions:

1. Preheat oven to 350 °F. Coat the muffin tins with vegetable oil. Mix or combine the flour, baking soda, baking powder, oats, sugar, and salt in a bowl. Mix milk, dry milk, egg, and vegetable oil in another bowl.

2. Pour the bowl of wet fixing into the bowl of dry fixing and mix partially. Add the blueberries and mix until the consistency turns lumpy. Scoop blueberry batter into the muffin tins.

3. Bake within 30 minutes until the muffins turn golden brown on the edges. Serve warm immediately or put it in an airtight container and store it in the refrigerator to chill.

Nutrition: Calories 150
Sodium 180 mg
Fats 5 g
Carbohydrates 22 g
Proteins 4 g
Fibers 1 g

Banana Bread

Preparation time: 15 minutes Cooking time: 60 minutes Servings: 14
Ingredients:

- Vegetable oil cooking spray
- ½ cup brown rice flour
- ½ cup amaranth flour
- ½ cup tapioca flour
- ½ cup millet flour
- ½ cup quinoa flour
- ½ cup of raw sugar
- ¾ cup egg whites
- 1/8 teaspoon iodized salt 1 teaspoon baking soda
- tablespoons grapeseed oil 2 pieces of mashed banana

Directions:

1. Preheat oven to 350 °F. Coat a loaf pan with a vegetable oil cooking spray, dust evenly with a bit of flour, and set aside. In a bowl, mix the brown rice flour, amaranth flour, tapioca flour, millet flour, quinoa flour, and baking soda

2. Coat a separate bowl with vegetable oil, then mix eggs, sugar, and mashed bananas. Pour the bowl of wet fixing into the bowl of dry fixing and mix thoroughly. Scoop the mixture into the loaf pan. Bake within an hour.

3. To check the doneness, insert a toothpick in the center of the loaf pan; if you remove the toothpick and it has no batter sticking to it, remove the bread from the oven. Slice and serve immediately and store the remaining banana bread in a refrigerator to prolong shelf life.

Nutrition: Calories 150
Sodium 150 mg
Fats 3 g
Fibers 2 g
Proteins 4 g
Sugar 7 g

Poached Pears

Preparation time: 15 minutes Cooking time: 30 minutes Servings: 4
Ingredients:

- ¼ cup apple juice extract
- ½ cup fresh raspberries
- cup of orange juice extract 1 teaspoon cinnamon, ground 1 teaspoon ground nutmeg
- tablespoons orange zest
- 4 whole pears, peeled, destemmed, core removed

Directions:

1. In a bowl, combine the fruit juices, nutmeg, and cinnamon, and then stir evenly. In a shallow pan, pour the fruit juice mixture, and set to medium fire.

2. Adjust the heat to simmer within 30 minutes; turn pears frequently to maintain poaching, do not boil. Transfer poached pears to a serving bowl; garnish with orange zest and raspberries.

Nutrition: Calories 140
Fats 0.5 g
Proteins 1 g
Carbohydrates 34 g
Fibers 2 g
Sodium 9 mg

Pumpkin with Chia Seeds Pudding

Preparation time: 60 minutes Cooking time: 0 minutes Servings: 4
Ingredients:
- For the Pudding:
- ½ cuporganic chia seeds
- ¼ cup raw maple syrup 1 ¼ cup low-fat milk
- cup pumpkin puree extract For the Toppings:
- ¼ cup organic sunflower seeds
- ¼ cup coarsely chopped almonds
- ¼ cup blueberries

Directions:

1. Add all the ingredients for the pudding in a bowl and mix until blended. Cover and store in a chiller for 1-hour. Remove from the chiller, transfer contents to a jar and add the ingredients for the toppings. Serve immediately.

Nutrition: Calories 189
Sodium 42 mg
Fats 7 g
Potassium 311 mg
Carbohydrates 27 g
Fibers 4 g
Proteins 5 g
Sugar 18 g

Milk Chocolate Pudding

Preparation time: 15 minutes Cooking time: 15 minutes Servings: 4

Ingredients:
- ½ teaspoon vanilla extract 1/3 cup chocolate chips 1/8 teaspoon salt
- 2 cups nonfat milk
- tablespoons cocoa powder 2 tablespoons sugar
- tablespoons cornstarch

Directions:

1. Mix cocoa powder, cornstarch, sugar, and salt in a saucepan and whisk in milk; frequently stir over medium heat.

2. Remove, put the chocolate chips and vanilla extract, stir until the chocolate chips and vanilla melt into the pudding. Pour contents into serving bowls and store in a chiller. Serve chilled.

Nutrition: Calories 197
Sodium 5 mg
Fats 5 g
Carbohydrates 9 g
Proteins 0.5 g

Minty Lime and Grapefruit Yogurt Parfait

Preparation time: 15 minutes Cooking time: 0 minutes Servings: 6
Ingredients:
- A handful of torn mint leaves 2 teaspoons grated lime zest
- tablespoons lime juice extract
- tablespoons raw honey 4 large red grapefruits
- cups reduced-fat plain yogurt

Directions:

1. Cut the top and lower part of the red grapefruits and stand the fruit upright on a cutting board. Discard the peel with a knife and slice along the membrane of each segment to remove the skin.

2. Mix yogurt, lime juice extract, and lime zest in a bowl. Layer half of the grapefruit and yogurt mixture into 6 parfait glasses; add another layer until the glass is filled and then drizzle with honey and top with mint leaves. Serve immediately.

Nutrition: Calories 207
Sodium 115 mg
Fats 3 g
Cholesterol 10 mg
Carbohydrates 39 mg

Sugar 36 g
Fibers 3 g

Peach Tarts

Preparation time: 15 minutes Cooking time: 55 minutes Servings: 8
Ingredients:
Tart Ingredients:
- ¼ cup softened butter
- ¼ teaspoon ground nutmeg 1 cup all-purpose flour
- 3 tablespoons sugar Filling Ingredients:
- ¼ teaspoon ground cinnamon
- ¼ cup coarsely chopped almonds 1/8 teaspoon almond extract
- 1/3 cup sugar
- 2 pounds peaches medium, peeled, thinly sliced

Directions:

1. Preheat oven to 375 °F. Mix butter, nutmeg, and sugar in a bowl until light and fluffy. Add and beat in flour until well-blended. Place the batter on an ungreased fluted tart baking pan and press firmly on the bottom and topsides.

2. Put it in the medium rack of the preheated oven and bake for about 10 minutes until it turns to a crust. In a bowl, coat peaches with sugar, flour, cinnamon, almond extract, and almonds.

3. Open the oven, put the tart crust on the lower rack of the oven, and pour in the peach filling; bake for about 40-45 minutes. Remove, cool, and serve; or cover with a cling wrap and refrigerate to serve chilled.

Nutrition: Calories 222
Sodium 46 milligrams
Fats 8 g
Cholesterol 15 mg
Carbohydrates 36 g
Sugar 21 g
Fibers 3 g
Proteins 4 g

Raspberry Nuts Parfait

Preparation time: 15 minutes Cooking time: 10 minutes Servings: 1
Ingredients:
- ¼ cup frozen raspberries
- ¼ cup frozen blueberries
- ¼ cup toasted, thinly sliced almonds 1 cup

nonfat, plain Greek yogurt
- 2 teaspoons raw honey

Directions:

1. First, layer Greek yogurt in a parfait glass; add berries; layer yogurt again, top with almonds and more berries; drizzle with honey. Serve chilled.

Nutrition: Calories 378
Sodium 83 mg
Fats 15 g
Fibers 6 g
Carbohydrates 35 g
Proteins 30 g
Sugar 25 g

Strawberry Bruschetta

Preparation time: 15 minutes Cooking time: 0 minutes Servings: 12
Ingredients:
- 1 loaf sliced Ciabatta bread 8 ounces goat cheese
- cup basil leaves
- containers of strawberries, sliced 5 tablespoons balsamic glaze

Directions:
Wash and slice strawberries; set aside. Wash and chop the basil leaves; set aside. Slice the ciabatta bread and spread some goat cheese evenly on each slice; add strawberries, balsamic glaze, and top with basil leaves. Serve on a platter.
Nutrition: Calories 80
Sodium 59 mg
Fats 2 g
Carbohydrates 12 g
Proteins 3 g

Vanilla Cupcakes with Cinnamon-Fudge Frosting

Preparation Time: 10 minutes Cooking Time: 18 minutes Servings: 1 dozen Ingredients:
- 11/2 cups white whole-wheat flour 3/4 cup sugar
- 3/4 teaspoon sodium-free baking powder
- 1/2 teaspoon sodium-free baking soda 1 cup nondairy milk
- 6 tablespoons canola oil
- tablespoon apple cider vinegar 1 tablespoon pure vanilla extract
- Frosting:
- cups powdered sugar
- 1/3 cup unsweetened cocoa powder

- 4 tablespoons non-hydrogenated vegetable shortening 4 tablespoons nondairy milk
- teaspoon ground cinnamon 1 teaspoon pure vanilla extract

Directions:

1. Warm oven to 350 F. Line a 12-muffin tin with paper liners and put aside. Mix or combine the flour, sugar, baking powder, and baking soda into a mixing bowl. Add the remaining batter fixing and stir just until combined.

2. Split the batter evenly between the muffin cups, then bake within 18 minutes. Remove, then put on a wire rack to cool. Beat until fluffy the frosting fixings into a mixing bowl. Frost cupcakes. Serve immediately.

Nutrition:
Calories: 347
Fat: 7 g
Protein: 13 g
Sodium: 46 mg
Fiber: 4 g
Carbohydrates: 60 g
Sugar: 3 g

Chocolate Cupcakes with Vanilla Frosting

Preparation time: 15 minutes Cooking time: 20 minutes Servings: 12
Ingredients:
- 11/2 cups white whole-wheat flour 1 cup of sugar
- teaspoons sodium-free baking soda
- 1/4 cup unsweetened cocoa powder 1 cup of water
- 4 tablespoons canola oil
- 4 tablespoons unsweetened applesauce 1 tablespoon pure vanilla extract
- 1 teaspoon distilled white vinegar
- Frosting:
- 11/2 cups powdered sugar
- 4 tablespoons non-hydrogenated vegetable shortening 21/2 tablespoons nondairy milk
- 1 tablespoon pure vanilla extract

Directions:

1. Warm oven to 350°F. Prepare a 12-muffin tin with paper liners and set aside. Measure the flour, sugar, and baking soda into a mixing bowl and whisk well to combine. Put the rest of the batter ingredients and stir

just until combined.

2. Divide the batter evenly into the muffin cups. Bake within 20 minutes or until a toothpick inserted in the center of cupcakes comes out clean.

3. Remove, then put on a wire rack to cool. Mix the frosting fixing into a clean mixing bowl, then frost cupcakes. Serve immediately.

Nutrition:
Calories: 272
Fat: 9 g
Protein: 2 g
Sodium: 2 mg
Fiber: 1 g
Carbohydrates: 45 g
Sugar: 32 g

Chocolate Chip Banana Muffin Top Cookies

Preparation time: 15 minutes Cooking time: 15 minutes Servings: 16
Ingredients:
- 1 cup quick oats
- 1 cup white whole-wheat flour 1/4 cup sugar
- 1 tablespoon sodium-free baking powder 1 teaspoon ground cinnamon
- ripe medium bananas, mashed
- tablespoons canola oil
- 1 tablespoon pure vanilla extract 3/4 cup chocolate chips

Directions:

1. Preheat oven to 350°F. Put aside a baking sheet with parchment paper. Measure the oats, flour, sugar, baking powder, and cinnamon into a mixing bowl and whisk. Put the rest of the fixing and stir just until combined.

2. Using a medium-sized ice cream scoop, scoop the batter onto the prepared baking sheet, leaving an inch or two between cookies. Bake within 15 minutes. Remove, then put on a wire rack to cool. Serve immediately.

Nutrition: Calories: 150
Fat: 6 g
Protein: 2 g
Sodium: 0 mg
Fiber: 1 g

Carbohydrates: 23 g
Sugar: 10 g

Lemon Cookies

Preparation time: 15 minutes Cooking time: 10 minutes Servings: 36
Ingredients:

- 21/2 cups white whole-wheat flour 11/2 cups sugar
- tablespoon sodium-free baking powder
- 3/4 cup canola oil
- large lemons, juice, and grated zest 1 tablespoon pure vanilla extract

Directions:

1. Preheat oven to 350°F. Mix the flour, sugar, plus baking powder into a mixing bowl. Put the rest of the fixing and stir to form a stiff dough.

2. Drop by rounded tablespoons onto an ungreased baking sheet. Bake within 10 minutes. Remove, then let cool on sheet for a few minutes before transferring to a wire rack to cool fully. Serve immediately.

Nutrition: Calories: 106
Fat: 5 g
Protein: 1 g
Sodium: 0 mg
Fiber: 0 g
Carbohydrates: 15 g
Sugar: 8 g

Peanut Butter Chocolate Chip Blondies

Preparation time: 15 minutes Cooking time: 20 minutes Servings: 24
Ingredients:

- 1/4 cup salt-free peanut butter 3/4 cup light brown sugar
- 1/2 cup unsweetened applesauce
- 1/4 cup canola oil 2 egg whites
- tablespoon pure vanilla extract
- teaspoons sodium-free baking powder 1 cup unbleached all-purpose flour
- 1/2 cup white whole-wheat flour
- 1/2 cup semisweet chocolate chips

Directions:

1. Preheat oven to 400°F. Oiled and flour a 9" × 13" baking pan and set aside. Measure the peanut butter, sugar, applesauce, oil, egg whites, and vanilla into a mixing bowl and stir well to combine.

2. Add the baking powder and mix. Gradually add in the flours, stirring well. Fold in the chocolate chips. Spread batter in prepared pan and smooth to even.

3. Bake within 20 minutes. Remove, then let it cool. Cool before cutting into bars and serving.

Nutrition: Calories: 18
Fat: 5 g
Protein: 2 g
Sodium: 7 mg
Fiber: 1 g
Carbohydrates: 17 g
Sugar: 10 g

Ginger Snaps

Preparation time: 15 minutes Cooking time: 10 minutes Servings: 18
Ingredients:

- 4 tablespoons unsalted butter 1/2 cup light brown sugar
- 2 tablespoons molasses
- 1 egg white
- 21/2 teaspoons ground ginger 1/4 teaspoon ground allspice
- 1 teaspoon sodium-free baking soda 1/2 cup unbleached all-purpose flour 12 cup white whole-wheat flour
- 1 tablespoon sugar

Directions:

1. Warm oven to 375°F. Put aside a baking sheet with parchment paper.

2. Put the butter, sugar, plus molasses into a mixing bowl and beat well.

3. Mix the egg white, ginger, and allspice. Mix in the baking soda, then put the flours, then beat.

4. Roll the dough into small balls. Put the balls on a prepared baking sheet and press down using a glass dipped in the tablespoon sugar.

Once the glass presses on the dough, it will moisten sufficiently to coat with sugar. Bake within 10 minutes. Let it cool, then serve.
Nutrition: Calories: 81
Fat: 2 g
Protein: 1 g
Sodium: 6 mg
Fiber: 0 g
Carbohydrates: 14 g

Sugar: 8 g

Carrot Cake Cookies

Preparation time: 15 minutes Cooking time: 12 minutes Servings: 36
Ingredients:

- 3 medium carrots, shredded
- 11/2 cups white whole-wheat flour 3/4 cup oat flour
- 3/4 cup light brown sugar 1 egg white
- 1/3 cup canola oil
- 1 tablespoon pure vanilla extract
- 1 teaspoon sodium-free baking powder 11/2 teaspoons ground cinnamon
- 1/2 teaspoon ground nutmeg 1/4 teaspoon ground ginger 1/8 teaspoon ground cloves

Directions:

1. Preheat oven to 375°F. Prepare and line a baking sheet with parchment paper and set aside. Place all the ingredients into a mixing bowl and stir well to combine. The dough will be quite sticky.

2. Put onto a lined baking sheet. Bake within 12 minutes. Remove, then transfer cookies to a wire rack to cool. Store in an airtight container.

Nutrition: Calories: 67
Fat: 2 g
Protein: 1 g
Sodium: 7 mg
Fiber: 0 g
Carbohydrates: 10 g
Sugar: 4 g

Chewy Pumpkin Oatmeal Raisin Cookies

Preparation time: 15 minutes Cooking time: 16 minutes Servings: 48
Ingredients:

- cup pumpkin purée 12/3 cups sugar
- tablespoons molasses
- 11/2 teaspoons pure vanilla extract 2/3 cup canola oil
- tablespoon ground flaxseed
- teaspoons Ener-G Baking Soda Substitute 1 teaspoon ground cinnamon
- 1/2 teaspoon ground nutmeg
- 1 cup unbleached all-purpose flour 1 cup white whole-wheat flour 11/3 cups rolled or quick oats
- 1 cup seedless raisins

Directions:

1. Preheat oven to 350°F. Spray 2 baking sheets lightly with oil and set aside. Measure the ingredients into a large mixing bowl and stir using a rubber spatula.

2. Scoop batter out by tablespoons—a small retractable ice cream scoop works wonderfully here—and place on the prepared baking sheets.

3. Put sheets on the middle rack in the oven and bake 16 minutes. Remove, then transfer cookies to a wire rack to cool. Repeat process with remaining batter. Cool, and serve.

Nutrition: Calories: 97
Fat: 3 g
Protein: 1 g
Sodium: 1 mg
Fiber: 0.6 g
Carbohydrates: 16 g
Sugar: 9 g

Easy Apple Crisp

Preparation time: 15 minutes Cooking time: 25 minutes Servings: 8
Ingredients:

- 6 medium apples
- 1 tablespoon lemon juice 1/3 cup sugar
- 1/2 cup rolled or quick oats
- 1/2 cup white whole-wheat flour 1/2 cup light brown sugar
- 1 tablespoon pure vanilla extract 1 teaspoon ground cinnamon 1/2 teaspoon ground ginger
- 3 tablespoons unsalted butter

Directions:

1. Preheat oven to 425°F. Take out a 2-quart baking pan and set aside.

2. Slice each apple into 16 wedges. Put into a mixing bowl, place the lemon juice and sugar, and toss well to coat.

3. Turn batter out into the baking pan, then set aside. Place the oats, flour sugar, vanilla, and spices into a mixing bowl and stir to combine.

4. Slice the butter into the mixture using your hands and process until a wet crumb has formed. Sprinkle mixture over the fruit. Bake within 25 minutes. Remove, then let it cool and serve.

Nutrition: Calories: 232

Fat: 5 g
Protein: 2 g
Sodium: 5 mg
Fiber: 2 g
Carbohydrates: 46 g
Sugar: 34 g

Mango Crumble

Preparation time: 15 minutes Cooking time: 25 minutes Servings: 8
Ingredients:

- 2 barely ripe mangoes
- 2 tablespoons light brown sugar 1 tablespoon cornstarch
- 11/2 teaspoons minced fresh ginger 1/2 cup unbleached all-purpose flour 1/2 cup white whole-wheat flour
- 1/2 cup sugar
- 1 teaspoon ground cinnamon 1/4 teaspoon ground ginger 3 tablespoons unsalted butter

Directions:

1. Preheat oven to 375°F. Take out an 8-inch square baking pan and set aside. Peel mangoes and cut into 1-inch chunks. Place in a mixing bowl.

2. Add the brown sugar, cornstarch, and minced ginger and toss to coat. Put the batter out into the baking pan and spread to even. In another bowl, whisk the flours, sugar, cinnamon, and ginger.

3. Slice the butter into pieces, and put it in the bowl. Work the butter into the mixture using your hands until it resembles damp sand and sticks when squeezed. Sprinkle mixture evenly over the fruit.

4. Bake within 25 minutes, until fruit is tender. Remove, and put on a wire rack to cool. Serve warm or cool.

Nutrition: Calories: 190
Fat: 5 g
Protein: 3 g
Sodium: 3 mg
Fiber: 2 g
Carbohydrates: 37 g
Sugar: 23 g

Homemade Banana Ice Cream

Preparation time: 5 minutes Cooking time: 0 minutes Servings: 4
Ingredients:

- 4 ripe bananas

Directions:

1. Place bananas in the freezer and freeze until solid. Remove bananas

2. from the freezer, peel, and slice into chunks. Pulse chunks into a blender or food processor. Scoop mixture out and serve immediately.

Nutrition: Calories: 105
Fat: 0 g
Protein: 1 g
Sodium: 1 mg
Fiber: 3 g
Carbohydrates: 26 g
Sugar: 14 g

Vegan Rice Pudding

Preparation time: 15 minutes Cooking time: 20 minutes Servings: 8
Ingredients:

- 1-quart vanilla nondairy milk
- 1 cup basmati or jasmine rice, rinsed 1/4 cup sugar
- 1 teaspoon pure vanilla extract 1/8 teaspoon pure almond extract 1/2 teaspoon ground cinnamon 1/8 teaspoon ground cardamom

Directions:

1. Mix all of the fixings into a saucepan and stir well to combine. Bring to a boil over medium-high heat. Adjust heat to low and simmer, stirring very frequently, about 15–20 minutes. Remove from heat and cool. Serve sprinkled with additional ground cinnamon if desired.

Nutrition: Calories: 148
Fat: 2 g
Protein: 4 g
Sodium: 48 mg
Fiber: 1 g
Carbohydrates: 26 g
Sugar: 10 g

Beetroot and Berry Smoothie

Preparation time: 5 minutes Cooking time: 0 minutes Servings: 1
Ingredients:

- 1/2 cup pineapple juice
- 1/2 cup low-fat vanilla yogurt 1/2 cup frozen strawberries 1/4 cup frozen blueberries
- 1/4 cup beetroot (peeled, washed, and sliced)

Directions:

1. Combine all the ingredients in a blender and blend until you obtain a smooth puree. Serve cold.

Nutrition: Calories 218 g
Fat 1.9 g
Carbohydrates 40.7 g
Protein 8.4 g
Sodium- 121 mg

Berry Blast

Preparation time: 15 minutes Cooking time: 40 minutes Servings: 1
Ingredients:

- 4 cups blueberries (2 cups fresh and 2 cups frozen) 1 cup rolled oats
- tsp cinnamon
- tbsp all-purpose flour 2 tsp unsalted butter
- 1 tbsp maple syrup

Directions:

1. Coat a pie pan with cooking spray and set it aside. Put the blueberries on the pie plate. Preheat the oven to 250 degrees Fahrenheit.

2. Combine the flour, butter, oats, maple syrup, and cinnamon in a large mixing bowl and whisk until you obtain a grainy mixture.

3. Transfer the oats mixture to the pie pan and bake for forty minutes until the mixture is golden brown. Serve warm.

Nutrition: Calories 824 g
Fat 15.2 g
Carbohydrates 166.6 g
Protein 16.9 g
Sodium 65 mg

Oats and Fruit Bar Cracker

Preparation time: 15 minutes Cooking time: 0 minutes Servings: 3
Ingredients:

- 1 cup quinoa
- cup oats
- 1/2 cup figs (dried) 1/2 cup honey
- 1/2 cup almonds (chopped) 1/2 cup apricots (dried)
- 1/2 cup wheat germ
- 1/2 cup pineapple (dried and chopped) 1 tbsp cornstarch

Directions:

1. Mix the fixing in a mixing bowl until you

obtain a well-balanced mixture. Put the batter on a baking tray or plate and flatten it. Ensure that the mixture is at least one inch thick. Let it cool before you cut it into pieces and serve.

Nutrition: Calories 766 g
Fat 15.7 g
Carbohydrates 144.2 g
Protein 22.2 g
Sodium 12 mg

Colorful Pops

Preparation time: 15 minutes Cooking time: 0 minutes Servings: 6
Ingredients:

- cups of watermelon, strawberries, and cantaloupe (diced) 2 cups pure apple juice
- 2 cups fresh blueberries
- 6 craft sticks
- 6 paper cups

Directions:

1. Mix all the fruit in a mixing bowl. Divide the fruit salad into the paper cups and pour the apple juice. Ensure that the apple juice only covers half the paper cup. Deep-freeze the cups for an hour or until they are partially frozen.

2. Remove the cups and add the sticks to the cups, and deep freeze for one more hour. Serve them as colorful pops!

Nutrition: Calories 83 g
Fat 0.2 g
Carbohydrates 20.8 g
Protein 0.7 g
Sodium 8 mg

Pumpkin Pie Recipe

Preparation time: 15 minutes Cooking time: 50 minutes Servings: 2
Ingredients:

- 1 cup ginger snaps
- 8 ounces canned pumpkin 1/4 cup egg whites
- 1/4 cup erythritol
- 1 tsp pumpkin pie spice
- 6 ounces evaporated skim milk Cooking spray

Directions:

1. Preheat the oven to 300 degrees Fahrenheit. Oiled a glass pie pan with cooking spray. Crumble the ginger snaps and pat them into

the glass pan. Mix the rest of the fixing in a mixing bowl and pour it into the prepared glass pie pan.

2. Bake the dish for fifty minutes or until a knife inserted in the center comes out clean. Transfer the pie pan into the refrigerator and allow it to cool. Serve cold.

Nutrition: Calories 792 g

Fat 16.6 g

Carbohydrates 172.7 g

Protein 20 g

Sodium 1181 mg

Walnut and Oatmeal Chocolate Chip Cookies

Preparation time: 15 minutes Cooking time: 20 minutes Servings: 4

Ingredients:

- cup rolled oats
- 1/4 cup all-purpose flour
- 1/4 cup whole-wheat pastry flour 1/2 tsp ground cinnamon
- 1/4 tsp baking soda 1/4 tsp salt
- 1/4 tsp tahini
- 1tbsp unsalted butter (cubed) 1/2 cup erythritol
- 1/2 cup maple syrup
- 2 eggs (one whole and one egg white) 1/2 tbsp vanilla extract
- 1/2 cup bittersweet chocolate chips 1/4 cup chopped walnuts

Directions:

1. Place racks in the oven's upper and lower parts and preheat the oven to 300 degrees Fahrenheit. Prepare or arrange two lined baking sheets with parchment paper. Combine the oats, whole-wheat flour, all-purpose flour, baking soda, cinnamon, and salt in a bowl and whisk.

2. Beat butter and tahini in a large mixing bowl and blend until you obtain a paste. Add maple syrup and granulated sugar to the bowl and continue to beat until you get a well-combined mixture. Note that the mixture will still be slightly grainy.

3. Now, add the vanilla extract, egg white, and whole egg to the bowl and continue to whisk until you obtain a well-combined mixture.

4. Stir in the oat's mixture, chocolate chips,

and walnuts into the bowl. Wet your hands slightly, roll one tablespoon of the batter into a small ball, and place it on the baking sheet. Flatten the ball out but ensure that the sides do not crack. Continue with the remaining batter and leave at least a two-inch space between each cookie.

5. Bake the cookies for twenty minutes or until golden brown. Cool the cookies for two minutes before you transfer them onto the wire rack to cool completely.

Directions: Nutrition: Calories 530 g

Fat 14.8 g

Carbohydrates 98.6 g

Protein 10.6 g

Sodium 280 mg

Apple Dumplings

Preparation time: 10 minutes Cooking time: 30 minutes Servings: 6

Ingredients:

Dough:

- 1 tablespoon butter
- 1 teaspoon honey
- cup whole-wheat flour
- tablespoons buckwheat flour 2 tablespoons rolled oats
- 2 tablespoons brandy or apple liquor Apple filling:
- 6 large tart apples, thinly sliced
- teaspoon nutmeg
- tablespoons honey Zest of one lemon

Directions:

1. Warm oven to heat at 350 degrees F. Combine flours with oats, honey, and butter in a food processor. Pulse this mixture for few times, then stirs in apple liquor or brandy. Mix until it forms a ball. Wrap it in a plastic sheet.

2. Refrigerate for 2 hours. Mix apples with honey, nutmeg, and lemon zest, then set it aside. Spread the dough into ¼ inch thick sheet. Cut it into 8-inch circles and layer the greased muffin cups with the dough circles.

3. Divide the apple mixture into the muffin cups and seal the dough from the top. Bake for 30 minutes at 350 degrees F until golden brown. Enjoy.

Nutrition:

Calories 178

Fat 5.7 g
Cholesterol 15 mg
Sodium 114 mg
Carbs 12.4 g Fiber 0.2g Sugar 15 g
Protein 9.1 g

Berries Marinated in Balsamic Vinegar

Preparation time: 10 minutes Cooking time:
0 minutes
Servings: 2 Ingredients:
- 1/4 cup balsamic vinegar 2 tablespoons brown sugar 1 teaspoon vanilla extract 1/2 cup sliced strawberries 1/2 cup blueberries
- 1/2 cup raspberries 2 shortbread biscuits

Directions:

1. Combine balsamic vinegar, vanilla, and brown sugar in a small bowl. Toss strawberries with raspberries and blueberries in a bowl. Pour the vinegar mixture on top and marinate them for 15 minutes. Serve immediately.

Nutrition: Calories 176
Fat 11.9 g
Cholesterol 78 mg
Sodium 79 mg
Carbs 33 g
Fiber 1.1 g
Sugar 10.3 g
Protein 13 g

Lemon Pudding Cakes

Preparation time: 10 minutes Cooking time: 40 minutes Servings: 4
Ingredients:
- 2 eggs
- 1/4 teaspoon salt 3/4 cup sugar
- 1 cup skim milk
- 1/3 cup freshly squeezed lemon juice 3 tablespoons all-purpose flour
- tablespoon finely grated lemon peel 1 tablespoon melted butter

Directions:

1. Warm oven at 350 degrees F. Grease the custard cups with cooking oil. Whisk egg whites with salt and ¼ cup sugar in a mixer until it forms stiff peaks. Beat egg yolks with ½ cup sugar until mixed.

2. Stir in lemon juice, milk, butter, flour, and lemon peel. Mix it until smooth. Fold in the egg white mixture. Divide the batter into the custard cups. Bake them for 40 minutes

until golden from the top. Serve.
Nutrition: Calories 174
Fat 10.2 g
Cholesterol 120 mg
Sodium 176 mg
Carbs 19 g
Fiber 1.9 g
Sugar 11.4 g
Protein 12.8 g

Mixed Berry Whole-Grain Coffee Cake

Preparation time: 10 minutes Cooking time: 30 minutes Servings: 6
Ingredients:
- 1/2 cup of skim milk 1 tbsp vinegar
- tbsp canola oil
- 1 tsp vanilla
- 1 egg
- 1/3 cup of packed brown sugar
- 1 cup of whole-wheat pastry flour 1/2 tsp baking soda
- 1/2 tsp ground cinnamon
- 1/8 tsp salt
- 1 cup of frozen mixed berries
- 1/4 cup of low-fat granola, slightly crushed

Directions:

1. Warm oven to heat at 350 degrees F. Grease an 8-inch baking pan with cooking spray and dust it with flour. Combine milk with vanilla, oil, vinegar, brown sugar, and egg until smooth.

2. Add baking soda, cinnamon, salt, and flour. Mix well. Fold in half of the berries and transfer the batter to the pan. Top it with the berries and granola. Bake for 30 minutes until golden brown. Serve.

Nutrition: Calories 135 Fat 24g
Cholesterol 61 mg
Sodium 562 mg
Carbs 23 g
Fiber 1.7 g
Sugar 39 g Protein 11g

Strawberries and Cream Cheese Crepes

Preparation time: 10 minutes Cooking time: 10 minutes Servings: 2
Ingredients:
- 4 tbsp cream cheese, softened 2 tbsp powdered sugar, sifted 2 tsp vanilla extract
- 2 pre-packaged crepes, each about 8 inches

in diameter 8 strawberries, hulled and sliced

Directions:

1. Set the oven to heat at 325 degrees F. Grease a baking dish with cooking spray. Mix cream cheese with vanilla plus powdered sugar in a mixer. Spread the cream cheese mixture on each crepe and top it with 2 tablespoons strawberries.

2. Roll the crepes and place them in the baking dish. Bake them within 10 minutes until golden brown. Garnish as desired. Serve.

Nutrition: Calories 144
Fat 4.9 g
Cholesterol 11 mg
Sodium 13 mg
Carbs 19.3 g
Fiber 1.9 g
Sugar 9.7 g
Protein 3.4 g

Healthy Blueberry & Banana Muffins

Preparation Time: 30 minutes Cooking Time: 25 minutes Servings: 12
Ingredients:
- 3/4 cup mashed ripe banana
- 3/4 cup + 2 tbsp almond milk, unsweetened 1 teaspoon apple cider vinegar
- 1/4 cup pure maple syrup
- teaspoon pure vanilla extract 1/4 cup coconut oil, melted 1/2 teaspoon baking soda
- teaspoons baking powder 4 tablespoons coconut sugar 1 1/2 teaspoons cinnamon
- 2 cups white spelt flour 1 1/4 cups of blueberries
- 1/2 cup walnut halves, chopped

Directions:

1. Prepare lined 12-muffin tin with muffin liners and preheat oven to

2. 350oF. In a large mixing bowl, whisk well-mashed bananas, almond milk, vinegar, maple syrup, vanilla, melted coconut oil, baking soda, baking powder, coconut sugar, and cinnamon.

3. Whisk well until thoroughly incorporated. Fold in spelt flour. Add blueberries and walnut halves. Evenly divide batter into prepared muffin tins. Bake within 25

minutes. Cool completely. Serve.
Nutrition: Calories: 226.5 Protein: 5g
Carbs: 33.4g Fat: 8.1g Sodium: 67mg

Tart Raspberry Crumble Bar

Preparation Time: 50 minutes Cooking Time: 45 minutes Servings: 9
Ingredients:
- 1/2 cup whole toasted almonds 1 3/4 cups whole wheat flour 1/4 tsp salt
- 3/4 cup cold butter, unsalted, cut into cubes 3 tbsp cold water, or more if needed
- 1/2 cup granulated sugar
- 18-ounce fresh raspberries

Directions:

1. Pulse almonds using a food processor until chopped coarsely. Transfer to a bowl. Add flour and salt into the food processor and pulse until a bit combined. Put butter, then pulse until you have a coarse batter. Evenly divide batter into two bowls.

2. In the first bowl of batter, knead well until it forms a ball. Wrap in cling wrap, flatten a bit, and chill for an hour for easy handling. In the second bowl of batter, add sugar. In a pinching motion, pinch batter to form clusters of streusels. Set aside.

3. When ready to bake, warm oven to 375oF and lightly grease an 8x8- inch baking pan with cooking spray. Discard cling wrap and evenly press dough on the bottom of the pan, up to 1-inch up the pan's sides, making sure that everything is covered in dough.

4. Evenly spread raspberries. Top with streusel. Bake within 45 minutes. Remove from oven and cool within 20 minutes before slicing into 9 equal bars. Serve and enjoy or store in a lidded container for 10-days in the fridge.

Nutrition: Calories: 235.7
Protein: 4.4g Carbs: 29.1g Fat: 11.3g Sodium: 73mg

Easy Strawberry Sheet Cake

Preparation Time: 1 Hour Cooking Time: 60 minutes Servings: 16
Ingredients:
- 9 tablespoons unsalted butter 3/4 teaspoon salt
- 1 1/2 cups granulated sugar, divided

- 1 large egg
- 1 large egg yolk
- 1/2 teaspoons vanilla extract 3/4 cup low-fat milk
- 1/4 teaspoons baking powder 2 1/4 cups whole wheat flour
- 1 1/2 pounds fresh and a bit overripe strawberry, hulled and halved

Directions:

1. Oiled a 9x13-inch baking pan with cooking spray and preheat oven to

2. 350oF. Remove 3 tbsp of sugar and set aside. In a blender, blend well butter, salt, sugar, egg, egg yolk, vanilla extract, milk, and baking powder until smooth and creamy.

3. Add flour and blend until thoroughly incorporated. Scrape down sides of the blender and blend once more. Pour batter evenly into prepared pan. Evenly spread halved strawberries on top of batter. Sprinkle the set aside 3 tbsp sugar on top of strawberries.

4. Pop in the oven and bake within 45 minutes or until golden brown. Remove from oven and cool within 20 minutes before slicing into 16 equal pieces. Serve.

Nutrition: Calories: 182.4 Protein: 5g
Carbs: 25.3g Fat: 6.8g Sodium: 163mg

Easy Coconut-Carrot Cake Balls

Preparation Time: 10 minutes Cooking Time: 0 minutes Servings: 16
Ingredients:
- 3/4 cup carrot, peeled and finely shredded 1 cup packed Medjool date, pitted
- 1 ¾ cups raw walnuts
- 3/4 tsp ground cinnamon 1/2 tsp ground ginger
- pinch ground nutmeg
- tsp vanilla extract 5 tbsp almond flour 1/4 cup raisins
- ¼ cup desiccated coconut flakes

Directions:

1. In a food processor, process dates until it clumps. Transfer to a bowl. In the same food processor, process walnuts, cinnamon, ginger, and nutmeg. Process until it resembles a fine meal.

2. Add the processed dates, extract, almond flour, and shredded carrots. Pulse until you form a loose dough but not mushy. Do not over-pulse. Transfer to a bowl.

3. Pulse desiccated coconut into tinier flakes and transfer to a small plate. Divide the carrot batter into 4 and then divide each part into 4 to make a total of 16 equal-sized balls. Roll it in the coconut flakes, place in a lidded container, and refrigerate for 2 hours before enjoying.

Nutrition: Calories: 77.9 Protein: 1.5g
Carbs: 3.8g Fat: 6.3g Sodium: 8mg

Banana Delight

Preparation Time: 15 minutes Cooking Time: 12 minutes Servings: 4
Ingredients:
- 1 tbsp sodium-free baking powder 1 tbsp sugar
- 1 cup flour
- 1 tbsp oil
- ¼ cup egg substitute
- ½ tsp nutmeg
- 1 cup banana (chopped) 1 tbsp oil
- ½ cup skim milk

Directions:

1. In a bowl, mix and stir baking powder, sugar, and flour. Mix oil, egg, and milk, then add nutmeg and banana in a separate bowl. Add the mixture into the bowl of dry ingredients.

2. In a hot frying pan, drop just by tablespoonfuls and fry for about 2 to 3 minutes. Wait until it is golden brown, then drain and serve.

Nutrition: Calories: 210.1 Protein: 5.7g Carbs: 37.6g Fat: 4.1g Sodium: 141mg

Healthy Banana-Choco Ice Cream

Preparation Time: 10 minutes Cooking Time: 0 minutes Servings: 4
Ingredients:
- 3 medium bananas, peeled and frozen 3 tbsp Unsweetened Cocoa Powder 1/2 tsp peppermint extract

Directions:

1. Place all the fixing in a blender and puree until it resembles soft-serve ice cream. Evenly divide into 4 bowls. Serve and

enjoy

Nutrition: Calories: 88 Protein: 1.7g Carbs: 22.6g Fat: 0.8g Sodium: 2.0 mg

Healthy Chocolate Mousse

Preparation Time: 10 minutes Cooking Time: 0 minutes Servings: 4

Ingredients:

- 1 large, ripe avocado
- 1/4 cup sweetened almond milk 1 tbsp coconut oil
- 1/4 cup cocoa or cacao powder 1 tsp vanilla extract

Directions:

1. Process all the fixing using a food processor until smooth and creamy. Chill within 4 hours. Serve and enjoy.

Nutrition: Calories: 125 Protein: 1.2g Carbs: 6.9g Fat: 11.0g
Sodium: 22.0 mg

Almond Rice Pudding

Preparation time: 25 minutes Cooking time: 20 minutes Servings: 6

Ingredients:

- 3 cups 1% milk 1 cup white rice 1/4 cup sugar
- teaspoon vanilla
- 1/4 teaspoon almond extract Cinnamon
- 1/4 cup toasted almonds

Directions:

1. Mix milk plus rice in a medium saucepan. Bring them to a boil. Reduce heat and simmer for 20 minutes with the lid on until the rice is soft.

2. Remove, then put the sugar, vanilla, almond extract, and cinnamon. Put toasted almonds on top, then serve warm.

Nutrition: Calories 180
Fat 1.5 g
Carbohydrates 36 g
Protein 7 g
Fiber 1 g
Sodium 65 mg
Potassium 1 mg

Apples and Cream Shake

Preparation time: 10 minutes Cooking time: 0 minutes Servings: 4

Ingredients:

- cups vanilla low-fat ice cream 1 cup apple

sauce

- 1/4 teaspoon ground cinnamon
- 1 cup fat-free skim milk

Directions:

1. In a blender container, combine the low-fat ice cream, applesauce, and cinnamon. Cover and blend until smooth. Add fat-free skim milk. Cover and blend until mixed. Pour into glasses. Serve immediately.

Nutrition: Calories 160
Fat 3 g
Carbohydrates 27 g
Protein 6 g
Fiber 1 g
Sodium 80 mg
Potassium 46 mg

Baked Stuffed Apples

Preparation time: 10 minutes Cooking time: 8 minutes Servings: 4

Ingredients:

- 4 Jonagold apples
- 1/4 cup flaked coconut
- 1/4 cup chopped dried apricots 2 teaspoons grated orange zest 1/2 cup orange juice
- 2 tablespoons brown sugar

Directions:

1. Peel the apples 1/3, then hollow out the center with a knife. Arrange, peeled end up, in microwave-safe baking dish. Combine coconut, apricots, and orange zest. Divide to fill centers of apples evenly.

2. Mix orange juice plus brown sugar, then put over apples. Microwave on high within 8 minutes or until apples are tender. Cool before serving.

Nutrition: Calories 192
Fat 2 g
Carbohydrates 46 g
Protein 1 g
Fiber 6 g
Sodium 19 mg

Carrot-Cake Smoothie

Preparation Time: 5 minutes Cooking Time: 0 minute Servings: 2

Ingredients:

- 1 frozen banana, peeled and diced
- 1 cup carrots, diced (peeled if preferred) 1 cup nonfat or low-fat milk
- ½ cup ice

- ¼ cup diced pineapple, frozen
- ½ teaspoon ground cinnamon Pinch nutmeg
- ½ cup nonfat or low-fat vanilla Greek yogurt Optional toppings: chopped walnuts, grated carrots

Directions:

1. Add all of the fixing listed to a blender and process until smooth and creamy. Serve immediately with optional toppings as desired.

Nutrition: Calories: 180
Fat: 1 g
Cholesterol: 5 mg
Sodium: 114 mg
Carbs: 36 g
Fiber: 4 g
Sugar: 25 g
Protein: 10 g

Easy Cinnamon Baked Apples

Preparation Time: 5 minutes Cooking Time: 45 minutes Servings: 4
Ingredients:

- 4 apples, cored, peeled, and sliced thin
- ½ tablespoon ground cinnamon
- ¼ cup brown sugar
- ¼ teaspoon ground nutmeg
- Optional: 2 teaspoons freshly squeezed lemon juice

Directions:

1. Preheat the oven to 375°F. Place apples in a mixing bowl and gently mix all the other ingredients. Put apples in a nonstick pan.

2. Bake within 45 minutes, stirring at least once every 15 minutes. Once they are soft, cook for another few minutes to thicken the cinnamon sauce. Serve.

Nutrition: Calories: 117
Fat: 1 g
Sodium: 4 mg
Carbs: 34 g
Fiber: 5 g
Sugar: 28 g
Protein: 0 g

Chocolate Cake in A Mug

Preparation Time: 5 minutes Cooking Time: 1 minute Servings: 1
Ingredients:

- 3 tablespoons white whole-wheat flour

- tablespoons unsweetened cocoa powder 2 teaspoons sugar
- 1/8 teaspoon baking powder 1 egg white
- ½ teaspoon olive oil
- tablespoons nonfat or low-fat milk
- ½ teaspoon vanilla extract Cooking spray

Directions:

1. Place the flour, cocoa, sugar, and baking powder in a small bowl and whisk until combined. Then add in the egg white, olive oil, milk, and vanilla extract, and mix to combine.

2. Oiled a mug with cooking spray and pour batter into mug. Microwave on high for 60 seconds or until set. Serve.

Nutrition: Calories: 217
Fat: 4 g
Cholesterol: 1 mg
Sodium: 139 mg
Carbs: 35 g
Fiber: 7 g
Sugar: 12 g
Protein: 11 g

Peanut Butter Banana "Ice Cream"

Preparation Time: 10 minutes Cooking Time: 0 minute Servings: 4
Ingredients:

- 2 tablespoons peanut butter
- 4 bananas, very ripe, peeled and sliced into ½-inch rings

Directions:

1. On a large baking sheet or plate, spread the banana slices in an even layer. Freeze for 1 to 2 hours. Puree the frozen banana until it forms a smooth and creamy mixture in a food processor or blender, scraping down the bowl as needed.

2. the peanut butter, pureeing until just combined. For a soft-serve ice cream consistency, serve immediately. For a harder consistency, place the ice cream in the freezer for a few hours before serving.

Nutrition: Calories: 153
Fat: 4 g
Sodium: 4 mg
Carbs: 29 g
Fiber: 4 g
Sugar: 15 g
Protein: 3 g

Banana-Cashew Cream Mousse

Preparation Time: 55 minutes Cooking Time: 0 minute Servings: 2

Ingredients:

- ½ cup cashews, presoaked 1 tablespoon honey
- 1 teaspoon vanilla extract
- 1 cup plain nonfat Greek yogurt
- 1 large banana, sliced (reserve 4 slices for garnish)

Directions:

1. Put the cashews in your small bowl, then cover with 1 cup of water. Dip at room temperature within 2 to 3 hours. Drain, rinse and set aside. Place honey, vanilla extract, cashews, and bananas in a blender or food processor.

2. Blend until smooth. Place mixture in a medium bowl. Fold in yogurt, mix well. Cover, then chill within 45 minutes. Portion mousse into 2 serving bowls. Garnish each with 2 banana slices.

Nutrition: Calories: 329

Fat: 14 g

Sodium: 64 mg

Carbs: 37 g

Fiber: 3 g

Sugar: 24 g

Protein: 17 g

Grilled Plums with Vanilla Bean Frozen Yogurt

Preparation Time: 10 minutes Cooking Time: 15 minutes Servings: 4

Ingredients:

- 4 large plums, sliced in half and pitted 1 tablespoon olive oil
- 1 tablespoon honey
- teaspoon ground cinnamon
- cups vanilla bean frozen yogurt

Directions:

1. Preheat the grill to medium heat. Brush the plum halves with olive oil. Grill, flesh-side down, for 4 to 5 minutes, then flip and cook for another 4 to 5 minutes, until just tender.

2. Mix the honey plus cinnamon in a small bowl. Scoop the frozen yogurt into 4 bowls. Place 2 plum halves in each bowl and drizzle each with the cinnamon-honey mixture.

Nutrition: Calories: 192

Fat: 8 g

Sodium: 63 mg

Carbs: 30 g

Fiber: 1 g

Sugar: 28 g

Protein: 3 g

Key Lime Cherry "Nice" Cream

Preparation Time: 10 minutes Cooking Time: 15 minutes Servings: 4

Ingredients:

- 4 frozen bananas, peeled
- 1 cup frozen dark sweet cherries Zest and juice of 1 lime, divided
- ½ teaspoon vanilla extract
- ¼ teaspoon kosher or sea salt

Directions:

1. Blend the fixing in a food processor and enjoy a frozen treat. Place the bananas, cherries, lime juice, vanilla extract, and salt in a food processor and purée until smooth, scraping the sides as needed.

2. Transfer the "nice" cream to bowls and top with the lime zest. For leftovers, place the "nice" cream in airtight containers and store them in the freezer for up to 1 month. Let thaw for 30 minutes, until it reaches a soft-serve ice cream texture.

Nutrition: Calories: 150

Fat: 0 g

Sodium: 147 mg

Carbs: 37 g

Fiber: 4 g

Sugar: 21 g

Protein: 2 g

Oatmeal Dark Chocolate Chip Peanut Butter Cookies

Preparation Time: 15 minutes Cooking Time: 10 minutes Servings: 24

Ingredients:

- 1½ cups natural creamy peanut butter
- ½ cup dark brown sugar 2 large eggs
- cup old-fashioned rolled oats 1 teaspoon baking soda
- ½ teaspoon kosher or sea salt
- ½ cup dark chocolate chips

Directions:

1. Preheat the oven to 350°F. Line a baking sheet with parchment paper.

2. Whip the peanut butter in the bowl of a stand mixer until very smooth. Continue beating and add the brown sugar, then one egg at a time, until fluffy.

3. Beat in the oats, baking soda, and salt until combined. Fold in the dark chocolate chips. Put the cookie dough on the baking sheet, about 2 inches apart. Bake within 8 to 10 minutes, depending on your preferred level of doneness.

Nutrition: Calories: 152
Fat: 10 g
Sodium: 131 mg
Carbs: 12 g
Fiber: 2 g
Sugar: 8 g
Protein: 4 g

Peach Crumble Muffins

Preparation Time: 25 minutes Cooking Time: 25 minutes Servings: 12
Ingredients:
For the crumble:

- tablespoons dark brown sugar 1 tablespoon honey
- 1 teaspoon ground cinnamon 2 tablespoons canola oil
- ½ cup old-fashioned rolled oats
- For the peach muffins:
- 1 teaspoon baking powder 1 teaspoon baking soda
- 1 teaspoon ground cinnamon
- ½ teaspoon ground ginger
- ½ teaspoon kosher or sea salt
- ¼ cup canola oil
- ¼ cup dark brown sugar 2 large eggs
- 1½ teaspoons vanilla extract
- ¼ cup plain nonfat Greek yogurt 3 peaches, diced (about 1½ cups)
- 1¾ cups whole-wheat flour or whole-wheat pastry flour

Directions:
In a small bowl, mix the brown sugar, honey, cinnamon, canola oil, and oats until combined for the crumble. For your muffins, mix the flour, baking powder, baking soda, cinnamon, ginger, and salt in a large bowl.

Beat the canola oil, brown sugar, and one egg at a time in a separate bowl, using a hand mixer until fluffy. Beat in the vanilla extract and yogurt. Put the flour mixture in the bowl and whisk until the ingredients are just combined.

1. Fold in the diced peaches with a spatula. Preheat the oven to 425°F. Oiled a 12-cup muffin tin with muffin liners. Fill each muffin well with batter about three-quarters of the way full. Scoop the crumble batter on top of each.

2. Bake for 5 to 6 minutes, then reduce the oven temperature to 350°F and bake for 15 to 18 additional minutes. Cool before removing from the muffin tin. Once completely cooled, serve.

Nutrition: Calories: 187
Fat: 8 g
Sodium: 216 mg
Carbs: 26 g
Fiber: 3 g
Sugar: 10 g
Protein: 4 g

Karen's Apple Kugel

Preparation time: 15 minutes Cooking time: 25 minutes Servings: 8
Ingredients:

- sheets unsalted matzo 2 cups of water
- tart green apples
- 1 tablespoon freshly squeezed lemon juice 3 tablespoons unsalted butter, melted
- 1/4 cup brown sugar
- 1/2 cup seedless raisins 3 egg whites
- 11/2 teaspoons ground cinnamon

Directions:

1. Preheat oven to 400°F. Take out an 8" × 11" baking dish and set aside. Place the matzo in an 8-inch square baking pan. Pour the water into the pan and set aside to rehydrate.

2. Peel apples, core, and cut into quarters. Cut each quarter crosswise into thirds and then lengthwise into slices no more than 1/4 inch thick. Transfer apples to a mixing bowl.

3. Check on the matzo. When soft, drain the matzo and squeeze out excess water. Place matzo into the mixing bowl. Put the rest of the fixing and stir well to combine.

4. Pour mixture into the 8" × 11" baking dish. Bake within 25 minutes. Remove from the

oven. Set on a wire rack to cool. Cut into portions and serve warm or cool.

Nutrition: Calories: 181
Fat: 4 g
Protein: 3 g
Sodium: 24 mg
Fiber: 2 g
Carbohydrates: 34 g
Sugar: 21 g

Peach Cobbler

Preparation time: 15 minutes Cooking time: 25 minutes Servings: 8
Ingredients:

- 6 ripe peaches, peeled and sliced 3 tablespoons sugar
- Juice of 1 fresh lemon
- 11/4 cups unbleached all-purpose flour 1/2 cup white whole-wheat flour
- 2/3 cup sugar
- 1 teaspoon sodium-free baking powder
- 4 tablespoons unsalted butter, melted and cooled 1 egg white
- 1/2 cup low-fat milk
- 1 tablespoon pure vanilla extract

Directions:

1. Preheat oven to 425°F. Take out a 9" × 13" baking dish and set aside. Put the sliced peaches into a mixing bowl, put sugar plus lemon juice, and toss well to coat. Transfer to the baking dish. Set aside.

2. Mix the flours, sugar, plus baking powder into a mixing bowl. Add the melted butter, egg white, milk, and vanilla and stir well to combine. Scoop batter over sliced peaches.

3. Put baking dish on middle rack in the oven, then bake for 25 minutes. Remove dish from oven and place on a wire rack to cool. Serve warm or cool.

Nutrition: Calories: 273
Fat: 6 g
Protein: 5 g
Sodium: 15 mg
Fiber: 3 g
Carbohydrates: 50 g
Sugar: 28 g

Blueberry Pudding Cake

Preparation time: 15 minutes Cooking time: 25 minutes Servings: 6
Ingredients:

- 3 cups blueberries
- 3/4 cup sugar, divided
- tablespoon freshly squeezed lemon juice 6 tablespoons unsalted butter, softened
- teaspoons pure vanilla extract
- 1 teaspoon freshly grated lemon zest 1 egg white
- 11/2 teaspoons sodium-free baking powder 2 tablespoons low-fat milk
- 2/3 cup white whole-wheat flour

Directions:

1. Preheat oven to 400°F. Oiled an 8-inch square baking pan lightly with oil and set aside. Place blueberries into a mixing bowl. Add 1/4 cup sugar and the lemon juice and toss well to coat.

2. Pour berries into the prepared baking pan, place on the middle rack in the oven, and bake for 5 minutes. Remove from the oven and set aside. Place the butter and remaining 1/2 cup sugar into a mixing bowl and beat to combine.

3. Add the vanilla, lemon zest, and egg white and mix well. Add the baking powder and milk and stir. Gradually add in the flour, mixing until combined.

4. Pour batter over the cooked blueberries. Bake within 20 minutes, until golden brown. Serve warm or cool.

Nutrition: Calories: 300
Fat: 12 g
Protein: 2 g
Sodium: 14 mg
Fiber: 2 g
Carbohydrates: 46 g
Sugar: 32 g

Peanut Butter Banana Bread Bites

Preparation Time: 10 minutes Cooking Time: 20 minutes Servings: 24
Ingredients:

- 1½ cups whole-wheat pastry flour 2 tablespoons ground flaxseed
- teaspoon baking powder
- ½ teaspoon kosher or sea salt
- ½ teaspoon ground cinnamon 3 ripe bananas, peeled
- large eggs
- 2 tablespoons canola oil

- ½ cup dark brown sugar 2 tablespoons honey
- ½ cup natural creamy peanut butter
- ¼ cup nonfat Greek yogurt 1 teaspoon vanilla extract
- ¼ cup unsalted roasted peanuts, crushed

Directions:

1. Preheat the oven to 350°F. Oiled a 24-cup mini muffin tin with cooking spray. In a bowl, whisk the flour, flaxseed, baking powder, salt, and cinnamon. Beat the bananas in a separate bowl with a hand mixer set on low.

2. Add the eggs, one at a time, then add the canola oil, brown sugar, and honey. Adjust the speed to medium and beat until fluffy. Add the peanut butter, Greek yogurt, and vanilla extract and mix until combined. Lower the speed to low, then beat in the dry ingredient mixture until just combined.

3. Put the mixture into each of the muffin wells about three-quarters of the way full. Tap it on the counter until the batter is evenly spread out.

4. Top with the crushed peanuts. Bake within 20 minutes, until a toothpick inserted into the center of a bite, comes out clean. Let rest on the counter until cooled. Remove the bites from the muffin tin. Serve.

Nutrition: Calories: 123
Fat: 5 g
Sodium: 81 mg
Carbs: 17 g
Fiber: 2 g
Sugar: 8 g
Protein: 3 g

Toasted Almond Ambrosia

Preparation Time: 10 minutes Cooking Time: 20 minutes Servings: 2
Ingredients:
- ½ Cup Almonds, Slivered
- ½ Cup Coconut, Shredded & Unsweetened 3 Cups Pineapple, Cubed
- 5 Oranges, Segment
- 2 Red Apples, Cored & Diced 2 Tablespoons Cream Sherry Mint Leaves, Fresh to Garnish
- Banana, Halved Lengthwise, Peeled & Sliced

Directions:

1. Start by heating your oven to 325, and then get out a baking sheet. Roast your almonds for ten minutes, making sure they're spread out evenly. Transfer them to a plate and then toast your coconut on the same baking sheet.

2. Toast for ten minutes. Mix your banana, sherry, oranges, apples, and pineapple in a bowl. Divide the mixture, not serving bowls and top with coconut and almonds. Garnish with mint before serving.

Nutrition: Calories: 177
Fat: 4.9 g
Sodium: 13 mg
Carbs: 36 g
Fiber: 0 g
Sugar: 0 g
Protein: 3.4 g

Apricot Biscotti

Preparation Time: 10 minutes Cooking Time: 50 minutes Servings: 4
Ingredients:
- Tablespoons Honey, Dark 2 Tablespoons Olive Oil
- ½ Teaspoon Almond Extract
- ¼ Cup Almonds, Chopped Roughly 2/3 Cup Apricots, Dried
- 2 Tablespoons Milk, 1% & Low Fat
- 2 Eggs, Beaten Lightly
- ¾ Cup Whole Wheat Flour
- ¾ Cup All-Purpose Flour
- ¼ Cup Brown Sugar, Packed Firm 1 Teaspoon Baking Powder

Directions:

1. Start by heating the oven to 350, then mix your baking powder, brown sugar, and flours in a bowl. Whisk your canola oil, eggs, almond extract, honey, and milk. Mix until it forms a smooth dough. Fold in the apricots and almonds.

2. Put your dough on plastic wrap, and then roll it out to a twelve-inch- long and three-inch wide rectangle. Place this dough on a baking sheet, and bake for twenty-five minutes. It should turn golden brown. Allow it to cool, slice it into ½ inch thick slices, and then bake for another fifteen minutes. It should be crispy.

Nutrition: Calories: 291

Fat: 2 g
Sodium: 123 mg
Carbs: 12 g
Fiber: 0 g
Sugar: 0 g
Protein: 2 g

Apple & Berry Cobbler

Preparation Time: 10 minutes Cooking Time: 40 minutes Servings: 4
Ingredients:
Filling:

- Cup Blueberries, Fresh 2 Cups Apples, Chopped 1 Cup Raspberries, Fresh
- Tablespoons Brown Sugar 1 Teaspoon Lemon Zest
- 2 Teaspoon Lemon Juice, Fresh
- ½ Teaspoon Ground Cinnamon 1 ½ Tablespoons Corn Starch
- Topping:
- ¾ Cup Whole Wheat Pastry Flour 1 ½ Tablespoon Brown Sugar
- ½ Teaspoon Vanilla Extract, Pure
- ¼ Cup Soy Milk
- ¼ Teaspoon Sea Salt, Fine 1 Egg White

Directions:

1. Turn your oven to 350, and get out six small ramekins. Grease them with cooking spray. Mix your lemon juice, lemon zest, blueberries, sugar, cinnamon, raspberries, and apples in a bowl. Stir in your cornstarch, mixing until it dissolves.

2. Beat your egg white in a different bowl, whisking it with sugar, vanilla, soy milk, and pastry flour. Divide your berry mixture between the ramekins and top with the vanilla topping. Put your ramekins on a baking sheet, baking for thirty minutes. The

top should be golden brown before serving.
Nutrition: Calories: 131
Fat: 0 g
Sodium: 14 mg
Carbs: 13.8 g
Fiber: 0 g
Sugar: 0 g
Protein: 7.2 g

Mixed Fruit Compote Cups

Preparation Time: 5 minutes Cooking Time: 15 minutes Servings: 2
Ingredients:

- 1 ¼ Cup Water
- ½ Cup Orange juice
- 12 Ounces Mixed Dried Fruit 1 Teaspoon Ground Cinnamon
- ¼ Teaspoon Ground Ginger
- ¼ Teaspoon Ground Nutmeg
- 4 Cups Vanilla Frozen Yogurt, Fat-Free

Directions:

1. Mix your dried fruit, nutmeg, cinnamon, water, orange juice, and ginger in a saucepan. Cover, and allow it to cook over medium heat for ten minutes. Remove the cover and then cook for another ten minutes. Add your frozen yogurt to serving cups, and top with the fruit mixture.

Nutrition: Calories: 228
Fat: 5.7 g
Cholesterol: 15 mg
Sodium: 114 mg
Carbs: 12.4 g
Fiber: 0 g
Sugar: 0 g
Protein: 9.1 g

28-Day Meal Plan – Average Calories: 1074

	Breakfast	Lunch	Dinner	Total Calories
DAY 1	Spinach, Mushroom, and Feta Cheese Scramble Calories:236	Cod Soup Calories:344	Shrimp and Onion Ginger Dressing Calories:360	**940**
DAY 2	Apple Pancakes Calories:378	Sweet Potatoes and Zucchini Soup Calories:270	Fruit Shrimp Soup Calories:290	**938**
DAY 3	Super-Simple Granola Calories:254	Chickpea Cauliflower Tikka Masala Calories:323	Tofu & Green Bean Stir-Fry Calories:380	**957**
DAY 4	Energy Sunrise Muffins Calories:292	Peanut Vegetable Pad Thai Calories:393	Sweet Potato Cakes with Classic Guacamole Calories:369	**1054**
DAY 5	Spinach, Egg, And Cheese Breakfast Quesadillas Calories:453	Tofu & Green Bean Stir-Fry Calories:380	Chickpea Cauliflower Tikka Masala Calories:323	**1156**
DAY 6	Creamy Avocado and Egg Salad Sandwiches Calories:488	Caramelized Fennel and Sardines with Penne Calories:400	Peanut Vegetable Pad Thai Calories:393	**1281**
DAY 7	Breakfast Hash Calories:323	Air-Fryer Fish Cakes Calories:399	Eggplant Parmesan Stacks Calories:377	**1099**
DAY 8	Hearty Breakfast Casserole Calories:378	Lemon Herb Baked Salmon Calories:377	Roasted Vegetable Enchiladas Calories:335	**1090**
DAY 9	Creamy Apple-Avocado Smoothie Calories:200	Baked Salmon Foil Packets with Vegetables Calories:400	Lentil Avocado Tacos Calories:400	**1000**
DAY 10	Strawberry, Orange, and Beet Smoothie Calories:266	Lemon Garlic Chicken Calories:439	Tomato & Olive Orecchiette with Basil Pesto Calories:332	**1037**
DAY 11	Blueberry-Vanilla Yogurt Smoothie Calories:228	Mediterranean Turkey Breast Calories:537	Lima Beans Dish Calories:600	**1365**
DAY 12	Greek Yogurt Oat Pancakes Calories:318	Buffalo Chicken Salad Wrap Calories:300	Bean Spread Calories:298	**916**
DAY 13	Scrambled Egg and Veggie Breakfast Quesadillas Calories:445	Lemony Parmesan Shrimps Calories:252	Butter Corn Calories:279	**976**
DAY 14	Stuffed Breakfast Peppers Calories:136	Bean Salad with Orange Vinaigrette Calories:393	Lima Beans Dish Calories:600	**1129**

DAY 15	Apple-Apricot Brown Rice Breakfast Porridge Calories:260	Healthy Chicken Orzo Calories:518	Artichoke and Spinach Dip Calories:263	**1041**
DAY 16	Steel-Cut Oatmeal with Plums and Pear Calories:307	Mediterranean Turkey Breast Calories:537	Sardine Bruschetta with Fennel and Lemon Crema Calories:400	**1244**
DAY 17	Baking Powder Biscuits Calories:118	Olive Capers Chicken Calories:433	Air-Fryer Fish Cakes Calories:399	**1055**
DAY 18	Creamy Oats, Greens & Blueberry Smoothie Calories:280	Buffalo Chicken Salad Wrap Calories:300	Herbed Seafood Casserole Calories:404	**984**
DAY 19	Banana & Cinnamon Oatmeal Calories:215	Lemon Garlic Chicken Calories:439	Roasted Vegetable Enchiladas Calories:335	**989**
DAY 20	No Cook Overnight Oats Calories:271	Peanut Vegetable Pad Thai Calories:393	Garlic Pepper Chicken Calories:462	**1126**
DAY 21	Avocado Cup with Egg Calories:206	Chickpea Cauliflower Tikka Masala Calories:323	Baked Salmon Foil Packets with Vegetables Calories:400	**926**
DAY 22	Instant Banana Oatmeal Calories:243	Air-Fryer Fish Cakes Calories:399	Grilled Chicken Calories:512	**1154**
DAY 23	Brown Sugar Cinnamon Oatmeal Calories:208	Healthy Chicken Orzo Calories:518	Quick Shrimp Scampi Calories:316	**1042**
DAY 24	Buckwheat Pancakes with Vanilla Almond Milk Calories:240	Lemon Garlic Chicken Calories:439	Lentil Avocado Tacos Calories:400	**1079**
DAY 25	Salmon and Egg Scramble Calories:120	Cod Soup Calories:344	Falling "Off" The Bone Chicken Calories:664	**1128**
DAY 26	Sweet Berries Pancake Calories:161	Bean Salad with Orange Vinaigrette Calories:393	Healthy Chicken Orzo Calories:518	**1072**
DAY 27	Breakfast Banana Split Calories:145	Mediterranean Turkey Breast Calories:537	Lima Beans Dish Calories:600	**1282**
DAY 28	Spinach, Mushroom, and Feta Cheese Scramble Calories:236	Bean Salad with Orange Vinaigrette Calories:393	Peanut Vegetable Pad Thai Calories:393	**1022**

Appendix 1 Measurement Conversion Chart

VOLUME EQUIVALENTS(DRY)

US STANDARD	METRIC (APPROXIMATE)
1/8 teaspoon	0.5 mL
1/4 teaspoon	1 mL
1/2 teaspoon	2 mL
3/4 teaspoon	4 mL
1 teaspoon	5 mL
1 tablespoon	15 mL
1/4 cup	59 mL
1/2 cup	118 mL
3/4 cup	177 mL
1 cup	235 mL
2 cups	475 mL
3 cups	700 mL
4 cups	1 L

WEIGHT EQUIVALENTS

US STANDARD	METRIC (APPROXIMATE)
1 ounce	28 g
2 ounces	57 g
5 ounces	142 g
10 ounces	284 g
15 ounces	425 g
16 ounces (1 pound)	455 g
1.5 pounds	680 g
2 pounds	907 g

VOLUME EQUIVALENTS(LIQUID)

US STANDARD	US STANDARD (OUNCES)	METRIC (APPROXIMATE)
2 tablespoons	1 fl.oz.	30 mL
1/4 cup	2 fl.oz.	60 mL
1/2 cup	4 fl.oz.	120 mL
1 cup	8 fl.oz.	240 mL
1 1/2 cup	12 fl.oz.	355 mL
2 cups or 1 pint	16 fl.oz.	475 mL
4 cups or 1 quart	32 fl.oz.	1 L
1 gallon	128 fl.oz.	4 L

TEMPERATURES EQUIVALENTS

FAHRENHEIT(F)	CELSIUS(C) (APPROXIMATE)
225 °F	107 °C
250 °F	120 °C
275 °F	135 °C
300 °F	150 °C
325 °F	160 °C
350 °F	180 °C
375 °F	190 °C
400 °F	205 °C
425 °F	220 °C
450 °F	235 °C
475 °F	245 °C
500 °F	260 °C

Appendix 2   Dirty Dozen and Clean Fifteen

The Environmental Working Group (EWG) is a nonprofit, nonpartisan organization dedicated to protecting human health and the environment Its mission is to empower people to live healthier lives in a healthier environment. This organization publishes an annual list of the twelve kinds of produce, in sequence, that have the highest amount of pesticide residue-the Dirty Dozen-as well as a list of the fifteen kinds ofproduce that have the least amount of pesticide residue-the Clean Fifteen.

THE DIRTY DOZEN

- The 2016 Dirty Dozen includes the following produce. These are considered among the year's most important produce to buy organic:

Strawberries	Spinach
Apples	Tomatoes
Nectarines	Bell peppers
Peaches	Cherry tomatoes
Celery	Cucumbers
Grapes	Kale/collard greens
Cherries	Hot peppers

- *The Dirty Dozen list contains two additional itemskale/collard greens and hot peppers-because they tend to contain trace levels of highly hazardous pesticides.*

THE CLEAN FIFTEEN

- The least critical to buy organically are the Clean Fifteen list. The following are on the 2016 list:

Avocados	Papayas
Corn	Kiw
Pineapples	Eggplant
Cabbage	Honeydew
Sweet peas	Grapefruit
Onions	Cantaloupe
Asparagus	Cauliflower
Mangos	

- *Some of the sweet corn sold in the United States are made from genetically engineered (GE) seedstock. Buy organic varieties of these crops to avoid GE produce.*

Appendix 3   Index

2

28-Day Meal Plan – Average Calories: 1074 157

A

Air-Fryer Fish Cakes 70
Almond and Tomato Balls 133
Almond Butter-Banana Smoothie 15
Almond Rice Pudding 150
Appendix 1   Measurement Conversion Chart 159
Appendix 2   Dirty Dozen and Clean Fifteen 160
Appendix 3   Index 161
Apple & Berry Cobbler 156
Apple Dumplings 146
Apple Pancakes 7
Apple Quinoa Muffins 20
Apple Salsa 65
Apple-Apricot Brown Rice Breakfast Porridge 12
Apples and Cream Shake 150
Apricot Biscotti 155
Apricot Chicken 88
Aromatic Whole Grain Spaghetti 41
Artichoke and Spinach Chicken 82
Artichoke and Spinach Dip 63
Arugula Salad 49
Asparagus Cheese Vermicelli 111
Avocado Cup with Egg 15
Avocado Side Salad 60
Avocado Tuna Bites 134
Avocado, Tomato, and Olives Salad 49

B

Baby Spinach and Grains Mix 63
Bacon Bits 21
Bagels Made Healthy 11
Baked Broccoli 58
Baked Cauliflower with Chili 58
Baked Chicken 86
Baked Chickpe -And-Rosemary Omelet 108
Baked Eggplant Parmesan 106
Baked Eggs in Avocado 103
Baked Falafel 41
Baked Fish & Potatoes 75
Baked Fish Served with Vegetables 78
Baked Potato with Thyme 57
Baked Salmon Foil Packets with Vegetables 74
Baked Stuffed Apples 150
Baking Powder Biscuits 14
Balsamic Cabbage 53
Banana & Cinnamon Oatmeal 11
Banana Bread 138
Banana Custard 134
Banana Delight 149
Banana-Cashew Cream Mousse 152
Banana-Peanut Butter and Greens Smoothie 13

Basil Olives Mix 49
Bean Salad with Orange Vinaigrette 125
Bean Soup 115
Bean Spread 64
Beef & Barley Soup 118
Beetroot and Berry Smoothie 144
Berries Marinated in Balsamic Vinegar 147
Berry Blast 145
Black Bean Burgers 99
Black Bean Soup 12 1
Black Bean Stew with Cornbread 39
Black-Bean and Vegetable Burrito 102
Black-Bean Soup 104
Black-Eyed Peas and Greens Power Salad 106
Blueberry Oat Muffins 138
Blueberry Pudding Cake 154
Blueberry Waffles 9
Blueberry-Vanilla Yogurt Smoothie 11
Breakfast Banana Split 16
Breakfast Fruits Bowls 17
Breakfast Hash 9
Broccoli Soup 115
Broccoli with Garlic and Lemon 97
Brown Rice and Chicken Soup 115
Brown Rice Casserole with Cottage Cheese 100
Brown Rice Pilaf 98
Brown Sugar Cinnamon Oatmeal 22
Brown Sugar Glazed Carrots 56
Brussels Sprouts Casserole 65
Buckwheat Pancakes with Vanilla Almond Milk 22
Buffalo Chicken Salad Wrap 89
Butter Corn 61
Butternut Squash Soup 121
Butternut-Squash Macaroni and Cheese 106

C

Cabbage Soup 119
Caramelized Fennel and Sardines with Penne 69
Carrot Cake Cookies 143
Carrot Cake Overnight Oats 13
Carrot Cakes 40
Carrot Muffins 16
Carrot-Cake Smoothie 109
Carrot-Cake Smoothie 150
Cauliflower Lunch Salad 28
Cauliflower Mashed Potatoes 108
Cereal with Cranberry-Orange Twist 14
CHAPTER 1: The Dietary Approach to Stop Hypertension
(DASH) Basics 2
CHAPTER 10: Vegetables 97
CHAPTER 11: Soups 113
CHAPTER 12: Salads 125
CHAPTER 13: Snacks 132
CHAPTER 14: Desserts 136
CHAPTER 2: Benefits of Dash Diet 4
CHAPTER 3: Breakfast 7
CHAPTER 4: Lunch 25

CHAPTER 5: Dinner 29
CHAPTER 6: Mains 34
CHAPTER 7: Side Dishes 48
CHAPTER 8: Fish and Seafood 66
CHAPTER 9: Poultry 82
Chewy Pumpkin Oatmeal Raisin Cookies 143
Chia Seeds Breakfast Mix 17
Chicken & Rice Soup 122
Chicken and Tortilla Soup 123
Chicken Corn Chowder 122
Chicken Divan 93
Chicken Sliders 89
Chicken Squash Soup 114
Chicken Thighs and Apples Mix 82
Chicken Tikka 94
Chicken Tortellini Soup 93
Chicken Tortillas 84
Chicken with Mushrooms 96
Chicken with Noodles 91
Chicken with Potatoes Olives & Sprouts 84
Chicken Wrap 45
Chicken, Bamboo, and Chestnuts Mix 26
Chicken, Pasta and Snow Peas 91
Chicken, Tomato and Green Beans 84
Chickpea & Kale Soup 121
Chickpea Cauliflower Tikka Masala 34
Chickpea Curry 42
Chickpeas and Curried Veggies 64
Chili Beans 64
Chili Broccoli 54
Chilled Cucumber-And-Avocado Soup with Dill 108
Chipotle Squash Soup 113
Choco Banana Cake 137
Chocolate Cake in A Mug 151
Chocolate Chip Banana Muffin Top Cookies 12
Chocolate Coconut Bombs 133
Chocolate Cupcakes with Vanilla Frosting 141
Chocolate Truffles 136
Chopped Tuna Salad 66
Chunky Black-Bean Dip 98
Chunky Tomatoes 41
Cilantro Lime Rice 52
Cioppino 69
Citrus-Glazed Salmon with Zucchini Noodles 67
Clam Chowder 122
Classic Hummus 109
Cobb Pasta Salad 131
Coconut Arugula Soup 119
Coconut Avocado Soup 119
Coconut Curry Sea Bass 76
Coconut Turkey Mix 32
Cod and Cauliflower Chowder 66
Cod Soup 27
Collard, Sweet Potato and Pea Soup 114
Colored Iceberg Salad 59
Colorful Pops 145
Corn Mix 59
Corn Salad with Lime Vinaigrette 52
Corn Stuffed Peppers 111
Creamy Apple-Avocado Smoothie 11
Creamy Avocado and Egg Salad Sandwiches 9

Creamy Broccoli Cheddar Rice 51
Creamy Cauliflower Mash 48
Creamy Chicken Breast 25
Creamy Chicken Fried Rice 93
Creamy Haddock with Kale 80
Creamy Low-Sodium Coleslaw 126
Creamy Oats, Greens & Blueberry Smoothie 11
Creamy Pumpkin Pasta 38
Crispy Cashew Chicken 92
Crispy Coconut Bombs 133
Crispy Potato Skins 109
Cucumber Soup 118
Cumin Brussels Sprouts 55
Curry Vegetable Noodles with Chicken 44

D

Delicious Lemon Chicken Salad 85
Dill and Lemon Cod Packets 76
Dill Chicken Salad 47

E

Easy Apple Crisp 143
Easy Carrots Mix 56
Easy Cinnamon Baked Apples 151
Easy Coconut-Carrot Cake Balls 149
Easy Lunch Salmon Steaks 26
Easy Shrimp 79
Easy Steamed Alaskan Cod 76
Easy Strawberry Sheet Cake 148
Easy Veggie Muffins 16
Edamame Salad with Corn and Cranberries 129
Egg White Breakfast Mix 19
Eggplant Parmesan Stacks 35
Energy Sunrise Muffins 8
Escarole with Bean Soup 113
Espresso Fat Bombs 133

F

Falling "Off" The Bone Chicken 83
Faux Mac and Cheese 134
Feisty Chicken Porridge 83
Fennel Salad with Arugula 59
Fish Amandine 75
Fish in A Vegetable Patch 79
Fish Stew 32
Flax Banana Yogurt Muffins 21
Flounder with Tomatoes and Basil 68
French Toast with Applesauce 13
Fresh Corn, Pepper, and Avocado Salad 125
Fruit Pizza 21
Fruit Shrimp Soup 31
Fruited Quinoa Salad 40

G

Garlic and Lemon Soup 117
Garlic and Pumpkin Soup 120
Garlic and Tomatoes on Mussels 78

Garlic Cottage Cheese Crispy 132
Garlic Mushroom Chicken.......................................85
Garlic Pepper Chicken 86
Garlic Potato Pan 53
Garlic Potato Salad 125
Ginger Sesame Salmon...80
Ginger Snaps 142
Ginger Zucchini Avocado Soup 119
Glazed Eggplant Rings 42
Gnocchi with Tomato Basil Sauce 38
Golden Mushroom Soup...120
Greek Flatbread with Spinach, Tomatoes & Feta...............101
Greek Lemon and Chicken Soup 120
Greek Yogurt Oat Pancakes 12
Green Goddess Crab Salad with Endive 70
Grilled Chicken 85
Grilled Mahi-Mahi with Artichoke Caponata 68
Grilled Pineapple Strips 136
Grilled Plums with Vanilla Bean Frozen Yogurt 152

H

Halibut in Parchment with Zucchini, Shallots, and Herbs........68
Ham and Pea Soup 123
Harissa Bolognese with Vegetable Noodles 44
Hassel back Eggplant...46
Healthy Banana-Choco Ice Cream 149
Healthy Blueberry & Banana Muffins 148
Healthy Chicken Orzo 86
Healthy Chocolate Mousse 150
Healthy Tahini Buns 134
Healthy Vegetable Fried Rice 107
Hearty Breakfast Casserole 10
Hearty Buttery Walnuts 132
Hearty Ginger Soup 116
Hearty Lentil Soup 103
Herbed Seafood Casserole 73
Homemade Banana Ice Cream 144
Honey Crusted Chicken 87
Honey Spiced Cajun Chicken 94
Hot Brussels Sprouts 55
Hot Chicken Wings 92

I

Indian Chicken Stew 25
Ingenious Eggplant Soup 116
Instant Banana Oatmeal...15
Introduction 1
Italian Chicken..94
Italian Roasted Cabbage...61
Italian Sausage & Fennel Soup 117
Italian Stuffed Portobello Mushroom Burgers 37
Italian Wedding Soup 117

J

Jack-o-Lantern Pancakes 21
Jalapeno Black-Eyed Peas Mix...................................55

K

Kale Verde 113
Kale-Poppy Seed Salad 129
Karen's Apple Kugel 153
Key Lime Cherry "Nice" Cream 152

L

Leeks Soup 28
Lemon and Cilantro Rice 63
Lemon Asparagus 48
Lemon Cookies 142
Lemon Fat Bombs..132
Lemon Garlic Chicken 86
Lemon Garlic Shrimp 74
Lemon Herb Baked Salmon 73
Lemon Pudding Cakes 147
Lemon Salmon with Kaffir Lime 78
Lemongrass and Chicken Soup 25
Lemon-Parsley Chicken Breast 96
Lemony Parmesan Shrimps 77
Lentil Avocado Tacos 35
Lentil Quinoa Gratin with Butternut Squash 100
Lentil-Stuffed Zucchini Boats 105
Light Balsamic Salad 27
Lima Beans Dish 60
Lime Carrots 48
Lime Shrimp and Kale 30
Loaded Baked Sweet Potatoes 104
Loaded Tofu Burrito with Black Beans 102
Loving Cauliflower Soup 116

M

Mango Crumble..144
Mango Rice Pudding..137
Mediterranean Chickpea Salad 60
Mediterranean Pop Corn Bites.................................132
Mediterranean Toast..15
Mediterranean Turkey Breast 95
Mexican-Style Potato Casserole 38
Milk Chocolate Pudding 139
Minestrone...120
Minty Lime and Grapefruit Yogurt Parfait.....................139
Mixed Berry Whole-Grain Coffee Cake 147
Mixed Fruit Compote Cups.....................................156
Mixed Vegetarian Chili 110
Monkfish with Sautéed Leeks, Fennel, and Tomatoes 69
Moroccan-Inspired Tagine with Chickpeas & Vegetables 97
Mushroom Cakes 42
Mushroom Florentine 45
Mushroom Risotto with Peas 101
Mushroom Sausages 54
Mushroom Shallot Frittata 23
Mushrooms and Cheese Omelet 18
Mushrooms and Turkey Breakfast 18
Mussels and Chickpea Soup 31
Mustard Chicken Tenders 87

N

No Cook Overnight Oats 14
No-Bake Breakfast Granola Bars 23
No-Mayo Potato Salad 51

O

Oatmeal Banana Pancakes with Walnuts 14
Oatmeal Dark Chocolate Chip Peanut Butter Cookies 152
Oats and Fruit Bar Cracker 145
Oaxacan Chicken 90
Olive Capers Chicken 95
Orchid Salad 127
Oregano Chicken Thighs 84
Oven Roasted Asparagus 57
Oven-Fried Chicken Breasts 88
Oven-Roasted Beets with Honey Ricotta 56

P

Paella 41
Paella with Chicken, Leeks, and Tarragon 87
Pan-Fried Salmon with Salad 42
Paprika Brussels Sprouts 55
Parmesan and Chicken Spaghetti Squash 88
Parmesan Endives 48
Parsley Cod Mix 30
Parsley Fennel 62
Parsley Red Potatoes 54
Parsley Seafood Cocktail 29
Pasta with Tomatoes and Peas 107
Pea Soup 124
Peach and Carrots 62
Peach Cobbler 154
Peach Crumble Muffins 153
Peach Tarts 140
Peanut Butter & Banana Breakfast Smoothie 23
Peanut Butter Banana "Ice Cream" 151
Peanut Butter Banana Bread Bites 154
Peanut Butter Chocolate Chip Blondies 142
Peanut Vegetable Pad Thai 36
Persimmon Salad 59
Pesto Chicken Breasts with Summer Squash 84
Pesto Omelet 19
Pesto Shrimp Pasta 71
Pilaf with Bella Mushrooms 62
Pineapple Oatmeal 16
Poached Pears 138
Poached Salmon with Creamy Piccata Sauce 72
Portobello-Mushroom Cheeseburgers 107
Pumpkin and Black Beans Chicken 82
Pumpkin Cookies 17
Pumpkin Muffins 18
Pumpkin Pie Fat Bombs 133
Pumpkin Pie Recipe 145
Pumpkin Soup 119
Pumpkin with Chia Seeds Pudding 139
Purple Potato Soup 28

Q

Quick Shrimp Scampi 71
Quinoa and Scallops Salad 29
Quinoa Bowls 19
Quinoa Curry 63
Quinoa-Stuffed Peppers 100

R

Radish and Olives Salad 49
Raspberry Nuts Parfait 140
Raspberry Peach Pancake 12
Red Beans and Rice 103
Red Velvet Pancakes with Cream Cheese Topping 23
Refreshing Watermelon Sorbet 132
Rice with Chicken 26
Roasted Brussels Sprouts 97
Roasted Carrot Soup 118
Roasted Carrots 57
Roasted Chicken Thighs 95
Roasted Chickpeas 109
Roasted Garlic Soup 118
Roasted Okra 56
Roasted Turnips 50
Roasted Vegetable Enchiladas 36
Rosemary Roasted Chicken 82

S

Salad Niçoise 128
Salmon and Cabbage Mix 32
Salmon and Egg Scramble 15
Salmon Cakes with Bell Pepper Plus Lemon Yogurt 67
Salmon Wrap 47
Salsa Chicken 26
Salsa Chicken Chili 87
Sardine Bruschetta with Fennel and Lemon Crema 66
Savory Lobster Roll 78
Savory Yogurt Bowls 8
Scrambled Egg and Veggie Breakfast Quesadillas 12
Seared Scallops with Blood Orange Glaze 70
Shrimp and Broccoli Soup 32
Shrimp and Onion Ginger Dressing 30
Shrimp Cocktail 31
Shrimp Fra Diavolo 74
Simple Cheese and Broccoli Omelets 8
Simple Green Salad 129
Simple Mediterranean Chicken 95
Slow Cooked Potatoes with Cheddar 58
Smashed Brussels Sprouts 52
Soup for The Day 113
Sour Cream Green Beans 55
Southwest Tofu Scramble 102
Southwestern Bean Salad with Creamy Avocado Dressing .. 131
Southwestern Bean-And-Pepper Salad 108
Southwestern Beet Slaw 126
Southwestern Chicken and Pasta 88
Southwestern Vegetables Tacos 112
Soy Sauce Green Beans 61
Spaghetti Squash with Maple Glaze & Tofu Crumbles 104

Spanish Rice 50
Spiced Broccoli Florets 60
Spicy Brussels Sprouts 57
Spicy Chicken with Minty Couscous 91
Spicy Tofu Burrito Bowls with Cilantro Avocado Sauce..........34
Spinach and Endives Salad 49
Spinach Muffins 17
Spinach, Egg, And Cheese Breakfast Quesadillas 7
Spinach, Mushroom, and Feta Cheese Scramble 22
Squash Salad with Orange 58
Squid and Shrimp Salad...29
Steamed Blue Crabs 79
Steamed Fish Mediterranean Style 76
Steamed Fish with Scallions and Ginger.................................80
Steamed Salmon Teriyaki 75
Steamed Tilapia with Green Chutney 80
Steamed Veggie and Lemon Pepper Salmon 80
Steel-Cut Oatmeal with Plums and Pear 13
Stevia Peas with Marjoram 61
Stewed Cod Filet with Tomatoes 77
Stir-Fried Steak, Shiitake, and Asparagus 64
Strawberries and Cream Cheese Crepes 147
Strawberry Bruschetta 140
Strawberry Sandwich 19
Strawberry, Orange, and Beet Smoothie 11
Stuffed Breakfast Peppers...12
Stuffed Chicken Breasts 89
Stuffed Eggplant Shells 111
Stuffed Pepper Soup 123
Stuffed Tex-Mex Baked Potatoes 105
Summer Barley Pilaf with Yogurt Dill Sauce 99
Super-Simple Granola 7
Sweet Almond and Coconut Fat Bomb 133
Sweet and Sour Vegetable Noodles 45
Sweet Berries Pancake 19
Sweet Butternut...54
Sweet Potato Balls 42
Sweet Potato Cakes with Classic Guacamole 34
Sweet Potato Rice with Spicy Peanut Sauce 98
Sweet Potato Soup 27
Sweet Potato Toast Three Ways 10
Sweet Potatoes and Apples..50
Sweet Potatoes and Zucchini Soup 25
Sweet Potato-Turkey Meatloaf 90
Sweet-Ginger Scallops...77

T

Tabouleh Salad..127
Taco Soup...117
Tangy Three-Bean Salad with Barley...............................130
Tart Apple Salad with Fennel and Honey Yogurt Dressing 127
Tart Raspberry Crumble Bar...148
Tasty Cauliflower..62
Tasty Grilled Asparagus 7
Tasty Tofu and Mushroom Soup 116 57

teel Cut Oat Blueberry Pancakes..22
Teriyaki Chicken Wings...92
Tex-Mex Cole Slaw 53
Thai Chicken Thighs 82
Thai Pasta Salad 127
The Ultimate Faux-Tisserie Chicken 83
Toasted Almond Ambrosia 155
Tofu & Green Bean Stir-Fry 36
Tom Kha Gai 122
Tomato & Olive Orecchiette with Basil Pesto 37
Tomato Soup 26
Tuna and Carrots Casserole...77
Tuna Salad-Stuffed Tomatoes with Arugula 72
Tuna Sandwich 40
Turkey Ginger Soup 123
Turkey Sausage and Mushroom Strata 20
Turkey Wrap 45
Turmeric Endives...48
Tuscan-Style Tuna Salad 72

V

Vanilla Cupcakes with Cinnamon-Fudge Frosting 12
Vegan Chili 40
Vegan Rice Pudding 144
Vegetable Cheese Calzone 110
Vegetable Noodles with Bolognese 43
Vegetable Pasta..43
Vegetable Red Curry...98
Vegetarian Kebabs 46
Vegetarian Lasagna 39
Veggie and Beef Soup..114
Veggie Quiche Muffins 20
Veggie Scramble 17
Veggie Variety 43
Veggie Wrap 46
Very Berry Muesli..20

W

Walnut and Oatmeal Chocolate Chip Cookies.....................146
Warm Asian Slaw...130
Warm Kale Salad 126
Wedge Salad with Creamy Blue Cheese Dressing 130
White Beans Stew 46
White Beans with Spinach and Pan-Roasted Tomatoes.......104
White Chicken Chili 90
Whole-Wheat Couscous Salad with Citrus and Cilantro.......128

Z

Zesty Zucchini Muffins..137
Zucchini Pancakes 19
Zucchini Pepper Kebabs 110
Zucchini Tomato Bake 51

Printed in Great Britain
by Amazon